Dallas Cowboys
in the Hall of Fame

Dallas Cowboys in the Hall of Fame

Their Remarkable Journeys to Canton

David Thomas

ROWMAN & LITTLEFIELD
Lanham • Boulder • New York • London

Published by Rowman & Littlefield
A wholly owned subsidiary of The Rowman & Littlefield Publishing Group, Inc.
4501 Forbes Boulevard, Suite 200, Lanham, Maryland 20706
www.rowman.com

Unit A, Whitacre Mews, 26-34 Stannary Street, London SE11 4AB

British Library Cataloguing in Publication Information Available

Library of Congress Cataloging-in-Publication Data

Names: Thomas, David, 1968 June 21-
Title: Dallas Cowboys in the Hall of Fame : their remarkable journeys to
  Canton / David Thomas.
Description: Lanham : ROWMAN & LITTLEFIELD, [2016] | Includes bibliographical
  references and index.
Identifiers: LCCN 2015039186| ISBN 9781442255685 (hardcover : alk. paper) |
  ISBN 9781442255692 (ebook)
Subjects: LCSH: Dallas Cowboys (Football team)—History. | Football
  players—United States—Biography.
Classification: LCC GV956.D3 T56 2016 | DDC 796.332/64097642812—dc23
LC record available at http://lccn.loc.gov/2015039186

∞™ The paper used in this publication meets the minimum requirements of
American National Standard for Information Sciences—Permanence of Paper
for Printed Library Materials, ANSI/NISO Z39.48-1992.

Printed in the United States of America

Contents

Introduction

$\mathcal{T}$he road from the home of the Dallas Cowboys to Canton, Ohio, is nearly a 1,200-mile trip. For members of the Pro Football Hall of Fame, however, the trip to the home of football's ultimate club is a journey years—even decades—in the making.

As would be expected for a franchise that has made eight Super Bowl appearances—winning five—the Cowboys have produced more than their share of members of that club. Twenty-two Cowboys have been inducted into the Hall of Fame. Fifteen were inducted as Cowboys, while seven others played smaller portions of their careers wearing the helmet bearing a star on each side. Twenty were players, one was a coach, and one an executive. That range is fitting for a franchise that, for much of its existence, has been known for representing excellence on the field, on the sideline, and in the front office.

From 1960, when the Cowboys took the field for the first time, to 2006, Dallas fans had the opportunity to watch at least one future hall of famer. For all but one of those forty-seven seasons, the Cowboys sported at least two future hall of famers. Each year of the 1970s, when Dallas played in five of the decade's 10 Super Bowls, there were never fewer than six Cowboys who were on the road to Canton.

It is difficult to discuss hall of famers without mentioning their numbers, because statistics are the measuring stick of sports. And, naturally, the Cowboys in the Hall of Fame racked up impressive statistics.

Emmitt Smith rushed for 18,355 yards. Bob Lilly was selected to 11 Pro Bowls, including 10 consecutively. Bob Hayes averaged 20.0 yards per reception during his career. Deion Sanders scored 18 touchdowns via kickoff, punt, and interception returns. Tony Dorsett rushed for at least 100 yards in 43 games as a Cowboy.

But hall of famers are more than a collection of impressive statistics. They are people, and while their paths merged while they worked with teammates toward a common goal on the football field, they each followed their own unique journeys to the Hall of Fame.

Dorsett was a heralded star. Smith faced doubters who claimed that at the next level—whatever that level may be—his size would limit him. Roger Staubach was not a starting quarterback until his senior year in high school and then placed his football career on hold to serve his country, fully aware that football might not be waiting for him when his military service ended. Larry Allen survived tough streets and a path rarely taken to the NFL. Tom Landry was inducted into the Hall of Fame the year after he left coaching. Rayfield Wright, inexplicably, did not enter the Hall until 27 years after he retired. Bob Hayes had already passed away when his induction finally came.

Yet, from such diverse backgrounds, 22 men who called the Cowboys their team earned a place in football's most exclusive group. They all wore the star, and they wore it well.

These are the stories of their unique journeys to the Hall of Fame.

Troy Aikman

A Winner

Troy Kenneth Aikman
Class: 2006 (Harry Carson, John Madden, Warren Moon, Reggie White, Rayfield Wright)
Seasons with Cowboys: 1989–2000
Other NFL teams: None
Positions: Quarterback
Colleges: Oklahoma, UCLA

On the day he signed his first contract with the Dallas Cowboys, Troy Aikman said he hoped that within five years, the team's fans would be comparing him with Roger Staubach. Five years later, he had won the same number of Super Bowls as Staubach, and there still was one more Vince Lombardi Trophy that Aikman would hoist.

It was none other than Staubach himself who would later rank Aikman as the best draft pick in franchise history.

"Troy Aikman resurrected the Cowboys," Staubach said as Aikman prepared to enter the Hall of Fame as part of the class of 2006.

Throughout Aikman's career, he was lauded for his pinpoint passing accuracy, arm strength, leadership, and willingness to sacrifice individual numbers for team success. There was one word, however, that was most often employed to describe what Aikman did best: *win*.

When Norv Turner, the Cowboys' offensive coordinator from 1991 to 1993, presented Aikman at the Hall of Fame induction ceremony, he told of being asked by an interviewer a couple of years earlier whom he would choose as his starting quarterback if given only one game to coach. Turner easily picked the quarterback for whom he called plays for two Super Bowl championships.

"The interviewer politely asked me why," Turner told the crowd. "I said, 'Because I want to win.'"

Wise choice.

No quarterback to that point in NFL history had won more games in a decade than Aikman did in the 1990s, when he led the Cowboys to 90 victories in his starts. That figure does not include the 11 postseason games the Cowboys won under Aikman, who often was at his best in games that mattered most. Aikman owned a 3–0 record in Super Bowls and a 3–1 mark in NFC Championship Games.

Troy Aikman won his way to Canton. But if not for a family move, he might have set his sights on Cooperstown instead.

BIG-LEAGUE DREAMS

Baseball was Aikman's first love growing up in Cerritos, California. Although he began playing football at age seven, he dreamed of playing baseball for the University of Southern California and pursuing a major-league career. When he was 12, his parents moved to the small town of Henryetta, Oklahoma (population approximately 6,000), where football reigned as the supreme sport.

Aikman did not tell coaches at Henryetta Middle School that he had played quarterback on his youth teams in California, and they inserted him into the lineup at fullback. After his eighth-grade year, he informed his coaches he had experience at quarterback. With one look at his powerful throwing arm, the coaches moved him forward a few steps in the backfield, and his days of receiving handoffs were over.

Aikman began playing on varsity as a sophomore, and even though the Fighting Hens' run-based, split-back veer offense did not present Aikman with many opportunities to show off his arm, he quickly gained recognition among the state's best quarterbacks. After football season, he became a starter on the basketball team—the only sophomore starter alongside four seniors.

Yet, some Henryetta coaches considered baseball to be the sandy-haired Aikman's best sport. The more snaps Aikman took under center for the Hens, however, the future he possessed in football became more and more clear. After one game, an opposing coach told Aikman, "We'll be watching you someday on *Monday Night Football*."

At 6-foot-3, Aikman was his team's largest player—larger even than the linemen—and played inside linebacker as a sophomore before moving to defensive back for his junior and senior seasons. His junior year, he led the Hens to their first playoff berth in 25 years. His senior season, Henryetta finished 6–4 and missed the playoffs.

Among the college coaches recruiting Aikman were in-state rivals Jimmy Johnson of Oklahoma State and Oklahoma's Barry Switzer. After Switzer assured Aikman that the Sooners would pass more with him as their quarterback, Oklahoma and its history of playing for national championships won out.

But before Aikman set foot on the (OU) campus, he had an opportunity to become a professional baseball player. On the eve of the 1984 draft, a New York Mets scout called Aikman and asked how much money it would take to sign him to a baseball contract. Football scholarship in hand, Aikman answered $200,000, and the Mets did not draft him.

Aikman played little as a freshman at Oklahoma, completing only six of 20 passes. He became the starter for his sophomore season. Although the Sooners won their first three games under Aikman, he struggled a little. He appeared to be turning a corner in the fourth game, against the University of Miami team, that year coached by Jimmy Johnson. (Future teammate Michael Irvin also was on the field for the Hurricanes that day.) Aikman completed six of his first seven passes for 131 yards and a touchdown before suffering a broken ankle that ended his season.

That injury also turned out to be the end of his career with the Sooners. Freshman Jamelle Holieway replaced Aikman and impressively ran the wishbone offense—the Sooners had been lining up in the I formation with Aikman—as he led Oklahoma to the national championship. Aikman, unhappy that Switzer had not kept his word to pass more, decided to leave Oklahoma.

He landed at UCLA, where, after sitting out one season, as mandated by NCAA transfer rules, he showed he was ready to become the quarterback that coaches—including Switzer—had said he would be: a NFL quarterback.

Aikman finished third in voting for the 1988 Heisman Trophy, behind Barry Sanders and Rodney Peete. He sported a 20–4 record in his two seasons as a starting quarterback for the Bruins, leading them to victories in the Aloha and Cotton Bowl games.

Only losses to crosstown rival USC in the final games of the 1987 and 1988 regular seasons had prevented UCLA from playing in the prestigious Rose Bowl as the Pac-10 conference champion. "The only athletic regret I have," Aikman would say years later, after his NFL career had concluded, "is that at UCLA I failed to take our team to the Rose Bowl. That's the only thing I can look back and think, 'Wow, I wish I had been able to do that.'"

Along with the invitation to play in the Cotton Bowl during Aikman's senior season came the opportunity for the Bruins to practice in Texas Stadium, the home of the Dallas Cowboys. The Cowboys had finished that season 3–13, securing them the first overall pick in the 1989 draft. Coach Tom

Landry and Gil Brandt, the team's vice president of player personnel, watched Aikman practice one day. Afterward, when Brandt asked Landry if he wanted to come back and watch Aikman again the following day, Landry answered, "No, I've seen enough. He's our choice."

COWBOYS COME CALLING

The Cowboys needed a franchise quarterback. An injury had cut short Danny White's season in 1986, and he had been benched in favor of Steve Pelluer for the final part of the 1987 season. Pelluer started 14 games during the 3–13 season of 1988.

Aikman, being billed as the best quarterback prospect since John Elway five years earlier, seemed to be a no-brainer pick for the Cowboys. But on February 25, 1989, Jerry Jones, an oil and gas millionaire from Arkansas, purchased the Cowboys, fired Landry, and replaced him with none other than Johnson, Jones's teammate on the University of Arkansas's 1964 national championship team.

Johnson had twice attempted to woo Aikman into being his quarterback—out of high school when Johnson was at Oklahoma State and again at Miami when Aikman decided to leave Oklahoma. But this time it would be Johnson who held the power of choice. And this time, he got his quarterback.

The new-look Cowboys ensured there would be no draft-day surprise when they signed Aikman to a NFL rookie-record, six-year, $11.2 million contract three days before the draft. Almost three months later, however, the Cowboys did pull off a big surprise when they selected Steve Walsh in the supplemental draft at the price of the team's first-round pick in the 1990 draft. Walsh had been Johnson's final quarterback at Miami, winning 23 of 24 games in two seasons. Walsh admitted to being surprised by being drafted by the team that already owned Aikman.

When Johnson stated that he did not select Walsh to trade him, speculation began of a high-profile quarterback competition between Aikman and Walsh. The speculation was further fueled by Johnson's statement that "Any time you have competition, it makes your players better."

Aikman and Walsh spent more than a full season together on the Dallas roster. Aikman won the starting job in 1989, becoming the first Cowboys rookie quarterback to start a season opener since Staubach in 1969. But Aikman suffered a broken wrist in the fourth game. Walsh started four games in Aikman's place, including the Cowboys' lone win during what would turn out to be a 1–15 season. Aikman reassumed the starting position upon his return later in the year, and after the third game of the 1990 season, Walsh was traded to the New Orleans Saints for first-, second-, and third-round picks.

That trade made clear that Aikman would indeed be the Cowboys' quarterback for a long time.

QUARTERBACK OF THE 1990S

The year before the Cowboys drafted Aikman, they had selected Michael Irvin with the 11th overall pick. In 1990, they would have had the top overall pick again except for the supplemental-draft selection of Walsh. During that draft, they pulled off a trade with the Pittsburgh Steelers for the 17th pick and selected Florida running back Emmitt Smith.

With Aikman, Smith, and Irvin, the "Triplets," as they would become known, were in place. For three consecutive drafts, the Cowboys managed to land with their first pick a player who would become a member of the Pro Football Hall of Fame.

The turnaround came quickly. A four-game winning streak in November and December propelled the Cowboys, who had started the 1990 season 3–7, into position to make the playoffs during the final two weeks of the season. Then Aikman suffered a separated shoulder in the next-to-last game, a 17–3 loss to the Philadelphia Eagles, and without him, Dallas lost 26–7 in Atlanta to end the season. Their 7–9 record left them one game behind the wild-card Saints.

The five-year postseason drought ended the following year. (Since making the playoffs for the first time in 1966, the Cowboys had not previously missed the playoffs in back-to-back years.) Aikman again missed the final part of the season because of injury, but Steve Beuerlein stepped in and led Dallas into the playoffs and to a wild-card win at Chicago. Aikman returned for the NFC Divisional round, where the Cowboys' season ended with a 38–6 loss at Detroit. Aikman was rewarded for his campaign with the first of six consecutive Pro Bowl selections.

From that point onward, the Cowboys began earning their label as the NFL's team of the 1990s, winning three of the next four Super Bowls, and Aikman began earning his reputation as a player at his best in the biggest of games.

"If you look at Troy's greatest plays, they came in the most critical situations," Turner said during his speech inducting Aikman, continuing,

> If you look at his greatest games, they came against the best teams, and they came in the playoffs. Troy is one of the most unselfish players to have

played. He knew the things he had to do to give his team the best chance to win. In an era of super egos, he never let his get in the way of winning. Super Bowls were more important than statistics.

From 1992 to 1995, Aikman led the Cowboys to a 10–1 playoff record, including a 7–1 record against teams quarterbacked by Brett Favre, Steve Young, and Jim Kelly. The only hiccup came in the NFC Championship Game after the 1994 season, the season in which Switzer had replaced Johnson as Cowboys head coach.

During those 11 playoff games, Aikman averaged 265 yards passing per contest, completed 68.3 percent of his passes, and threw 21 touchdowns compared to 8 interceptions. Interestingly, for a player known more for winning than individual statistics, the Cowboys' lone postseason loss during that run came in a game in which Aikman produced some of his biggest numbers. In a 38–28 loss to Young's 49ers in the NFC Championship Game played in January 1995, Aikman completed 30 of 53 passes for 380 yards, with two touchdowns and three interceptions.

The Cowboys went 3–0 in Super Bowls under Aikman, and he was selected MVP of Super Bowl XXVII, played at the Rose Bowl, the home field of his college alma mater. All three championships came prior to age 30. Only Joe Montana and Terry Bradshaw have started at quarterback for more Super Bowl victories.

"There are some things that reflect talent that can be shown," Irvin said of Aikman. "But there are some that can't be so easily shown. The ability to lead and demand greatness out of your players—that's a talent Troy had that people couldn't see."

THE DREAM THAT CAME TRUE

Aikman played 12 seasons in the NFL, all with Dallas. He retired at the age of 34, after spending the latter portion of his career battling concussions and a degenerative back condition. His career ended unceremoniously when he was waived by the Cowboys in March 2001, one day before a $7 million bonus and seven-year contract extension were scheduled to kick in.

He left Dallas owning nearly every major franchise passing record. In the end, he had more Super Bowl victories than Staubach (3–2), more conference championships (4–3), more passing yards (32,942–22,700), and a better completion percentage (61.5–57.0).

Aikman also developed a close friendship with the player he had admired, partnering with Staubach in 2005 to form a NASCAR team they named

Hall of Fame Racing. He has said that he considers the Cowboys' success in the 1990s a continuation of the success that Staubach created with America's Team in the 1980s.

Aikman's Hall of Fame credentials were never questioned. Although often asked to sign "HOF" along with his name when giving autographs, he would not do so until his inclusion became official out of respect for those already in the Hall. His election occurred in 2006, his first year of eligibility, with Aikman already firmly established as commentator on Fox's lead team for NFL broadcasts.

The first hall of famer from the Jones–Johnson era of the Cowboys was the youngest of a class that also consisted of Harry Carson, John Madden, Warren Moon, Reggie White, and former Cowboy Rayfield Wright. Furman Fisher, sports columnist for the *Atlanta Journal Constitution*, called it the strongest class in his 29 years on the selection committee.

In his 20-minute enshrinement speech, Aikman shared the words Turner had told him numerous times after a close loss or a game when Aikman had thrown a costly interception.

"Sometimes we have to remind ourselves," Aikman recalled Turner reminding him, "that these are the jobs we've always dreamed of having."

The one-time sandy-haired kid with a big-league dream never forgot that.

"For as long as I can remember, all I ever wanted was to play pro sports," Aikman said as an abundance of Cowboys jersey–wearing fans listened to his speech in Canton. "A lot of kids want that, but very few actually get the chance. I was able to live a dream. I played professional football."

CAREER HIGHLIGHTS

Won three Super Bowl championships in three appearances.

First quarterback to win three Super Bowls in a four-year span.

Named MVP of Super Bowl XXVII.

Selected to play in six Pro Bowls (1992–1997).

Compiled more victories (90) during the 1990s than any other quarterback.

Set 45 Cowboys passing records.

Led the Cowboys to six NFC East titles (1992–1996, 1998).

Led the Cowboys to four NFC Championship Games (1992–1995).

Named the 1997 Walter Payton NFL Man of the Year.

Named a consensus All-American at UCLA in 1988.

Compiled a 20–4 record as a starter at UCLA, including going 2–0 in
   bowl games.
Won the 1988 Davey O'Brien National Quarterback Award.
Placed third in the 1988 Heisman Trophy voting.
Member of National Football Foundation Hall of Fame.
Chosen as the number-one overall pick in the 1989 NFL Draft.

FIVE COWBOYS MEMORIES

1. *November 12, 1989*

After missing the previous five games with a broken finger, Troy Aikman
passed for a NFL rookie-record 379 yards and two touchdowns, including a
75-yard pass to James Dixon that gave the Cowboys a 20–17 lead against the
Phoenix Cardinals. But as was par for the course in a 1–15 season, Dallas lost
when the Cardinals struck for their own long touchdown pass in the final
minute. Aikman's passing yardage exceeded the career high of Roger Staubach and was the fifth-best in franchise history at the time. After the game,
Phoenix coach Gene Stallings tracked Aikman down and told him, "Great
job. I enjoyed watching you play."

2. *January 17, 1993*

The Cowboys had not played in a Super Bowl since 1979, and general consensus was that they were still one season away from making their return.
But on a muddy Candlestick Park field, Aikman led the Cowboys to a 30–20
victory over the San Francisco in the NFC Championship Game to propel
Dallas into the Super Bowl. Aikman completed 24 of 34 passes for 322 yards
and two touchdowns without throwing an interception. His second half
was the most impressive. After being shoved around and sacked four times
before halftime, Aikman responded by completing 13 of his 26 passes for
208 yards and both of his touchdowns. The first—a 15-yard pass to Emmitt
Smith—came after Aikman engineered a 14-play, 79-yard drive that chewed
exactly nine minutes off the clock. On that drive, the Cowboys converted
four of four third downs in stretching their lead to 24–13. The 49ers came
back to score a touchdown that again cut the Dallas lead to four. This time,
the Cowboys answered quickly. A 70-yard pass to Alvin Harper set up a
six-yard pass from Aikman to Kelvin Martin that stretched the margin back
to the final score of 30–20.

3. January 31, 1993

In his first extended playoff run, Aikman had never been better. In fact, as far as the postseason was concerned, no NFL quarterback had ever been better. Aikman put the wraps on a historic postseason by being named MVP of Super Bowl XXVII after completing 22 of 30 passes for 273 yards and four touchdowns, as Dallas routed the Buffalo Bills, 52–17. His performance gave him a 116.7 quarterback rating during the postseason, easily breaking the previous record held by Bart Starr. For the third consecutive playoff game, Aikman did not throw an interception. No Super Bowl–winning quarterback had attempted as many passes in a postseason (89) without being picked off. Three of Aikman's touchdowns against the Bills came in the first half, when the Cowboys opened a 28–10 lead. The icing on the cake came early in the fourth quarter, with a 45-yard scoring strike to Alvin Harper that made the outcome evident. "Troy didn't do anything exceptional," said tight end Jay Novacek, who caught Aikman's first TD pass. "Troy was just Troy."

4. January 8, 1995

A sprained knee and a coinciding late-season slump had created rare questions about Aikman entering the postseason. He answered with an exclamation-mark performance in a surprisingly easy 35–9 defeat of the Green Bay Packers in the NFC Divisional round. Aikman completed 23 of 30 passes for a Cowboys playoff-record 337 yards. Included among his two touchdown passes was a 94-yard scoring strike to Alvin Harper in the first quarter that was the longest completion in NFL postseason history. After the game, offensive lineman Mark Tuinei referred to Aikman as "Mr. January." The nickname fit, considering Aikman improved his all-time postseason record as a starter to 7–0 and led the Cowboys into their third consecutive NFC Championship Game.

5. September 12, 1999

In what he called probably the "wildest" game of his career, Aikman threw a career-high five touchdown passes and led Dallas to an overtime victory against Washington in a game where the Cowboys trailed by 21 points early in the fourth quarter. Aikman passed for 362 yards in the season opener, with the final 76 yards coming on the game-winning pass to Raghib "Rocket" Ismail in overtime. The comeback stunned the Redskins Stadium crowd of 79,237—the largest crowd to watch a sporting event in Maryland outside of the Preakness Stakes. Aikman's first two touchdown passes—both to tight end David LaFleur—gave the Cowboys a 14–3 lead in the second quarter. But 32 unanswered points by the Redskins left Dallas trailing 35–21 entering the

Statistics

Regular Season

Season	Team	G	Passing						Rushing			
			Cmp	Att	Int	Yds	TD	Pct	No.	Yds	Avg	TD
1989	Dallas	11	155	293	18	1,749	9	52.9	38	302	7.9	0
1990	Dallas	15	226	399	18	2,579	11	56.6	40	172	4.3	1
1991	Dallas	12	237	363	10	2,754	11	65.3	16	5	0.3	1
1992	Dallas	16	302	473	14	3,445	23	63.8	37	105	2.8	1
1993	Dallas	14	271	392	6	3,100	15	69.1	32	125	3.9	0
1994	Dallas	14	233	361	12	2,676	13	64.5	30	62	2.1	1
1995	Dallas	16	280	432	7	3,304	16	64.8	21	32	1.5	1
1996	Dallas	15	296	465	13	3,126	12	63.7	35	42	1.2	1
1997	Dallas	16	292	518	12	3,283	19	56.4	25	79	3.2	0
1998	Dallas	11	187	315	5	2,330	12	59.4	22	69	3.1	2
1999	Dallas	14	263	442	12	2,964	17	59.5	21	10	0.5	1
2000	Dallas	11	156	262	14	1,632	7	59.5	10	13	1.3	0
Totals		165	2,898	4,715	141	32,942	165	61.5	327	1,016	3.1	9

Postseason

Season	Team	G	Passing						Rushing			
			Cmp	Att	Int	Yds	TD	Pct	No.	Yds	Avg	TD
1991	Dallas	1	11	16	1	114	0	68.8	2	0	0.0	0
1992	Dallas	3	61	89	0	795	8	68.5	9	38	4.2	0
1993	Dallas	3	61	82	3	686	5	74.4	7	28	4.0	0
1994	Dallas	2	53	83	4	717	4	63.9	2	11	5.5	0
1995	Dallas	3	53	80	1	717	4	66.3	8	6	0.8	0
1996	Dallas	2	37	65	4	343	1	56.9	3	4	1.3	1
1998	Dallas	1	22	49	3	191	1	44.9	1	0	0.0	0
1999	Dallas	1	22	38	1	286	0	57.9	0	0	0.0	0
Totals		16	320	502	17	3,849	23	63.7	32	87	2.7	1

Others—Receiving: 2-minus 19.

fourth quarter. Emmitt Smith's one-yard run made it 35–21. Then Aikman hooked up with Michael Irvin on two touchdown passes in the final four minutes to force overtime and set up the heroics with Ismail. "He is a great quarterback," Washington rookie cornerback Champ Bailey said. "He knew exactly what he was doing at the end and just picked us part."

• 2 •

Larry Allen

Quiet Strength

Larry Christopher Allen
Class: 2013 (Cris Carter, Curley Culp, Jonathan Ogden, Bill Parcells, Dave Robinson, Warren Sapp)
Seasons with Cowboys: 1994–2005
Other NFL teams: San Francisco 49ers (2006–2007)
Positions: Guard, tackle
Colleges: Butte College, Sonoma State

*L*arry Allen once walked a path that could have led him to prison or death. Instead, he wound up on a road that marched him directly to Canton.

The big, tough kid from the streets of Compton, California, avoided the trouble that ensnared those around him and, with a far-from-prestigious athletic resume, made it to America's Team and became one of the most dominant offensive linemen in NFL history.

Along the way, the quiet Allen rarely spoke to the media. His feats of strength on and off the field spoke loud enough for him. And then there were plenty of others willing to speak on his behalf.

New York Giants defensive end Michael Strahan said, "It got to the point where you'd see guys pull up with some fake injury in the fourth quarter the week before he'd have to play Larry. It's sad. You're watching film and he hurts so many guys on film that his opponents don't want to deal with him."

Teammate Nate Newton commented, "He could run block. He could pass block. He could pull. He was a 10 on every scale. There was nothing he couldn't do. He had strength, agility, feet, work ethic. He is a top-five lineman of all time who could play in any era, face mask or no masks."

13

Hall of Fame coach and broadcaster John Madden stated, "I don't remember any battle Larry Allen ever lost. I don't remember anyone giving him a tough time. There weren't any great battles, because he was superior."

FROM STREETS TO GRIDIRON

The toughest battles for the lineman who helped clear the way for teammate Emmitt Smith to become the NFL's all-time leading rusher came as a child growing up in southern Los Angeles County.

As an infant, Allen contracted meningitis, and doctors gave him 24 hours to live. At age 10, he was stabbed multiple times in the head and shoulder by a 12-year-old neighbor when he stepped into a fight to take up for his little brother, Von. Soon after that, Allen's parents split, leaving his mother, Vera, to care for him and Von alone.

It was so common for the Allens to hear gunfire outside their Compton home that they would roll out of their beds and remain flat on the floor until the shooting stopped. Then they would get back into their beds and go right back to sleep.

"I developed a lot of quickness that way," Allen quipped.

Allen had a propensity for getting into fights. To try to keep her oldest son out of trouble, Vera moved frequently. Allen attended five middle schools and four high schools.

One of those changes in schools came when Allen tried to join a gang. His mother sent him to the rival gang's high school, telling her son, "We'll see how bad you really are." That move kept him out of any gangs.

At 15, Allen and a friend entered the drug-selling business.

"For about two hours," Allen said.

Allen and his friend had no money. Neither did their mothers. They did, however, both own trendy Starter-brand jackets that they gave to a dope dealer in exchange for rock cocaine the two intended to sell.

Recalled Allen, "So we're standing and talking and saying, 'We're going to be rich, we're going to have cars and all this.'"

Then a police car came driving down the street, and Allen and his friend threw aside the rock cocaine and ran. They lost both the cocaine and their jackets, and the two agreed to an immediate end to their drug-selling days.

"I didn't want to be a gang-banger or drug dealer," Allen says. "It wasn't for me. I wanted to do something for myself."

Football became that something.

Allen liked football and watched it on television growing up, but because his family could not afford for him to play in Pop Warner leagues, he was limited to playing pickup games on the streets and in parks.

His grandmother, Berkely Dotson, a hardworking owner of three restaurants, told Allen, "Larry, you need to find out what you're good at and go do it."

Allen joined the football team at Edison High School in Stockton, east of San Francisco, for his junior year and learned that the football field was a good place for him to take out his aggressions. That season marked the first time he had played organized football. For his senior year, he transferred seven miles northwest to Vintage High School in Napa. There, he moved from the defensive line to the offensive line.

Allen's size and strength attracted the attention of NCAA Division I-A programs, but he did not graduate from his high school and was ineligible to play at the NCAA level.

ATTRACTING THE SCOUTS

Craig Rigsbee was preparing for his first season as head coach of Butte College, a community college in the Northern California city of Chico, when four high school seniors were brought to his home as potential football players.

Rigsbee, who had recently been promoted from offensive line coach, did not need to take a second look at Allen. The coach has recounted how Allen was wider than his front door and appeared to weigh close to 360 pounds.

"Okay," Rigsbee thought to himself, "this is exactly what I need."

Rigsbee became more than Allen's coach; he became a father figure, helping Allen secure his GED so he would be eligible to play. Rigsbee also arranged for Allen to have a job on campus for spending money and taught him how to drive. Rigsbee's wife, Karla, showed Allen how to shop for groceries with the money he had received for financial aid. Both helped the player learn how to manage the little money he did have.

Allen received All-American accolades his sophomore season at Butte and again drew plenty of interest from major universities.

Sonoma State line coach Frank Scalercio was among the coaches who had watched him and dreamed of having him anchor his offensive line for the next two years. Scalercio, however, figured there was no chance that his small Division II school would be able to woo Allen.

The first time Scalercio saw Allen play, he had actually gone to that game to watch two other players. But Allen was the player who stood out most by dominating a junior college All-American defensive lineman who wound up playing at USC. Scalercio left the game convinced that Allen would go to a Division I school.

But Allen failed to complete his associate degree at Butte and, again, was ineligible to play in Division I. Rigsbee encouraged him to complete his two-year degree and play at Division II Sacramento State, but Allen opted to return to Compton to live with his father, with whom he had spent little time until that point.

Allen did not enroll in a school, costing him an opportunity to play football that season. Allen reached out to Rigsbee, who remembered Scalercio's interest in him and placed a call on his former lineman's behalf.

Scalercio could not reach Allen by phone, but the possibility of bringing him to Sonoma State warranted extra effort. Scalercio sent one of his players who lived near Los Angeles looking for Allen on local basketball courts. The player found Allen and told him Scalercio wanted to talk to him. The efforts paid off when Allen decided to play for the Cossacks. The decision proved beneficial for Allen, too, who has cited Scalercio as a father figure.

Allen knew that playing in Division II, he would have to be a dominant player to catch the attention of NFL scouts. He accomplished that.

His first season at Sonoma State, he left a lasting impression on a University of California Davis coach. Then-assistant head coach Fred Arp has told the story of how his All-Conference defensive end came to him on the sideline on the Cossacks' first offensive series and suggested the coach change defensive schemes immediately or there was no way the Davis defense could survive Allen.

Years later, one particular play still stood out to Arp. Allen, at 315 pounds, ran over the All-Conference player who had recommended changing defenses, continued downfield and knocked down an All-Conference linebacker, and kept going until he had dispatched of the free safety.

"So on one play he obliterated our three best defensive players," said Arp, who called Allen the best offensive lineman in the history of the Northern California Athletic Conference. "Quick, good body control, great instincts for the game. One of those guys who never says a word, just goes out and does his job."

In a game against Cal State Northridge, his coaches credited Allen with 22 knockdowns.

Sonoma State's highest-profile opponent during Allen's two years there was I-AA Weber State in the 1993 season opener. Although the Cossacks lost 40–28, Scalercio later recalled how Allen had "decimated" the Wildcats' defensive linemen throughout the game.

Allen's awe-inspiring performances were not limited to games.

Lenny Wagner, Sonoma State's linebacker coach while Allen played there, considered Allen an offensive lineman with the speed and aggression of a linebacker. One visual that has remained with Wagner is a play during practice in which Allen sprinted 40 yards downfield to block a defender.

"I'd spend all day teaching these guys how to play linebacker," Wagner said. "Then, in practice, one of them would do everything right, and Larry would come and knock him on his back. They'd say, 'Coach, that doesn't work.' I'd tell them, 'Well, Larry is different. He's going to be in the Hall of Fame one day.'"

Allen was chosen as a Division II first-team All-American. If a conference award can be more impressive than being named an All-American, Allen may have achieved that when the NCAC's coaches selected him the conference's Offensive Player of the Year—an extremely rare award for an offensive lineman.

Those feats earned Allen invitations to participate in two all-star games following his senior season: the Senior Bowl and the East–West Shrine Game. He was the only Division II player in the East–West game, where he displayed his versatility to NFL scouts by playing both right tackle and left tackle.

"You don't see many guys from small schools that do the things he did out there that week," said Larry Lacewell, director of pro and college scouting for the Dallas Cowboys.

VERSATILE, DURABLE, DOMINANT

Allen further impressed scouts when he ran the 40-yard dash in 5.18 seconds at the Indianapolis Combine and later clocked a 4.94. It was a rare display of speed for someone who came in at 6-foot-3 and 325 pounds, and part of the reason Allen projected to an early second-round pick or, perhaps, a late first-round choice.

The Cowboys traded up five spots in the first round, to number 23 overall, to choose Arizona State defensive end Shante Carver with their first pick. Their second and final pick of the draft's first day would come in the second round, the 46th overall pick—a slot they held as compensation for losing quarterback Steve Beuerlein and receiver Kelvin Martin through free agency.

Dallas had just won its second consecutive Super Bowl championship, with three offensive linemen—guard Nate Newton, center Mark Stepnoski, and tackle Erik Williams—making the Pro Bowl. But with free-agent uncertainty along the line, the Cowboys considered trading down and selecting two offensive linemen later in the draft. With Allen available, however, they instead chose to make him the first player ever drafted out of Sonoma State.

Allen celebrated by dashing out of his apartment and jumping into a swimming pool with his clothes on. He signed a four-year, $1.7 million contract with the Cowboys and told his mother he would buy her a house "wherever she wants to buy it."

Allen made his debut in the Cowboys' fifth game the ensuing season, starting at left tackle for an injured Mark Tuinei. He made nine other starts that season, at guard and tackle, to begin a record of longevity at four different positions on the Cowboys' line.

He started all 16 games during the 1995 through 1998 seasons. All four were Pro Bowl campaigns. In 1999, he missed five games because of an injury but still secured a fifth-straight Pro Bowl selection. All total, Allen started 16 games in nine of his 12 seasons with the Cowboys, starting 170 of his 176 games wearing the Cowboys' star. His 10 Pro Bowl selections remain tied with Mel Renfro for most by a Cowboys offensive player and second overall, one behind linebacker Lee Roy Jordan's 11.

Along the way, Allen built a reputation as a mostly quiet player in front of the media. It was not that he was mean or disliked the media; he just preferred not to talk. Instead, he allowed his play on the field to talk for him.

But there was one off-the-field moment that people still talk about with Allen: During the 2001 off-season, with teammates gathered around and cheering him on, he bench-pressed a whopping 700 pounds. In typical Allen fashion, he stood up from the bench, smiled, and laughed, but did not say a word.

"I would have never thought that a guy could naturally lift that type of weight," said Newton, a fellow offensive lineman whose size had earned him the nickname the "Kitchen."

"Absurd," said Cowboys fullback Daryl Johnston, Allen's teammate for six seasons.

With Allen's combination of size, strength, and speed, it is easy to see why he became one of the best—and most-feared—pulling offensive linemen in NFL history.

Hall of Fame offensive lineman Jonathan Ogden of the Baltimore Ravens said, "I saw [defensive linemen] physically develop cramps because they didn't want this guy coming at them."

That was part of Allen's game plan.

"My thought process when I was playing the game was I wanted to make the guy quit," he said. "Tap out."

Allen succeeded to the point that the phrases "Allen-itis" and the "Larry Allen flu" were created to describe the conditions that caused players to tap out against Allen.

"There was no one that he couldn't handle, or no situation that he couldn't handle," Madden said. "He was big and strong and fast. When you say strong, he may have been the strongest guy who ever played."

A "LONG" FAREWELL

Allen's run with Dallas ended when he was cut for salary cap reasons following the 2005 season, a season in which, at age 34, he was one of two Cowboys to play every snap and yielded a mere 2.5 sacks. At the time, owner Jerry Jones called the decision to cut Allen a "tough one for me personally."

A week later, Jones still struggled with the move.

"It hurts a lot," Jones said. "I was so proud of him as a Dallas Cowboy, as much as any player we've ever had. I have so much respect for him. You hear about Bob Lilly as the best left defensive tackle ever to play the game. I'm convinced that Larry can get some of that kind of recognition as well."

Allen left as the last player to have won a Super Bowl ring with the Cowboys. He returned to California, signing with the San Francisco 49ers. He played two more years there, earning his 11th and final Pro Bowl invitation in the 2006 season. In 2007, he started all 16 games and was named a Pro Bowl alternate.

Allen walked away from the NFL in the summer of 2008, but not before signing a ceremonial contract with Jones so he could retire as a Cowboy.

During his days with the Cowboys, Allen would look up into the Texas Stadium seats and read the names in the Ring of Honor. He joined that select group in 2011, at the new Cowboys Stadium. Jones introduced Allen that day, telling the crowd, "No one has ever said less as a player than Larry." Allen then took the microphone and gave an acceptance speech that lasted 13 seconds.

There was not much to be said, either, when Allen's name first came up for induction into the Pro Football Hall of Fame in 2013. Discussions of finalists' merits can be drawn out and intense. But when the selection committee considered Allen's case in his first year of eligibility, his ticket to Canton had been punched after only nine minutes—only the 11th linemen ever voted in on the first ballot.

Far removed from the days of jumping into an apartment complex swimming pool to celebrate being drafted, Allen responded to the news that he would be entering the Hall by breaking down and crying.

His mother would not be there for his induction—she had died a year earlier, at age 59. She had been the one who had steered him off the path that could have led him to prison or death. But his father, Larry Sr., had reentered his life and said he would be there to see his son inducted.

Of course, speculation was heavy on how long Allen's acceptance speech would be. His oldest daughter, Jayla, helped him write a speech that he anticipated would take him seven to 10 minutes to deliver. In time and in content, the quiet giant's speech exceeded expectations.

Wearing sunglasses that hid tears, Allen spoke for an emotion-filled 16 minutes. As he neared his conclusion, he summed things up by saying, "My goal was simple: to earn a seven-letter word called 'respect.' The respect of my teammates, opponents, and the NFL. Today, my mission is complete. I also played hard, whistle to whistle, to make my opponents submit. And today, I'm submitting to you."

Well said.

CAREER HIGHLIGHTS

Selected to play in 10 Pro Bowls, more than any other offensive player in Cowboys franchise history (tied with Mel Renfro for second-most Pro Bowl selections, one behind Lee Roy Jordan).

Named All-Pro seven times—six times at guard (1995–1997, 1999–2001) and once at tackle (1998).

Selected to the NFL's All-Decade Teams for the 1990s and 2000s.

Third player in NFL history to earn a Pro Bowl berth at multiple positions on the offensive line (1998). Finished his career with 11 Pro Bowl selections.

Played on the Super Bowl XXX championship team.

Played on teams that won two NFC championships and four NFC East titles.

Played every offensive line position except center.

Started all 16 regular-season games in nine of his 12 seasons in Dallas and his final 48 games with the Cowboys.

Blocked for eight of Emmitt Smith's 11 1,000-yard rushing seasons.

Started as offensive lineman when Emmitt Smith set the Cowboys' single-season rushing record in 1996, and when Frank Gore broke the San Francisco 49ers' single-season rushing record in 2006.

FIVE COWBOYS MEMORIES

1. October 9, 1994

Larry Allen made his first NFL start in the fifth game of his rookie season, a 38–3 defeat of the Arizona Cardinals. He started at left tackle for Mark Tuinei, who was suffering from back spasms. The Cowboys had Tuinei in uniform and ready to go into the game in case Allen struggled. Tuinei was not needed. Primarily going up against veteran Clyde Simmons, Allen did not permit a sack. He admitted to being a "little shaky" at the start of the game, especially when he took the field with the likes of Nate Newton, Erik Williams, Mark Stepnoski, Troy Aikman, Emmitt Smith, and Michael Irvin. "I almost puked right then and there in the middle of the huddle because I was so nervous," Allen said. He was rewarded for his performance with a game ball. Afterward, he said he had plenty of motivation in his first NFL start. "I want to prove," he said, "that somebody from a tiny school can make it in the NFL."

2. December 10, 2000

The Cowboys were a meager 4–9 late in the season, with the 7–6 Washington Redskins coming into Texas Stadium desperate for a win to remain in the playoff race six days after firing head coach Norv Turner. Allen and his offensive line mates cleared the way for the Cowboys to rush for 242 yards and three touchdowns on 43 carries, with Emmitt Smith gaining 150 yards, officially ending the Redskins' postseason hopes. Allen received a game ball, which he donated to the Pro Football Hall of Fame after being voted in.

3. January 15, 1995

Even though the Cowboys lost the NFC Championship Game at San Francisco's Candlestick Park, Allen's presence on the field showed his value to the Cowboys. He played most of the game on a sprained ankle, with the Cowboys deciding that a one-legged Allen was better than a fully healthy backup. The Cowboys lost to the 49ers, 38–28, in the teams' third consecutive meeting with a Super Bowl berth on the line.

4. December 19, 1994

For a player who paved the way for many touchdowns during his career, Allen became a hit for possibly saving a touchdown in a 24–16 Monday night victory at the New Orleans Saints. With the Cowboys leading 7–0 in the first quarter, Saint linebacker Darion Conner picked off a deflected pass at his team's 29-yard line and hit the left sideline for what had the looks of a game-tying touchdown return. But the 325-pound rookie, with a good angle on Conner, chased down the speedy linebacker for a diving tackle at the Cowboys' 15, causing both Allen and Conner to receive congratulatory helmet slaps from teammates as they made their way back to their respective sidelines. The Saints had to settle for a field goal on the possession. "This guy's got a rocket booster strapped to his back!" shocked ABC commentator Dan Dierdorf exclaimed as he watched the replay.

5. January 28, 1996

To cap his second season, Allen played in his only Super Bowl, a 27–17 defeat of the Pittsburgh Steelers, culminating a season in which he had started all 16 games and earned his first Pro Bowl selection. When he left Dallas after the 2005 season, he was the lone remaining Cowboy who had participated in Super Bowl XXX. After he retired, Allen was asked what he remembered most from the game. He said, "It was just winning the Super Bowl in my second season, and most guys don't even get one ring. That was pretty special."

Statistics

Season	Team	Games	Starts
1994	Dallas	16	10
1995	Dallas	16	16
1996	Dallas	16	16
1997	Dallas	16	16
1998	Dallas	16	16
1999	Dallas	11	11
2000	Dallas	16	16
2001	Dallas	16	16
2002	Dallas	5	5
2003	Dallas	16	16
2004	Dallas	16	16
2005	Dallas	16	16
2006	San Francisco	11	11
2007	San Francisco	16	16
Totals		203	197

· 3 ·

Tony Dorsett

"TD," for Sure

Anthony Drew Dorsett Sr.
Class: 1994 (Bud Grant, Jimmy Johnson, Leroy Kelly, Jackie Smith, Randy White)
Seasons with Cowboys: 1977–1987
Other NFL teams: Denver Broncos (1988)
Positions: Running back
College: Pittsburgh

*W*hen Tony Dorsett learned in 1994 that he had been voted into the Pro Football Hall of Fame, it did not take him long to determine who he wanted to introduce him on the day he was inducted.

"I suppose I thought about it for a minute, maybe two," Dorsett said. "Could there be anyone but Coach Landry for that occasion?"

Seven years earlier, Tom Landry might not have seemed to be that choice when he reduced Dorsett's playing time, leading the Cowboys' then-all-time leading rusher to request a trade from the only NFL franchise for which he had played. And even back in Dorsett's rookie season—long before his name would be mentioned as a Hall of Fame candidate—the running back had not minded questioning why Landry had not inserted him as a starter.

But in the end, given time to reflect on a 12-year career that saw Dorsett leave the game in the second spot on the NFL's list of all-time leading rushers, Landry was the obvious pick to deliver his induction speech.

23

"He's the reason I had the career I had," Dorsett explained. "At times, I criticized him because he didn't use me more. It did prolong my career, and I made the Hall of Fame. This is the way I'd like to thank him."

SIZE QUESTIONED

When the Cowboys drafted Dorsett out of the University of Pittsburgh in the first round of the 1977 draft, scouts questioned whether his 5-foot-11, 192-pound frame would prevent him from enjoying the success he had in college during an extended period of time in the NFL. Dorsett had already spent most of his lifetime dealing with those types of questions.

As a kid in Aliquippa, Pennsylvania, he and a friend placed rocks in their pockets hoping to reach the minimum weight required to play in a local youth league. The rocks were not enough, but that might have been the last time Dorsett's size stopped him.

"When I did start playing football, I was scared," he once recalled. "I remember the first time I ever touched the football. I was so afraid of getting hit, I took off like a little rabbit. Ended up running 75 yards for a touchdown."

Dorsett weighed 147 pounds as a sophomore starting at monster (a linebacker–defensive back hybrid position) for the Hopewell High School Vikings' defense. Before his junior year, he was promoted to tailback, ahead of the returning starter. On the Vikings' first offensive play of the season, Dorsett caught a short pass and dashed 75 yards to the end zone. He wound up scoring all three touchdowns in his team's season-opening 21–7 victory.

In his two seasons as tailback, Dorsett rushed for 2,500 yards, scored 42 touchdowns, and was selected All-State both years. He was named a *Parade* All-American following his senior season in 1972, during which he ran for 1,238 yards and 23 touchdowns for a 9–1 team.

"To be honest with you—and I wouldn't lie to you—I knew he was good," Hopewell head coach Butch Ross once told a sportswriter. "But every year he progressed, got better and better, got bigger and stronger and better. He had to overcome his stature. That aggressiveness is probably what prevailed over anything else."

His high school success drew the likes of Ohio State coach Woody Hayes and Arizona State coach Frank Kush to western Pennsylvania. Dorsett had plenty of colleges to choose from, but Pittsburgh won out, thanks largely to the nonstop efforts of head coach Johnny Majors and assistant coach Jackie Sherrill, even though they did not see Dorsett play for his high school team because Majors had not yet been hired at Pitt. Within hours of getting the job, he and Sherrill began recruiting Dorsett. Sherrill spent so much time on the

Hopewell campus that the school's principal jokingly gave him a form handed to substitute teachers. It worked—Pitt landed its prized recruit.

Majors first watched Dorsett in person at the summertime Big 33 all-star game, featuring the top high school players from Pennsylvania against a team of all-stars from Ohio. On one carry, a jaw-dropping move confirmed recruiting Dorsett was worth the effort.

"This is going to sound corny," Majors recalled, "but I went back to my hotel room and closed the door, and I screamed, 'Hallelujah, we've got a tailback!' I was just like a kid."

But, again, there were those who said Dorsett was too small to be a featured major college running back.

BIG THINGS AT PITT

Majors had a saying that resonated with Dorsett: "The little things make big things happen." Dorsett weighed 155 pounds his freshman season, but he immediately made big things happen.

In the Panthers' first scrimmage, he broke off an 80-yard touchdown run against his team's top defensive unit. Then, in the season opener against Georgia, with his smooth and explosive running style on full display publicly for the first time, he rushed for 100 yards on his way to a season total of 1,686 yards—the most ever by a college freshman and the first 1,000-yard season in Pitt history. He helped the Panthers improve from a 1–10 record the season before to a 6–4–1 mark and a Fiesta Bowl berth. He also became the first freshman consensus All-American since 1944.

"When you really talk about great running backs, you talk about how far that running back can take it," Sherrill said, adding,

> A lot of running backs get yardage, but the longest run they have is 15 or 20 yards. A great running back will put the ball in the end zone. Certainly, Tony separated himself from everyone on that. That's the thing that made him such a great player. The defensive team knew that, and yet they still couldn't stop him.

In the fourth game of his sophomore season, Dorsett broke Pitt's career rushing yardage record on his way to a 1,004-yard campaign. As a junior, he ran for 1,544 yards during the regular season, including a 303-yard game against Notre Dame.

Dorsett capped his college career by rushing for 2,150 yards and 22 touchdowns, as the Panthers finished the 1976 regular season with an 11–0 record. The university did not wait until he had finished his collegiate career before retiring his number 33, doing so at halftime of his final regular-season game.

Before the Panthers played for the national championship in the Sugar Bowl, Dorsett became the first Pitt player to win the Heisman Trophy. He received 701 of 842 first-place votes and easily outdistanced runner-up Ricky Bell for college football's top honor.

He put an exclamation point on his career with a Sugar Bowl–record 202 yards rushing in a 27–3 defeat of fifth-ranked Georgia, wrapping up the Panthers' first national championship. With 6,082 rushing yards in four years at Pitt—not including bowl games—Dorsett claimed the title of the NCAA Division I-A all-time leading rusher. His record stood for 22 years. He also was the first major college back to rush for at least 1,000 yards four times and gain at least 1,500 yards three times.

"He never ceased to amaze me," Majors said. "Everything he did was dramatic, without trying to be showy. He was the greatest four-year [college] player I've ever seen, and the greatest four-year player I've ever coached."

IMPRESSIVE ROOKIE SEASON

The Dallas Cowboys, coming off a NFC championship and their 10th post-season appearance in 11 years, coveted Dorsett so much that they traded up to the second spot in the first round to take him.

Second-year franchises Tampa Bay and Seattle held the top two picks. The Buccaneers made known their desire to draft USC running back Ricky Bell. The Cowboys traded a first-round pick and three second-round picks to the Seahawks in exchange for the opportunity to draft Dorsett. The four players Seattle chose in those spots were Steve August, Tom Lynch, Pete Cronan, and Terry Beeson. That trade remains one of the most one-sided deals in NFL Draft history.

Cowboys coach Tom Landry was a patient man. During Dorsett's rookie season, he was more patient than Tony liked, as he decided to bring his new player along slowly.

Dorsett was charged with simple assault stemming from a fight with a bartender about six weeks after the draft, although the charges were later dropped. He missed curfew during training camp. He was set back by a minor knee sprain in a scrimmage. And there were concerns about his attitude.

Dorsett received four carries in the season opener, then seven and 10 carries in the next two games, respectively. In week 4, he ripped off a 77-yard touchdown run and finished with 141 yards on 14 carries in a 30–24 win at St. Louis, giving the Cowboys a 4–0 start to the season.

It wasn't until the 10th game, however, that Landry named Dorsett as his full-time starter. Two weeks later, he rushed for 206 yards and two touchdowns on 23 carries in a 24–14 defeat of the Philadelphia Eagles.

Adding Dorsett to an offense already blessed with Roger Staubach and Drew Pearson enabled the Cowboys to repeat as NFC East champs, with a 12–2 record. Despite starting only four games, Dorsett was voted the NFL Offensive Rookie of the Year after finishing the regular season with 1,007 rushing yards; he remains the only Cowboys rookie to rush for 1,000 yards—and a franchise-rookie record 12 touchdowns.

During that postseason, Dorsett rushed for four touchdowns, including the Cowboys' first score in their 27–10 victory against the Denver Broncos in Super Bowl XII, which earned the franchise its second Lombardi Trophy.

"I think during the years he was with us, there was only one player more important, and that was Roger Staubach," team president and general manager Tex Schramm said. "He was one of the main factors in reenergizing us and getting us back to winning the second Super Bowl. Dorsett provided us an added dimension with his speed and ball-carrying ability."

"When he came to us," Staubach said, "we hadn't had a strong running attack for about three years."

Dorsett took care of that.

END OF RUN IN DALLAS

Although the Cowboys would play in, and lose, only one more Super Bowl during Dorsett's 11 seasons in Dallas, he remained the big-play threat reflected in his nickname, "TD."

Dorsett rushed for at least 1,000 yards the next four years, giving him 11 consecutive 1,000-yard seasons dating to high school. The streak was stopped by the player's strike that shortened the 1982 regular season to nine games. He rushed for 745 yards that season. Oddly, that was the only season that Dorsett led the NFC in rushing yardage. That also was the season during which Dorsett's signature moment occurred.

In the final game of the regular season—actually played in January 1983—Dorsett turned in the first 99-yard touchdown run in NFL history.

Following the strike season, he topped 1,000 yards each year from 1983 to 1985, rushing for more than 1,300 yards twice. In '83, he earned the last of his four Pro Bowl appearnces.

The 1985 season turned out to be his last great year. Despite financial problems that led to the Internal Revenue Service seizing two of his homes and his decision to hold out of training camp until his contract was renegotiated, Dorsett gained 1,307 yards on the ground and accounted for 1,756 yards of total offense and 10 touchdowns on a 10–6 team that tied for the NFC East title but was shut out, 20–0, by the Los Angeles Rams in its first playoff game.

The Cowboys had drafted New Jersey Generals running back Herschel Walker in the 1985 draft, speculating that the United States Football League would shut down. Then, before the 1986 season, they signed Walker to a larger contract than Dorsett's.

The thought of Dorsett and Walker in the same backfield conjured the nickname the "Dream Backfield." But the pairing never lived up to the hype, and the Cowboys began a five-year absence from the playoffs that was the franchise's longest streak since missing the postseason in its first six years of existence.

Dorsett and Walker shared the workload in their first season together, 1986. Dorsett, who battled through knee and ankle injuries, got the ball 184 times for 748 yards, while Walker carried 151 times for 737 yards. The Cowboys finished 7–9 and in third place in the NFC East.

The next season, Dorsett took a backseat to Walker, who led the NFL with 1,606 yards from scrimmage (891 rushing, 715 receiving). Dorsett started only six games and had career lows in every major offensive category, including rushing for 456 yards and one touchdown. In four games from week 9 to week 13—missing one game with a shoulder injury—he totaled just 23 carries for 97 yards.

In his final game as a Cowboy, a win against the St. Louis Cardinals for a final record of 7–8, Dorsett did not play because of bad reactions to medicine he was given for back spasms. He had already made public a month earlier his desire to be traded, and not playing in the 1987 finale seemed like it would be an inglorious end to a glorious Cowboys career.

The Cowboys' all-time leading rusher, with 12,036 yards, got his wish the following June, when he was traded to the Denver Broncos for a conditional fifth-round draft pick, which the Cowboys used the next year to select defensive tackle Jeff Roth, who did not make the team.

Landry would later claim that Dorsett, Ed "Too Tall" Jones, and Randy White were three of the most significant players of that era for the Cowboys.

"Without those three players, we wouldn't have been at the high level we were in the late '70s and early '80s," Landry said. "I don't think any player we drafted came to our team with more of a celebrity type of feeling than Tony, and his presence on the field improved the confidence of the team."

CONTENT IN RETIREMENT

Dorsett arrived in Denver 34 years old but determined he could still carry the load in the NFL. He rushed for more than 100 yards in two of his first four games but played sparingly the second half of the season. He still led the Broncos with 703 yards and five touchdowns rushing. During a workout the following summer, he suffered a knee injury that proved to be a career-ender.

Dorsett retired with 12,739 career rushing yards, second only to Walter Payton, and 3,554 yards receiving and 90 touchdowns.

"Very few players have ever had the skill and balance to change direction without a loss of speed," said Dan Reeves, who not only was Dorsett's head coach in Denver but also a Cowboys assistant for his first four years in the NFL. "Only O. J. Simpson, Gale Sayers, and a couple of others, and even Sayers cut kind of jerky. Tony does it so smoothly."

It was no surprise when he was voted into the Hall of Fame in 1994, the first year his name appeared on the ballot, alongside Cowboys teammate Randy White. He was the second Cowboys offensive player voted in, following Staubach.

Dorsett remained convinced that he had not been used enough during his career. When asked about his career rushing yardage, he replied, "If I would have gotten the ball more, I would have gotten more than that."

But, in hindsight, he could see that Landry had been doing what he thought best to make sure that Dorsett enjoyed a long, effective career.

"I'm retired and content," he said, continuing,

> I'm not as moody and irritable as when I was a player. I know who I am and what my capabilities are. But with 25 carries per game, I would have retired as the all-time leading rusher. There's no question in my mind. I think Walter Payton carried the football a thousand times more.
>
> I was screaming for it when I first came to the Cowboys: "More carries. More carries." But Coach Landry thought that because of my physical size, my career would have been short-lived if that had happened. Maybe he was right. I understand the logic. But it's hard for me to accept.

Said Landry,

> I wanted to protect him more than anything else because I saw so many running backs of great ability, and by five years they were beat up and they didn't have a career like Tony had. We started him out so he would have a long career. But Tony had a lot of pride, and that's the thing he was concerned about—he wanted to be the best.

And it was that "man in the hat," as Dorsett called Landry in his acceptance speech, who was the last of his coaches he expressed appreciation for the day he entered the Hall.

"He taught me the value of discipline, the value of setting goals, and methods on how to accomplish those goals," Dorsett said. "These are things you take with you long after you leave the athletic arena. Coach Landry and I also had a lot of, well, should I say, one-on-one conversations. Some football related, some not. But I guess I needed most of those talks, huh Coach?"

CAREER HIGHLIGHTS

Retired as the NFL's second-leading all-time rusher (12,739 yards), behind Walter Payton.

Caught 398 passes for 3,554 yards, for a total of 16,293 combined yards (also second-best all-time when he retired) and 91 total touchdowns.

Played in four Pro Bowls, five NFC Championship Games, and two Super Bowls.

Named NFL Offensive Rookie of the Year in 1977, when he became the only Cowboys rookie to rush for 1,000 yards (1,007).

Rushed for at least 1,000 yards in eight of his first nine NFL seasons.

Rushed for 1,383 yards and totaled 1,786 yards from scrimmage in 17 postseason games.

Rushed for at least 100 yards in 43 games with the Cowboys, with the team owning a 39–4 record in those games.

Set a NFL record that cannot be broken with a 99-yard touchdown run in January 1983.

Became the Cowboys' all-time leading rusher in the next-to-last game of his fifth season; his 12,036 yards remained a Cowboys record until broken by Emmitt Smith in 1998.

Rushed for a then-franchise record 1,646 yards in 1981.

Compiled an average of 4.37 career yards per carry, which still stands as the best by a Cowboy.

Led the Cowboys in rushing yards 10 consecutive seasons (1977–1986).

Ran for 3,432 receiving yards, the most by a Cowboys running back.

Awarded the Heisman Trophy in 1976, when he led the University of Pittsburgh to the national championship.

Named an All-American four times at Pitt, where he owns the career rushing record, with 6,526 yards.

Became the first running back from a major college with four 1,000-yard rushing seasons.

Had his number 33 retired at Pitt, the first player to have his number
retired by the university.

First player to win the Heisman Trophy, win a college national championship, win a Super Bowl, and be enshrined in both the College
Football Hall of Fame and the Pro Football Hall of Fame.

FIVE COWBOYS MEMORIES

1. January 3, 1983

In the final game of the regular season, and on *Monday Night Football* no less,
Tony Dorsett set a NFL record with a 99-yard touchdown run against the
Minnesota Vikings. A kickoff bobbled out of bounds by Tommy Newsome
stuck the Cowboys with the ball inside their one-yard line. The Cowboys had
only 10 players on the field because Dorsett had mistakenly waived fullback
Ron Springs out of the huddle and off the field. "I actually thought I was going to get the snot knocked out of my nose," Dorsett recalled. "When you're
backed up that far, the defense knows what you're going to do: run straight
ahead and get some breathing room." Dorsett took a handoff from Danny
White, broke through an opening in the middle of the line, cut right, and
broke two arm tackles inside the Cowboys' 15-yard line as he headed toward
the sideline. "Ninety-nine yards and a half," color analyst Don Meredith said
as Dorsett neared midfield. Dorsett picked up a couple of downfield blocks
from receiver Drew Pearson, broke through one final would-be tackle at the
20, and raced into the end zone and a permanent spot in the NFL record
book.

2. December 4, 1977

Dorsett made his first home start with Dallas memorable by rushing for a club-
record 206 yards on 23 carries and scoring two touchdowns in a 24–14 victory
against the Philadelphia Eagles. He became the first Cowboy to rush for 200
yards in a game and only the third rookie in NFL history to reach that mark.
After scoring on a one-yard run for the Cowboys' first points, he scored the
game-clinching touchdown in the fourth quarter on an 84-yard run that was
the longest in franchise history. Dorsett had entered the game with 659 yards
rushing for the season, and his performance put him in range of 1,000 with
two games remaining. He wound up reaching that mark, finishing his rookie
season with 1,007 yards.

3. December 28, 1980

Through the first seven playoff games of his career, Dorsett had not carried the ball 20 times in a game. That was not good enough for the man who always wanted the ball more. He got his wish in a wild-card game against the Los Angeles Rams, rushing 22 times for 160 yards, a franchise postseason record. He also caught three passes for 28 yards and scored a touchdown both rushing and receiving, avenging an embarrassing 24-point loss to the Rams two weeks earlier. Dorsett's first touchdown came on a 12-yard run that tied the score at 13–13 with 6:16 to play before halftime. In the third quarter, his 10-yard pass from Danny White gave the Cowboys a 20–13 lead and set Dallas on its way to victory. "In his earlier years here, I was concerned about his size, and I tried to make sure he could last the season and make his 1,000 yards," Landry said after the game. "But recently in the stretch drive, I've been using him much more, and he has responded to it. You couldn't have asked for a better running back today." Indeed, statistically, the Cowboys had not had a better running back in a playoff game.

4. September 4, 1978

The Cowboys hosted the Baltimore Colts for the 1978 season opener as the defending Super Bowl champions. Dorsett was coming off his Rookie of the Year debut season. Both backed up their previous season's performances in routing the Colts, 38–0, at Texas Stadium. Dorsett became the first Cowboy to gain 100 yards rushing and receiving in the same game, carrying the ball 15 times for 147 yards and catching three passes for 107 yards and a touchdown, and continuing the big-play ability he had displayed as a rookie. His touchdown came on a 91-yard pass play, on a Staubach pass that was tipped at the line of scrimmage. Dorsett hauled in the pass that was not intended for him, dodged three tacklers, and sprinted to the end zone. Although that was his lone touchdown of the day, he did break off runs of 46 and 78 yards.

5. October 13, 1985

Dorsett became the sixth player in NFL history to rush for 10,000 career yards against the team he grew up rooting for, the Pittsburgh Steelers. He entered the game 31 yards shy of the milestone and was held to three yards in the first half. But as part of a big second half, he rushed 19 yards on a sweep around the left end with 6:16 remaining in the third quarter to join Walter Payton, Jim Brown, Franco Harris, O. J. Simpson, and John Riggins in the 10,000-yard club. Despite the slow start, Dorsett finished with 113 yards on 21 carries and 82 receiving yards on four catches. He scored a touchdown rushing and

Statistics

Regular Season

Season	Team	G	Rushing				Receiving			
			No.	Yds	Avg	TD	No.	Yds	Avg	TD
1977	Dallas	14	208	1,007	4.8	12	29	273	9.4	1
1978	Dallas	16	290	1,325	4.6	7	37	378	10.2	2
1979	Dallas	14	250	1,107	4.4	6	45	375	8.3	1
1980	Dallas	15	278	1,185	4.3	11	34	263	7.7	0
1981	Dallas	16	342	1,646	4.8	4	32	325	10.2	2
1982	Dallas	9	177	745	4.2	5	24	179	7.5	0
1983	Dallas	16	289	1,321	4.6	8	40	287	7.2	1
1984	Dallas	16	302	1,189	3.9	6	51	459	9.0	1
1985	Dallas	16	305	1,307	4.3	7	46	449	9.8	3
1986	Dallas	13	184	748	4.1	5	25	267	10.7	1
1987	Dallas	12	130	456	3.5	1	19	177	9.3	1
1988	Denver	16	181	703	3.9	5	16	122	7.6	0
Totals		173	2,936	12,739	4.3	77	398	3,554	8.9	13

Postseason

Season	Team	G	Rushing				Receiving			
			No.	Yds	Avg	TD	No.	Yds	Avg	TD
1977	Dallas	3	51	222	4.4	4	4	48	12.0	0
1978	Dallas	3	47	262	5.6	1	8	68	8.5	0
1979	Dallas	1	19	87	4.6	0	0	0	0.0	0
1980	Dallas	3	45	252	5.6	2	11	95	8.6	1
1981	Dallas	2	38	177	4.7	2	4	48	12.0	0
1982	Dallas	3	68	266	3.9	0	7	52	7.4	0
1983	Dallas	1	17	59	3.5	0	4	12	3.0	0
1985	Dallas	1	17	58	3.4	0	8	80	10.0	0
Totals		17	302	1,383	4.6	9	46	403	8.8	1

Others—Passing: 2–8–1, 41 yards, 1 TD.

receiving. It was his touchdown on the ground—a 35-yard run on his last carry of the day—that sealed the Cowboys' 27–13 victory, improving their record to 5–1 and giving them an early two-game lead in the NFC East. The win was Dorsett's first against the Steelers, who had been 3–0 against Dallas with Dorsett in the backfield. "I had my doubts early in the first half, but anything good is worth waiting for," Dorsett said. "This is no doubt one of the highlights of my career."

Charles Haley

Five Rings

Charles Lewis Haley
Class: 2015 (Jerome Bettis, Tim Brown, Bill Polian, Junior Seau, Will Shields, Mick Tingelhoff, Ron Wolf)
Seasons with Cowboys: 1992–1996
Other NFL teams: San Francisco 49ers (1986–1991, 1999)
Positions: Defensive end/linebacker
College: James Madison

Charles Haley once said of champions, "They respect champions."

No player in the history of the NFL has been a Super Bowl champion more times than Haley, with his five rings, a record that still stands. During Haley's playing days, he recognized that his pursuit of greatness would bring conflict—not only with opponents, but also teammates and his own coaches.

"I had one standard when I stepped on the field: I kick butt, and I never turn that standard down. I'm going to step on toes. I'm going to step on feet. I will step on your neck if I have to."

His justification, as he looked back on his Hall of Fame career?

"I was just trying to win," he said.

During his 13 seasons on the field, at times he seemed more successful at winning championships than winning friends.

Consider the words of Tony Casillas, Haley's teammate for his first two seasons with the Dallas Cowboys:

> He was not a nice guy. He was hard on people. I think some people took that personally. There were times he pushed the envelope too much. And

you were like, "Charles, I had enough of your [butt] today." And he would keep poking you and keep poking you. I would be the first to tell you there were a lot of guys who didn't like him.

But then also consider the final words of Casillas to the reporter that day: "But everybody respected him."

Only after Haley's career had ended was the reason for his often mercurial personality discovered, when he was diagnosed with bipolar disorder. Cause determined, he set out in a new direction that led him to work on that likability problem and seek to mentor kids and young NFL players.

Haley's success in coming full circle was on display when he was inducted into the Hall of Fame in August 2015. Although he entered the Hall as a Cowboy—the franchise with which he won three of his five Super Bowl rings—he chose Eddie DeBartolo Jr. to introduce him. DeBartolo owned the San Francisco 49ers when they drafted Haley in 1986, and when the organization grew tired of Haley's disruptive ways, they traded him to Dallas in 1992.

Said DeBartolo of Haley, a few weeks before the defensive end's enshrinement, "I think his great legacy—besides being a Hall of Famer and great, great football player—is what he's going to do with the rest of his life in helping kids. That legacy probably is more important than the legacy that he aspired to in football."

HONORING HIS COMMITMENT

Haley either led the 49ers or shared the team lead in sacks his first six seasons with the franchise, averaging 10.6 per season and recording a career-high 16 in 1990, when he was named the NFC Defensive Player of the Year.

In watching Haley play at James Madison University (JMU), 49ers scouts drew comparisons to Fred Dean, a defensive end who, at the time, was putting the wraps on a Hall of Fame career in San Francisco.

"I don't want to put that burden on him," then-49ers defensive coordinator George Seifert said of Haley. "Fred Deans don't come around very often."

Nor, at that time, did future draft picks come through James Madison very often.

Haley signed with the Dukes out of William Campbell High School near Lynchburg, Virginia. Haley, who also was an All-District basketball player in high school, started three years for the William Campbell football team, earning All-District awards at linebacker and tight end, plus being selected All-Region on defense.

Then-JMU assistant coach Danny Wilmer recruited Haley. At the first game he watched Haley play, during Haley's senior season of 1981, Wilmer took note of two things: 1) Haley looked like a player who could make it to the NFL; 2) big-name programs were not in attendance.

James Madison, a NCAA Division I-AA program, received a commitment from Haley before the larger schools began pursuing him. Haley later received offers from better-known programs, but he stuck with his commitment to the Dukes.

During Haley's first practice at James Madison, it was apparent to coaches that he was ready to start as a freshman.

"We had high expectations for him coming in," head coach Challace McMillin said. "And after that first practice, I told our assistant coaches there was no doubt he was going to start and would be the best defensive player that we had had."

The Dukes had put together an 11–20 record the previous three seasons. They improved to 8–3 and were ranked nationally Haley's freshman year. Playing defensive end and outside linebacker, Haley was second on the team with 85 tackles, and he recorded five sacks.

Haley moved to inside linebacker during his sophomore season, where he led the Dukes with 143 tackles and sacked the quarterback four times. As a junior, he had a team-high 147 tackles, with three sacks, and received Associated Press All-America honorable mention recognition.

Following that season, a 49ers scout timed Haley at 4.55 seconds in the 40-yard dash—.04 faster than a wide receiver the team was seriously scouting. That receiver—John Taylor of Delaware State—and Haley would win two Super Bowls as 49ers teammates.

A new coaching staff moved Haley to outside linebacker, and he capped his college career with 131 tackles, 5 sacks, and 3 blocked kicks his senior season, as the Dukes finished the season with the 10th-ranked defense in I-AA. Haley was chosen as a first-team All-American.

"He was a great leader and a great example by what he did," said McMillin, who coached Haley for three seasons. "He was a very dedicated athlete who accepted challenges and responsibilities, and he was extremely hardworking. You could count on him to go really hard. He encouraged his teammates on and off the field."

In late April 1986, San Francisco made Haley the first James Madison player to be selected in the regular NFL Draft, taking him with the 96th pick. The 49ers offered him a $60,000 signing bonus.

"Boy," his mother told him, "there's nowhere for you to stay around this house, so you better make it."

TWO RINGS WITH SAN FRANCISCO

As in college, Haley did not need much to time to "make it" with San Francisco. But first, he had an encounter with St. Louis Rams offensive tackle Jackie Slater, who was in the 11th season of a 20-year Hall of Fame career. Haley attempted to bull-rush Slater, and the veteran lineman head-butted the rookie to the ground.

"He helped me reevaluate whether I wanted to be a football player or not," Haley said. "I went to the end of the bench, put my head in my hands, and I said, 'Okay, God, do I really want to do this?' I had never been hit like that before. But God told me to pull my head out of my butt, and let's go."

Haley bounced back from that experience to lead all rookies in the league with 12 sacks and was selected to the All-Rookie team. His second season, he led the 49ers with 6.5 sacks, despite starting only two games.

He became a full-time starter in 1988, and again led the team in sacks, with 11.5, and made his first of five Pro Bowls. With Haley arguably the defense's best player, the 49ers reached the postseason for the sixth consecutive year and won the Super Bowl for the third time in franchise history. The following year, Haley's 10.5 sacks tied for the team lead, and San Francisco went 14–2 in the regular season, en route to its second consecutive Super Bowl victory.

The 1990 season might have been Haley at his finest, when he recorded a career-high 16 sacks and was named the conference's top defensive player. The Niners won the NFC West again, with another 14–2 record, but lost 15–13 to the New York Giants in the NFC Championship Game.

San Francisco finished the 1991 regular season with a 10–6 mark, but they failed to make the postseason for the first time since 1982. By that point, Haley had begun to wear out his welcome in the Bay Area.

Among Haley's reported incidents were multiple fights with teammates, exposing himself to a female reporter, publicly criticizing Seifert (who had become head coach), and—following a loss to the Oakland Raiders—blaming quarterback Steve Young for the defeat and going ballistic to the point that former teammate Ronnie Lott had to be summonsed from the Raider locker room to settle him down.

On numerous occasions, Haley had demanded to be traded out of San Francisco, and when he got into another fight with a teammate during the 1992 preseason, the 49ers were ready to oblige.

Meanwhile, Jimmy Johnson's Dallas Cowboys were in need of a pass-rushing defensive end. The Cowboys had ranked 26th in sacks the previous season, with 23, and Johnson had told his team following its 38–6, second-round playoff loss at the Detroit Lions—during which Dallas had been torched for 337 passing yards—that he would make sure the pass-rush deficiencies would be addressed during the off-season.

Haley piqued the Cowboys' interest, and Johnson asked some of his players to call 49ers players and gather more information about him.

Johnson recalled,

> To a man, and of course everybody knew he was an outstanding player, but everybody said he had a passion for the game. He was smart. And he was an extremely hard worker. Regardless of his problems, I knew that if he was smart and would work hard and he had a passion for the game, that I could deal with him.

While Cowboys players were working their sources, owner Jerry Jones called 49ers general manager Carmen Policy to ask what it would take to acquire Haley.

"I was keenly aware that Charles had issues in San Francisco," Jones later said. "Most were."

The Cowboys decided to pull the trigger, sending the 49ers a second-round draft pick in 1993 and a third-rounder in 1994 for a 28-year-old, three-time Pro Bowler who was the NFC's active leader in sacks.

"I'd call it an attitude problem," Policy told reporters when asked after the trade to describe the problem with Haley. "Dallas is getting a good player. But sometimes his personality was so divergent from the team that he became a distraction. Let's just say it's in our best interest to have him play elsewhere."

Oakland Raiders owner Al Davis called Jones and told him, "You just won the Super Bowl."

THREE RINGS WITH DALLAS

In Dallas, Haley made an impression right away. Rookie safety Darren Woodson recalled being on a trainer's table getting taped up when Haley came in and did not want to wait to be taped.

"We had some words and almost had a scuffle, and everybody broke it up," Woodson said. "The next day he walks up to me, he says, 'I love your attitude. You got a little feistiness about you.'"

"He brought attitude, he brought accountability," offensive lineman Nate Newton said of Haley.

He also brought with him the 49ers' expectance to compete for a Super Bowl berth each season.

"When I got to the Cowboys," Haley said, "Jimmy was pushing guys, but they didn't know how to win. They didn't know how to prepare."

Once again, Haley made an immediate impact upon joining a new team.

The Dallas defense improved from 17th in the league in 1991 to number one in Haley's first season. And the Cowboys won their first Super Bowl in 15 years, routing the Buffalo Bills, 52–17, in Super Bowl XXVII.

The following season, the Cowboys again defeated the Bills in the Super Bowl to match the 49ers' feat of winning back-to-back championships.

When asked what difference Haley had made for the Cowboys, Newton simply answered, "Super Bowl. Super Bowl."

"We needed a pass rush," Newton said. "We had good corners that turned into great corners because Charles Haley was at that right defensive end."

A loss to San Francisco in the NFC Championship Game the next year prevented Dallas from going for three straight championships. Haley was chosen as NFC Defensive Player of the Year that season, after recording 12.5 sacks.

The Cowboys made it back to the Super Bowl the following season, 1995, and defeated the Pittsburgh Steelers, 27–17, to become the NFL's first franchise to win three Super Bowls in a four-year span.

Injuries were taking their toll on Haley, however. He appeared in only five games during the 1996 season and underwent season-ending back surgery that November. It was his second back surgery in 13 months.

With Haley's availability uncertain and his contract presenting salary-cap problems, he retired in July 1997.

Johnson had been correct about two things at the time of the trade with the 49ers: Haley was the pass-rusher the Cowboys needed, and he could handle Haley's personality.

That does not mean Haley was an angel with the Cowboys. He once showed up to a defensive meeting naked, and he picked on teammates to the point that they wanted to fight him.

After having a few run-ins with Johnson, Haley told his coach that he understood there were times when he needed to be corrected, but he asked Johnson to do so in private instead of front of the team. Johnson made no promises but said he would keep the request in mind.

"From that time forward, we had a great relationship," Johnson said.

"Jimmy let me play," Haley said. "And then when I needed it, he would say something. My thing is, I couldn't keep my mouth closed when he did. Jimmy was doing it for the betterment of the team. I was being selfish when it came to that. Everything else I did was about the team."

The Cowboys clearly reaped the benefits of the Haley trade, because with that deal, Dallas surpassed San Francisco as the NFC's best team.

"Charles was the difference-maker for us," Jones said. "He put the 1990s Cowboys over the top. He brought a personal spirit and a competitive drive to our organization that changed the course of Cowboys history."

Years later, DeBartolo called the trade his biggest mistake as 49ers owner, adding that he knew at the time the trade would "come back to haunt us."

"They talk about the trade that made Dallas a contender, when they made that big trade with Minnesota for Herschel Walker," DeBartolo said. "I don't think that's anything compared to when they stole Charles Haley from us."

When Haley retired from the Cowboys, Jones said, "[W]e couldn't spell Super Bowl until Charles joined us. He was our missing link."

NEW PERSPECTIVE

Haley made a comeback with San Francisco, returning in 1998 after a season off. He did not play in a game in 1998, and although he played in all 16 games in 1999, he started only one. Then he retired for good.

That began the wait for his election into the Hall of Fame.

Five times Haley made it to the finalists' round but failed to receive enough votes. In his case, the sixth time was the charm, in 2015.

It was a different Haley who became the sixth member of the Cowboys' last championship team to be honored in Canton. In 2002, he was diagnosed as bipolar. About a decade earlier, his wife Karen, whom he would later divorce, raised the possibility that he was bipolar, but he dismissed her suggestion to seek help. But with the diagnosis and proper medication, he gained a new perspective on his career.

"When I went into the NFL, I was a 22-year-old athlete that had an 11-year-old kid inside of me crying for help," he said. "But I refused to ask for it. I think the people that reached out to me were the people that saw me hurting and knew that I needed help and knew I was too dumb or too weak to ask for it. I realize at this stage of my life that it's better to mend fences than to burn them down."

He began devoting time to raising awareness and financial support for mental illness. He began working with young athletes, teaching them about the work ethic that had been instilled in him at a young age and enabled him to win more Super Bowls than any other player. His love for football shined through his love for teaching the game to youngsters.

He also began mentoring young NFL players, particularly rookies.

"Everybody thinks he's this crazy dude, and he is, but he has this crazy heart that he always tries to do everything for all the kids that he's around," said Michael Irvin, his Cowboys teammate and fellow Hall of Famer. "Now all the work that he does will also have that bright light of a Hall of Famer doing them. I think it should add to what he's done. He's been doing Hall of Fame stuff for a long while. Now he's getting a jacket to go with the work that he's been doing, and God blesses that."

That is how the postfootball Charles Haley is earning respect.

CAREER HIGHLIGHTS

Won five Super Bowls, the only player in NFL history to do so.

Won three Super Bowls during his first four seasons in Dallas.

Played on back-to-back Super Bowl–winning teams twice, in 1988–1989 with San Francisco and 1992–1993 with the Cowboys.

Named NFC Defensive Player of the Year in 1990 with San Francisco and 1994 with Dallas.

Selected to five Pro Bowls, including three with the Cowboys.

Held the record for career Super Bowl sacks (4.5) at the time of his retirement.

Recorded 11 career postseason sacks.

Played on teams that won 10 division championships.

Played in six NFC Championship Games, winning four.

Had six seasons with at least 10 sacks.

Ended his career with 100.5 sacks.

Selected All-Pro twice, once as a linebacker with the 49ers and once as a defensive end with the Cowboys.

Played for teams that had a 146–60-1 record, including 19–6 in the postseason; won at least 10 games in every season but one; and only missed the playoffs twice.

FIVE COWBOYS MEMORIES

1. January 28, 1996

In Charles Haley's fifth and final Super Bowl appearance, he became the first player in NFL history to play on five Super Bowl–winning teams. The Cowboys defeated the Pittsburgh Steelers, 27–17, in Super Bowl XXX, and it took an in-season decision to unretire for Haley to even play in the game. Haley injured his troublesome back against the Washington Redskins in early December. Doctors diagnosed a herniated disk, and Haley immediately announced that he would retire. He reconsidered later that week, underwent surgery, and missed the Cowboys' final three regular-season games and first two playoff games. He was cleared to play for the Super Bowl, and the team's leader in sacks during the regular season recorded one sack against the Steelers. It was a milestone sack, too, as it extended his own record for sacks in Super Bowls to 4.5. It also was his 11th career postseason sack—second-best in league history. Haley said he had never worn any of his Super Bowl rings, but that would change for number five. "I'm going to wear this one because it means so much to me," he said. "It's just a great feeling to endure all that I endured this season and get a ring."

2. January 31, 1993

The Cowboys acquired Haley via trade before the start of the 1992 season, hoping that he would be the missing defensive piece that would lead them to the Super Bowl. He was more than that. In Super Bowl XXVII, he registered a big sack that propelled the Cowboys to a 52–17 defeat of the Buffalo Bills. The Cowboys had fallen behind Buffalo, 7–0, when the Bills scored on their second possession. Dallas tied the score with a little more than two minutes to play in the first quarter on a Troy Aikman to Jay Novacek touchdown pass that had been set up by an interception. On the first play of Buffalo's ensuing possession, Jim Kelly dropped back to pass. Haley hit Kelly, knocking the football out of his hands and into the arms of defensive lineman Jimmie Jones at the Buffalo two-yard line. Jones took one step and lunged into the end zone for a 14–7 Cowboys lead, and with momentum on its side, Dallas was on its way to an easy victory. The win gave the Cowboys their first Super Bowl championship since 1977.

3. January 30, 1994

Super Bowl XXVIII brought a rematch with the Buffalo Bills. This time, however, victory would not come as easily. The Bills led Dallas, 13–6, at halftime. On the third play of the second half, defensive back James Washington returned a fumble 46 yards for a touchdown to tie the score. Following the kickoff, the Bills took over at their own 37. On third-and-eight, Haley and Jim Jeffcoat sacked Kelly for a 13-yard loss. A punt gave the Cowboys good field position, and Dallas drove for a go-ahead touchdown, with Emmitt Smith carrying the ball on seven of eight plays. In a span of barely more than two minutes, the game's momentum had completely swung to the Cowboys, who outscored Buffalo 24–0 after halftime in winning, 30–13. It was no coincidence that the Dallas defense led the second-half charge. Haley said after the game that the defense determined to come out aggressive to start the second half. "We just made a point among each of the defensive linemen that we weren't going to just sit there and wait to see whether they were going to run or pass," he said. "We were going to attack the line of scrimmage. We don't care what they do—we are going to play our football." With the Cowboys' victory, Haley earned his fourth Super Bowl ring in five years.

4. September 4, 1994

With Dallas coming off back-to-back Super Bowl championships, the Cowboys' defense used the 1994 season opener to send a message that complacency would not be a problem. The defense led the way in a 26–9 victory at the

Statistics

Regular Season

Season	Team	G	Tckl	Sacks	Int	Yds	TD	Fum	Yds	TD
1986	San Francisco	16	59	12.0	1	8	0	2	3	0
1987	San Francisco	12	25	6.5	0	0	0	0	0	0
1988	San Francisco	16	69	11.5	0	0	0	2	0	0
1989	San Francisco	16	57	10.5	0	0	0	1	3	1
1990	San Francisco	16	58	16.0	0	0	0	1	0	0
1991	San Francisco	14	53	7.0	0	0	0	1	3	0
1992	Dallas	15	39	6.0	0	0	0	0	0	0
1993	Dallas	14	41	4.0	0	0	0	1	0	0
1994	Dallas	16	42	12.5	1	1	0	0	0	0
1995	Dallas	13	31	10.5	0	0	0	0	0	0
1996	Dallas	5	6	1.0	0	0	0	0	0	0
1998	San Francisco	0	0	0.0	0	0	0	0	0	0
1999	San Francisco	16	5	3.0	0	0	0	0	0	0
Totals		169	485	100.5	2	9	0	8	9	1

Postseason

Season	Team	G	Sacks	Int	Yds	TD	Fum	Yds	TD
1986	San Francisco	1	1.0	0	0	0	0	0	0
1987	San Francisco	1	1.0	0	0	0	0	0	0
1988	San Francisco	3	3.5	0	0	0	1	0	0
1989	San Francisco	3	1.0	0	0	0	0	0	0
1990	San Francisco	2	1.0	0	0	0	0	0	0
1992	Dallas	3	1.0	0	0	0	0	0	0
1993	Dallas	3	1.5	1	0	0	0	0	0
1994	Dallas	2	0.0	0	0	0	0	0	0
1995	Dallas	1	1.0	0	0	0	0	0	0
1998	San Francisco	2	0.0	0	0	0	0	0	0
Totals		21	11.0	1	0	0	1	0	0

Pittsburgh Steelers, limiting Pittsburgh to 126 yards of total offense and sacking Neil O'Donnell nine times—the most sacks the Steelers had allowed in 10 seasons. Haley had four of those sacks, a career high, and was chosen the NFC Defensive Player of the Week. Coaches also credited him with 15 quarterback pressures, an unofficial statistic. Haley and the defense confused the Steelers offense all day. "I didn't even know where they were coming from at times," O'Donnell said after the game.

5. September 10, 1995

Haley earned two NFC Defensive Player of the Week honors with the Cowboys. The second came in the second game of 1995, a 31–21 home win against Denver. He sacked Bronco quarterback John Elway twice—both in the fourth quarter—for a total loss of 22 yards. One caused a fumble in Denver territory that teammate Chad Hennings recovered to set up a Chris Boniol field goal. Haley had five tackles in the game, and all were solo.

Bob Hayes

A Game-Changer

Robert Lee "Bullet Bob" Hayes
Class: 2009 (Randall McDaniel, Bruce Smith, Derrick Thomas, Ralph Wilson Jr., Rod Woodson)
Seasons with Cowboys: 1965–1974
Other NFL teams: San Francisco 49ers (1975)
Positions: Wide receiver
College: Florida A&M

"*B*ullet" Bob Hayes was a world-class sprinter. Receiving the postcareer accolades he deserved turned out to be a marathon.

Hayes retired from football after the 1975 season, but he wasn't inducted into the Cowboys' Ring of Honor until 2001. He died the following year, at age 59. In 2009, posthumously, he finally received the ultimate honor he had been waiting for: membership in the exclusive Pro Football Hall of Fame.

The day after Hayes passed away, former Cowboys president and general manager Tex Schramm said, "The situation with Bob Hayes and the Hall of Fame is one of the most tragic stories I've ever been associated with during my time in professional football."

Indeed, Hayes's candidacy for the Hall of Fame was discussed and debated—sometimes vehemently—for parts of three decades. But in the end, in what might have been his final opportunity to be voted in, his career was given the nod of approval he had spent the last part of his life seeking.

The most compelling case for inducting Hayes into the Hall of Fame centered on one basic fact: His speed changed the way the game was played.

Those arguing against his inclusion pointed to what they claimed were impressive career statistics but ones that came up short of Hall of Fame credentials. Then there were Hayes's off-field troubles following his career: He served 10 years in prison for selling drugs to an undercover officer.

Yet, according to Hall of Fame bylaws, the only criteria voters were to consider were a "nominee's achievements and contributions as a player, a coach, or a contributor in professional football." Noticeably absent, Hayes supporters argued, were references to personal character and statistics.

"There's a whole lot worse in the Hall of Fame than Bob Hayes's drug conviction," Hall of Fame voter Leonard Shapiro of the *Washington Post* argued in 2002. "L. T. [Lawrence Taylor] was a cocaine addict for a while. O. J. [Simpson] was a murderer, and they didn't kick him out. Our rules say off-the-field stuff shouldn't be counted."

But there were those who claimed that Hayes did not do enough on the field during his 10-year career.

Among those disagreeing was Herb Adderley, a Hall of Fame cornerback who had the unenviable task of covering Hayes as an opponent before he became a teammate and enjoyed watching Hayes slice through outmatched secondaries.

"He should have been in the Pro Football Hall of Fame his first year of eligibility," Adderley said. "There have been guys in the Hall of Fame that didn't contribute as much to their team as Bob Hayes did and wasn't as fast as Bob Hayes was. Bob Hayes revolutionized the game of football because of his speed."

NOT IN THE NUMBERS

The statistical case against Hayes included the following:

Hayes played in two Super Bowls and his team won one. He had only one reception, for 41 yards, in the Cowboys' 16–13 loss to the Baltimore Colts in Super Bowl V. The Cowboys won Super Bowl VI, defeating the Miami Dolphins, 24–3, but Hayes contributed little statistically that day. He caught two passes for 23 yards and had one rush for 16 yards. Two other Cowboys caught touchdown passes that day, Lance Alworth and Mike Ditka. Both men *were* voted into the Hall of Fame. In two appearances in football's biggest game, Hayes caught three passes for 64 yards.

Hayes lacked a "signature" postseason game, despite having plenty of opportunities. He played in six NFL/NFC Championship Games with the Cowboys. He caught eight passes in those games for 64 yards and did not score a touchdown. Statistically, he had only two notable performances among his 15 postseason games. In a 1967 game against the Cleveland Browns, which the Cowboys won, 52–14, Hayes caught five passes for 144 yards and scored on an 86-yard reception. He also returned three punts for 141 yards, including one return of 68 yards. In a Browns rematch the following year, a 31–20 Cowboys loss, Hayes caught five passes for 83 yards but did not score. After those two games, his next-best showing in the postseason was his four-catch, 44-yard-day against the Browns in 1969, when the Cowboys were blown out, 38–14.

In Hayes's 10 seasons, he caught 371 passes for 7,414 yards. Those totals came up short compared to receivers of his era who were voted into the Hall of Fame. Fred Biletnikoff came into the league in 1965, the same year as Hayes, and played 14 seasons for the Oakland Raiders. He caught 589 passes for 8,974 yards. Charley Taylor played 13 seasons during Hayes's era, with the Washington Redskins. He caught 649 passes for 9,110 yards. Lance Alworth played 11 seasons, from 1962 to 1972. His first nine years were with the San Diego Chargers, and he played his final two campaigns as Hayes's teammate with the Cowboys. Alworth ended his career with 542 receptions for 10,266 yards. Charlie Joiner entered the league in 1969 and played 18 seasons with the Houston Oilers, Cincinnati Bengals, and San Diego Chargers. Joiner's career totals: 750 receptions for 12,146 yards. The closest Hall of Fame receiver from that era, numbers-wise, was Paul Warfield. In 13 years with Cleveland and the Miami Dolphins (1964–1977), Warfield caught 427 passes for 8,565 yards. Warfield had the resume-booster of making eight Pro Bowls.

As Hayes's candidacy pushed into a new generation of the NFL that favored the passing game, Hayes's statistics began to look even smaller up against the likes of James Lofton (764/14,004), Steve Largent (819/13,089), Art Monk (940/12,721), Jerry Rice (1,549/22,895), Andre Reed (951/13,198), and even the Cowboys' own Michael Irvin (750/11,904). Yet, statistics were not supposed to be a criteria.

"WORLD'S FASTEST HUMAN"

Lost in the numbers was Hayes's impact on the game itself. His speed changed football and stood out long before he amazed the world at the 1964 Tokyo Olympic Games.

"I discovered him in my physical education class in seventh grade," said Earl Kitchings, who coached Hayes the two years he played football for the Matthew Gilbert High School Panthers in Jacksonville, Florida. "I noticed he had this natural ability for speed. He excelled at everything he did at the time."

Hayes was a running back on the 1958 team that went undefeated in winning the Florida black state championship and five decades later was voted Florida's best high school football team of the 1950s. The following season, Hayes was selected second-team All-Conference.

Kitchings recalled a game against Miami school Booker T. Washington, which boasted a defensive back who had been clocked at 9.6 seconds in the 100-yard dash. Hayes broke off a 94-yard touchdown run in that game, leaving the acclaimed defensive back in his wake as he sprinted for the end zone.

"Bob left him standing still," Kitchings said.

Hayes also played basketball and baseball at Gilbert. With his speed, he was a natural to play center field.

"I had my left fielder three feet from the left-field line and my right fielder three feet from the right-field line," Gilbert's baseball coach, Alvin White, said. "I stuck him in the middle. It was simple: He ran everything down."

And, of course, Hayes had to run track in high school. In his first meet, he won the 100, the 220, the 440, the 880, the sprint relay, the high jump, and the long jump.

He attended college at Florida A&M University, where he played football and ran track. As a halfback and kick returner, he led his team with 11 touchdowns in 1963. For his career, he averaged 20.3 yards per kickoff return and 26.2 yards on punt returns.

In 1962, competing in the Amateur Athletic Union national championship in St. Louis, Missouri, Hayes became the first person to run the 100-yard dash in 9.1 seconds. He ran that time twice at the meet, although one was wind-aided. His world-record time stood unbeaten for 11 years.

The following winter, Hayes staked claim to a share of the world indoor 60-yard dash mark, tying the record of 6.0 seconds four times in four weeks. He later became the first person to break the 6.0 barrier in that event and also broke the world outdoor record in the 200 meters (20.5).

The world received its introduction to Hayes in 1964, in Tokyo.

He entered the Olympic Games having won all of his 49 races dating to 1962. First, Hayes dominated in each of his four races in the 100 meters. In the semifinals, his time of 9.91 would have broken the world record had it not been wind-aided. In the finals, he matched the record of 10.0 seconds, defeating silver medalist Enrique Figuerola by a stunning seven feet.

Not only was Hayes's time set on a soft, cinder track, but he also won the race despite wearing a left shoe he had to borrow from teammate Tommy

Farrell. Roommate Joe Frazier had accidentally knocked one of Hayes's spikes out of his bag as he dug around for a piece of chewing gum.

Hayes's more impressive feat, however, came in the 4x100-meter relay. As the anchor leg, he received the baton in fifth place and two meters back of first place. He flew past the competition, and the U.S. team won by three meters in a world-record time of 39.0 seconds. Hayes's leg was unofficially timed at 8.6 seconds. It has widely been credited as the best 100 meters ever run.

After Hayes crossed the finish line, Jocelyn Delecour, of third-place France, told U.S. leadoff leg Paul Trayton, "You haven't got anything except Hayes." Drayton smiled and replied, "That's all we need, pal."

Hayes left Tokyo with the title "World's Fastest Human," and that speed is what changed the NFL.

IMMEDIATE IMPACT

Ten months before the Olympics, with Hayes a relative unknown with one more year to play at Florida A&M, the Cowboys took a flyer on the flyer, selecting Hayes in the seventh round of the NFL Draft as a future pick. Because Hayes was a redshirted junior, he was eligible to be drafted and then signed after his college eligibility had expired. At that point in the draft, Cowboys vice president of player personnel Gil Brandt recalled, Hayes met the qualification Schramm was looking for: He was the fastest player still available.

The Cowboys had to wait to see Hayes in uniform, but when he joined them for the 1965 season, his impact came—as seemingly everything did with Bullet Bob—quickly.

He scored touchdowns in each of his first two games, and in his fourth game, he torched the Philadelphia Eagles for 177 yards on eight catches and two touchdowns. His first touchdown came on a 49-yard catch-and-run, and the second covered 82 yards. It was the first of his four 100-yard receiving games in the 14-game season.

Hayes finished his rookie season with 46 receptions for 1,003 yards and 12 touchdowns, which tied for the NFL lead. He was the first Cowboy to gain 1,000 yards receiving in a season. He averaged 21.8 yards per catch, and his big-play ability was reflected in the distances of his 12 touchdown receptions: 45, 45, 49, 82, 24, 34, 28, 45, 44, 46, 65, and 33 yards. He also scored on an 11-yard touchdown rush and averaged 26.5 yards per kickoff return and 12.8 yards on punt returns.

And that is where the case for Hayes belonging in the Hall of Fame begins.

At the time, the Cowboys had not yet been labeled "America's Team." The excitement he brought to Dallas games led CBS to televise Cowboys games as much as possible.

"There was something special about him," Brandt said. "He brought charisma. He was the fastest man in the world. Everybody knew about him. He gave us a lift, an aura."

The Cowboys had an 18–46–4 record in the franchise's first five seasons. Their best records had been 5–8–1 in 1962 and 1964. In Hayes's rookie season of 1965, the team improved to 7–7. In his remaining nine seasons in Dallas, the Cowboys went 91–33–2, made the playoffs eight times, and played in two Super Bowls, winning one. Hayes played a big role in that turnaround.

He followed up his debut campaign by catching 64 passes for 1,232 yards and a league-leading 13 touchdowns in 1966. He totaled 998 yards (in 13 games) in 1967 and 909 yards in 1968. He had 10 touchdowns receiving.

Hayes burned traditional man-to-man coverages. Defenses had yet to begin moving defensive backs to match up with receivers. The right corner-back would cover the receiver across from him—regardless of who lined up there—the entire game, and the left cornerback would do the same on his side. Coach Tom Landry took advantage by playing matchup games with Hayes, lining him up in different positions, including the slot where he would be covered by a safety. Defenses had to change to try to contain him—or continue to be embarrassed.

Teams began double-teaming Hayes, with one defensive back jamming him at the line of scrimmage and a second waiting to cover him downfield. Zones became more popular, with the free safety designated to help cover Hayes.

"He changed the game with his speed," Hall of Fame coach Don Shula said. "He wasn't just the world's fastest human; he was a great athlete and football player. Put that together, and he made you change everything on your defense when you played the Cowboys."

Still, he put up big numbers. He averaged 20.0 yards per catch for his career. In 1970, he averaged 26.1 yards per reception. Of his 71 touchdown receptions, 19 came on plays of at least 50 yards.

Hayes averaged a touchdown every 5.2 receptions. That number compared favorably with Hall of Fame receivers from any era one could choose. Jerry Rice, the all-time leading receiver, scored a touchdown every 7.9 catches. Cris Carter averaged one every 8.5 catches. Charlie Joiner's figure was 11.5, while Steve Largent's was 8.2.

Dick LeBeau has coached defenses for more than four decades, earning the reputation as one of the most innovative defensive coaches in NFL history. Before he became a coach, he was a defensive back for the Detroit Lions and covered Hayes.

"He influenced what you see now with the deep ball and speed," LeBeau said. "These are all things the old guys remember as the evolution of the game."

POSTHUMOUS INDUCTION

Just as statistics were not supposed to be a criteria for the Hall of Fame, neither was character.

Hayes left the Cowboys after the 1974 season and played in three games with the San Francisco 49ers the next year before retiring. A heavy drinker, he also started using cocaine. Although he claimed he never dealt cocaine, he was arrested for selling a small amount of coke to an undercover police officer.

In 1979, he was sentenced to two concurrent five-year terms in federal prison. He served 10 months before being paroled.

"Going to prison destroyed my life," Hayes said.

It also appeared to have destroyed his chances of making the Hall of Fame.

In 2001, Cowboys owner Jerry Jones decided to give Hayes a spot in the Cowboys' Ring of Honor. Hayes had been battling health issues but was able to make it to Texas Stadium to receive that honor.

However, he would never have the chance to stand and accept the one honor he most desired. On September 18, 2002, Hayes died of kidney failure after battling prostate cancer and liver ailments. He was buried in a silver casket embossed with a big, blue star and draped with a white Olympic flag.

Former teammate Roger Staubach, who had not only campaigned to have Hayes join him in the Hall of Fame, but also loyally stayed beside Hayes through his life difficulties, was among those who eulogized the Jacksonville native.

"He was a great man," Staubach said. "He fought a tough fight, was a great athlete, and had a great heart."

During his 15 years of eligibility to be selected as a modern-era candidate, Hayes had never received enough votes to become a finalist. That meant his only means of entry would be through the Seniors Committee, which submitted one nominee per year for consideration. Through that process, Hayes became a finalist for the first time in 2004, but he failed to gain enough votes on the final ballot, prompting Paul Zimmerman of *Sports Illustrated* to resign from the committee in protest.

Former teammates continued to lead the charge for Hayes's inclusion, until finally, in 2009, in what likely would have been his last opportunity, Hayes made it into the Hall.

"In his last days he used to talk about the Hall of Fame," Bob Hayes Jr. said in his dad's stead on enshrinement day. "It hurts because he should have been here to witness this special occasion. But, unfortunately, he didn't make it to see it. I know wherever he is, he's smiling down. He's happy."

CAREER HIGHLIGHTS

Won two gold medals in the 1964 Olympic Games, in the 4x100-meter relay and the 100 meters, to earn the title "World's Fastest Human."

Became the first NFL player to own an Olympic gold medal and a Super Bowl championship ring.

Retired as the Cowboys' all-time leader in receptions (365), receiving yards (7,295), points scored (456), punt-return yards (1,158), highest punt-return average (11.1), and holder of season records for receiving yards (1,232 in 1966) and average yards per catch (26.1 in 1970).

Named first- or second-team All-NFL four times.

Selected to play in three Pro Bowls (1966–1968).

The only Cowboys rookie to lead the team in receptions (46) and receiving yards (1,003).

Recorded 23 games with at least 100 receiving yards.

Holds the Cowboys record for longest touchdown reception (95 yards versus Washington in 1966).

Holds the Cowboys record for career yards per reception (20.0), as well as career touchdown receptions (71).

Ranks first and second for longest punt returns in a playoff game (68 yards and 64 yards).

Held world records in the 60-, 100-, and 220-yard dashes. Also held the Olympic record for 100 meters.

Inducted into the USA Track and Field Hall of Fame in 1976.

He and Jim Thorpe are the only Olympic gold medalists in the Pro Football Hall of Fame.

FIVE COWBOYS MEMORIES

1. December 20, 1970

After scoring his franchise-record fourth touchdown in a 52–10 blowout of the Houston Oilers—on his 28th birthday, no less—Bob Hayes had the ball delivered to his wife in the Cotton Bowl seats. "It was my greatest day as a pro," he said "I'd like to give the credit to my wife. She's given me a lot of encouragement this season." In running up 187 receiving yards on six catches, Hayes scored on passes from Craig Morton of 38, 38, 15, and 59 yards. His touchdowns came in succession, as the Cowboys' lead increased from 10–3 in the first quarter to 38–3 in the third. With the win, Dallas ended the regular season with a 10–4 mark and won the NFC East by one game to clinch their fifth-consecutive playoff berth. Terrell Owens is the only other Cowboy with four touchdown receptions in one game.

2. November 13, 1966

Hayes had scored seven touchdowns in the first four games of the 1966 season. But then he had been shut out of the end zone for four consecutive weeks. He remedied that at D.C. Stadium in a 31–30 victory against Washington, scoring twice while racking up career highs with 246 yards and nine receptions. At the time, Hayes's 246 yards was the sixth-best day in NFL history. He matched his total of nine catches but never came close to duplicating his yardage total. His first score came on a 52-yard pass from Don Meredith, giving the Cowboys a 14–6 lead in the second quarter. He scored again on a 95-yard play in the third quarter. The play did not call for Hayes to go deep, but when he noticed two defenders giving him a cushion as he broke from the line of scrimmage, he continued on through the pair and hoped Meredith would read his adjustment. Meredith saw it, and the two connected for a big score. For his efforts, Hayes was selected Offensive Player of the Week by the Associated Press.

3. December 12, 1971

As a big baseball fan, Roger Staubach has claimed that one of his biggest thrills in football was throwing a touchdown pass to Hayes at Yankee Stadium. He actually threw two to Hayes that day—including a 46-yarder to start the scoring—and three overall in a 42–14 whitewashing of the New York Giants. But the play that stuck with Staubach throughout the years came in the second quarter, with the Cowboys up 21–0. Two-time Pro Bowl free safety Carl "Spider" Lockhart had drawn the assignment to guard Hayes with the Cowboys at their own 15-yard line. Staubach lifted a pass over Lockhart, which Hayes pulled in and ran for 85 yards into the Yankee Stadium end zone. "Once he caught the ball," Staubach recalled, "Spider couldn't have caught Bob if his life depended on it. He took off like a rocket." Big-play Bob also caught a 46-yard touchdown pass that day and finished with four receptions for 154 yards. The 10–3 Cowboys' sixth-straight victory was significant because it gave them a half-game lead over Washington in the NFC East.

4. October 10, 1965

It was a loss, but Hayes's efforts against the Philadelphia Eagles had the Cowboys in the lead in the third quarter at the Cotton Bowl. Hayes caught eight passes for 177 yards and two touchdowns, and also had a key punt return. Both of his touchdown receptions came in the first three quarters and from different quarterbacks. In the first quarter, he caught a pass from Craig Morton at the Eagles' 30-yard line and broke away for a 49-yard score that tied the game at 7–7. After Philadelphia had retaken the lead at 14–7 in the second quarter, his 47-yard punt return set up Danny Villanueva's 35-yard field goal. In the third quarter, he scored on an 82-yard play, in which he grabbed a bobbled pass from Jerry Rhome out of the air near the Philadelphia 40 and raced the rest of the way to give the Cowboys a 17–14 lead. The Eagles, however, scored 21 unanswered points and won, 35–24, to knock Dallas out of a tie for first place in the NFL East.

5. January 16, 1972

Far from Hayes's biggest game, Super Bowl VI still proved to be a crowning moment for him. With the Cowboys' 24–3 defeat of the Miami Dolphins in New Orleans, Hayes became the first athlete to win both a Super Bowl and an Olympic gold medal. In the victory, Hayes played more of a setup role. He caught two passes for 23 yards and carried the ball once for 16 yards. His 18-yard reception set up Mike Clark's nine-yard field goal in the first quarter to put up the game's first points. In the third quarter, with the Cowboys leading, 10–3, his run on an end-around gave Dallas the ball at Miami's six-yard line. Two plays later, Duane Thomas scored from three yards out, and the Cowboys held a safe 17–3 lead.

Statistics

Offense

	Regular Season		*Receiving*			
Season	*Team*	*G*	*Rec*	*Yds*	*Avg*	*TD*
1965	Dallas	13	46	1,003	21.8	12
1966	Dallas	14	64	1,232	19.3	13
1967	Dallas	13	49	998	20.4	10
1968	Dallas	14	53	909	17.2	10
1969	Dallas	10	40	746	18.7	4
1970	Dallas	13	34	889	26.1	10
1971	Dallas	14	35	840	24.0	8
1972	Dallas	12	15	200	13.3	0
1973	Dallas	13	22	360	16.4	3
1974	Dallas	12	7	118	16.9	1
1975	San Francisco	4	6	119	19.8	0
Totals		132	371	7,414	20.0	71

Postseason

Season	Team	G	Rec	Yds	Avg	TD
1966	Dallas	1	1	1	1.0	0
1967	Dallas	2	8	160	20.0	1
1968	Dallas	1	5	83	16.6	0
1969	Dallas	1	4	44	11.0	0
1970	Dallas	3	2	61	30.5	0
1971	Dallas	3	7	76	10.9	1
1972	Dallas	2	1	13	13.0	0
1973	Dallas	2	3	54	18.0	0
Totals		15	31	492	15.9	2

Special Teams

Regular Season		*Punt Returns*				*Kickoff Returns*			
Season	Team	No.	Yds	Avg	TD	No.	Yds	Avg	TD
1965	Dallas	12	153	12.8	0	17	450	26.5	0
1966	Dallas	17	106	6.2	0	0	0	0.0	0
1967	Dallas	24	276	11.5	1	1	17	17.0	0
1968	Dallas	15	312	20.8	2	1	20	20.0	0
1969	Dallas	18	179	9.9	0	3	80	26.7	0
1970	Dallas	15	116	7.7	0	0	0	0.0	0
1971	Dallas	1	5	5.0	0	1	14	14.0	0
1974	Dallas	2	11	5.5	0	0	0	0.0	0
Totals		104	1,158	11.1	3	23	581	25.3	0

Postseason		*Punt Returns*				*Kickoff Returns*			
Season	Team	No.	Yds	Avg	TD	No.	Yds	Avg	TD
1966	Dallas	3	−9	−3.0	0	0	0	0.0	0
1967	Dallas	3	141	47.0	0	0	0	0.0	0
1970	Dallas	4	17	4.3	0	1	16	16.0	0
1971	Dallas	2	2	1.0	0	0	0	0.0	0
Totals		12	151	12.6	0	1	16	16.0	0

· 6 ·

Michael Irvin

Contagious Confidence

Michael Jerome Irvin
Class: 2007 (Gene Hickerson, Bruce Matthews, Charlie Sanders, Thurman Thomas, Roger Wehrli)
Seasons with Cowboys: 1988–1999
Other NFL teams: None
Positions: Wide receiver
College: Miami (Florida)

$\mathcal{M}$ichael Irvin's beginning in football was humble, playing the game with his brothers on a Fort Lauderdale, Florida, street they converted into a makeshift football field with painted green lines.

In becoming the all-time leading receiver at the University of Miami and a first-round draft choice by the Dallas Cowboys in 1988, he was labeled as cocky, a showboat, and a hot dog. "Hot dog, no. Confident player, I'll say yes," Irvin said after being the Cowboys' top choice.

But in the end, when his career had come full circle with his enshrinement into the Pro Football Hall of Fame, Irvin stood before a supportive crowd a humble man, challenging his two sons to be better husbands, better fathers, and better role models than he believed he had been.

Polarizing at times, uniting at others, one thing remained a constant for Irvin: He could play football. And he knew it.

Irvin not only made the Cowboys a better team, he made them a different team.

When Dallas chose Irvin with the 11th pick of the 1988 draft, they had a combined record of 14–17 in the previous two seasons. They had not won a playoff game in six years. Their first two seasons with Irvin were rough—a 3–13 record his rookie year, 1–15 the next. But the poor campaigns positioned the Cowboys in the draft where they could add Troy Aikman and Emmitt Smith to the roster.

In the nine full seasons of the "Triplets," the Cowboys were 93–51 in the regular season, won outright or shared the NFC East title six times, qualified for the postseason seven times, had a 12–4 record in the playoffs, and won all three Super Bowls in which they played.

Without doubt, Michael Irvin was the heart and soul of those teams.

FOR HIS FATHER

Irvin's mother Pearl already had six children when she met Walter Irvin. Walter and Pearl both had come from large families—she was one of 13 children, he was one of eight. They had 11 more children together, for a total of 17.

When the Irvins first married, Walter joked that he wanted to have so many children that the couple would have to name their children Cornbread, Peas, and Mashed Potatoes. Fortunately for Michael, they hadn't had to resort to food names when he was born as number 15 in the family.

The Irvins lived in a three-bedroom home that often was not air conditioned. Milk was a luxury that did not last long in the household; the Irvin kids grew up accustomed to eating cereal in water.

"You talk about being disciplined. You talk about being somewhere on time," Irvin recalled. "If they said dinner is served at 6 o'clock, you'd be there at 5:45. You'd be there, or you'd wait until 7 o'clock the next morning to get something to eat."

Irvin's father was a minister and a roofer who preached right living and hard work.

"He was Superman," Irvin said. "People don't understand how hard he worked. He'd get up at 6 or 7 o'clock in the morning and come home at 8 o'clock at night, six days a week, then he'd go preach on Sundays."

Following a three-day suspension Irvin received at Piper High School during his sophomore year, his father decided he would transfer him for his junior year to St. Thomas Aquinas, a private school known for both its strong religious and educational environment and its staunch athletic program. Because St. Thomas had been accused of recruiting other schools' athletes, the Piper principal would not sign Irvin's transfer waiver, making him ineligible to participate in sports his junior year.

Aquinas football coach George Smith said, "[N]inety-nine out of 100 other kids would have left" his new school rather than sit out sports. But

Irvin stayed and focused on improving his grades. His new football coaches also took that time to transition him from an offensive and defensive lineman to a wide receiver.

"The next year," Smith said, "he was All-State in football, All-State in basketball, and went to the state track meet. That's the kind of talent he had."

Much of Irvin's motivation that year came from his father's death from a brain tumor. Irvin had driven his father to the hospital for his treatments, and as they rode together, Irvin would encourage his father to keep fighting by imagining aloud what his long-awaited first game at Aquinas would be like. Walter Irvin would promise his son he would be there to watch.

The week before Irvin's senior season began, Walter passed away.

Irvin ran from the house when he heard the news. His mother worried about her son until one of his football coaches called to say that Michael had run five miles to the school so he could be consoled by a priest.

With his father still watching him play, but from a different vantage point than Irvin had hoped for, he began pointing heavenward after scoring touchdowns. In the years that followed, many who did not know about Irvin's relationship with his father assumed that he was showboating on the field. Instead, he was paying tribute to the most important man in his life.

BACKING UP THE TALK

Irvin signed a football scholarship with the University of Miami Hurricanes, who had just won a national championship and then watched coach Howard Schnellenberger leave for the USFL. Oklahoma State coach Jimmy Johnson had been quickly hired to replace Schnellenberger, and Johnson's confident style proved a great match for Irvin. Johnson's team's swagger fit Irvin's growing image as the "Playmaker."

After sitting out his first year at Miami as a redshirt, Irvin stepped into a starting role and caught 46 passes and led the team with 840 receiving yards and nine receiving touchdowns. The Hurricanes finished 10–2 and defeated eventual national champion Oklahoma on the road.

In 1986, Irvin caught 53 passes for 868 yards and 11 touchdowns, as Miami went undefeated during the regular season and, with the national championship on the line, lost 14–10 to Penn State in the Fiesta Bowl.

The 1987 season figured to be a rebuilding year for the Hurricanes, who were ranked number 10 in the Associated Press preseason poll. But Miami had a high-powered offense that season, with—for the third consecutive year— Irvin leading his team in receiving yards, with 715 on 44 catches, to go along with his six touchdowns. Early in that campaign, Irvin surpassed Eddie Brown as Miami's all-time leader in receiving yards.

Miami finished the regular season unbeaten and ranked second to set up an Orange Bowl showdown with top-ranked Oklahoma for the national championship. In the run-up to the game, Irvin continued to entertain reporters with his lead-quote interview answers. In one session with the media, he revealed, "After I beat somebody on a pattern, I like to help them up and say, 'Hey, don't worry about it. I beat everybody.' I'm just trying to help the guy get his confidence back."

He also told reporters that he would not want to have to cover himself: "If I were a defensive back and the coach told me to cover Michael Irvin one-on-one, I'd say, 'No, Coach, I don't want to play. If I cover him man-to-man, those pro scouts are going to see it and I'm not going to get a shot in the NFL.'"

As he did throughout his career, Irvin backed up his talk. In Miami's 20–14 defeat of Barry Switzer's Sooners, he caught four passes for 57 yards and scored on a 23-yard touchdown pass from Steve Walsh that gave the Hurricanes a 17–7 lead.

With a national championship ring ordered and as owner of Miami records for receptions (143), receiving yards (2,423), and touchdown receptions (26), Irvin faced a decision: As a fourth-year junior, because of his redshirt year, he was eligible to turn pro and enter either the NFL's regular draft or supplemental draft. He declared for the regular draft in April, but there was a catch. If he did not graduate in May, the team that selected him would lose its pick.

That would not be a problem, however, because Irvin was only a few credits short of his degree, and he had promised his father that he would graduate.

The Cowboys needed a player like Irvin. They had suffered back-to-back losing seasons, their fan base was becoming increasingly discontent, and receiver Mike Sherrard—their number-one pick in 1986—would be missing his second consecutive season because of injuries.

Tim Brown of Notre Dame was expected to be the first receiver chosen, and he went to the Los Angeles Raiders with the sixth pick. The Green Bay Packers owned the next pick, and they called Irvin ahead of their selection. The native Floridian, however, did not want to play for a cold-weather team, and he knew that Johnson had been told that the Cowboys wanted to draft him. Irvin held the leverage of not having graduated yet and could drop one class to have his pick voided and then reapply for the supplemental draft. After talking to Irvin, the Packers decided to pick South Carolina wide receiver Sterling Sharpe instead.

The announcement that the Packers had selected someone else set off a celebration in the Irvin household that was topped four picks later when Irvin did indeed land with his father's favorite team. When that celebration had settled down, Irvin addressed the more than one hundred family members, friends, and neighbors crammed into the home.

"Somewhere up there," Irvin said as he looked up, "my dad's looking down and smiling. He's saying, 'I'm proud of you. Now, take care of your mother.'"

BIG PLAYER IN BIG GAMES

From his home after being drafted, Irvin served notice when he talked with the media that he would be bringing his confidence with him into the professional ranks.

"Danny White's going to be an All-Pro now that he's got the Playmaker to throw to," Irvin said of the Cowboys' veteran quarterback. "We're going to be the best combination since bread met butter."

Meanwhile, in Dallas, Cowboys president and general manager Tex Schramm was talking to the media about the newest Cowboy.

"I've heard that he's a flamboyant guy, which I like," Schramm said. "If a guy is going to be a star, I don't mind him being proud of it. I think he could do a lot for our team. We need a lift. If they see him doing things and getting the fans going, being an outgoing guy, that will spread."

Cowboys fans ate up Irvin's selection. When he flew into Dallas for the first time, about two hundred fans were waiting at the airport to cheer him. They were the first of more than a decade's worth of cheers for Irvin.

Irvin received the loudest cheers of any Cowboys player when, wearing the number 88 that had not been worn since Drew Pearson retired, he was introduced before the first preseason game at Texas Stadium.

Although Dallas won only three games his rookie season, the fans saw enough from Irvin to realize that the first key offensive player for a new era was in place. In his NFL debut, he was the first Cowboys rookie receiver to start since Bob Hayes in 1965. Plus, he scored on a 35-yard reception and caught three passes for 73 yards. In the third game, he caught six passes for 96 yards. Fittingly for the long and trying season, the Cowboys lost both of those games.

Irvin's biggest game as a rookie came in the next-to-last game, when he gained 149 yards on six passes and scored three times for all three of the Cowboys' touchdowns in a 24–17 victory at the Washington Redskins. It turned out to be the last of Tom Landry's 270 wins as coach.

In the biggest off-season change in Cowboys history, Arkansas oil and gas businessman Jerry Jones bought the team from Bum Bright, fired Landry, and hired Johnson, Irvin's college coach, to replace the legend. Then the Cowboys selected UCLA quarterback Troy Aikman with the first overall pick in the draft.

The 1989 season was the Cowboys' worst since the franchise's inaugural season. They went 1–15, and Irvin suffered a season-ending knee injury in the sixth game.

The Cowboys had forfeited their first pick in the 1990 draft by choosing Miami quarterback Steve Walsh in the previous year's supplemental draft. So Johnson traded back into the first round and, with the 21st pick, obtained from the Pittsburgh Steelers, chose Florida running back Emmitt Smith.

The Triplets were in place, and the Cowboys' historic run began with Irvin the team's spiritual and emotional leader.

With his size (6-foot-2, 207 pounds) and strength, Irvin became one of the league's best receivers at gaining yards after the catch. Norv Turner benefited from that in his three years as Dallas offensive coordinator. Then Turner learned what his opponents had suffered through when he went to Washington as head coach of the Redskins and had to play against the Cowboys twice each year.

"It was a real eye-opener when we had to line up and coach against those guys," Turner said. "All of a sudden, they ran out on the field, and I said, 'Damn, I forgot how big that sucker is. Look at him. We don't have a chance today.'"

Cris Carter, a Hall of Fame receiver who played with the Minnesota Vikings during Irvin's playing days, said Irvin's physical playing style changed the game.

"He was one of the first as far as a physical receiver," Carter said. "And you always had to double-cover him. To stop the Dallas Cowboys, you had to stop Michael Irvin."

That was especially true in big games. Irvin played in 16 postseason games—the equivalent of a NFL regular season. In those games, he totaled 87 receptions, 1,315 yards, and 8 touchdowns. He topped 100 yards in six playoff games. Only Jerry Rice had more career playoff receptions and receiving yards.

"The bigger the game," New York Giants coach Tom Coughlin said, "the better Irvin seemed to play."

INSPIRING EXAMPLE

Irvin's career also featured more than his share of off-the-field troubles. In March 1996, Irvin was found in a motel room with a former teammate and two self-employed models, drugs, and drug paraphernalia. He pleaded no contest to second-degree felony cocaine possession and was placed on four years' probation. The NFL suspended him for five games the ensuing season.

The next year, a young woman accused Irvin of holding a gun to her head while a teammate and another man raped her. Irvin was cleared of the charges.

In training camp in 1998, while still on probation, Irvin stabbed a teammate with a pair of scissors following an argument over a haircut. A district judge ruled the incident a matter of horseplay.

In 2000, after his playing days had ended, he was arrested on drug possession charges that were later dropped. In 2005, he was charged with misdemeanor possession of drug paraphernalia as the result of a traffic stop. Irvin said the paraphernalia was a friend's who he had been trying to help.

Those incidents delayed Irvin's entry into the Hall of Fame. Considered a candidate worthy of first-ballot admission, he admitted to possessing doubts about whether he would ever be voted in after being left out the first two years he was eligible. His mother kept assuring her son that God had a plan for him.

In the end, the timing of Irvin's election could not have been better. He was voted into the Hall in 2007, while the Super Bowl was in Miami.

On enshrinement day, Irvin delivered one of the more memorable Hall of Fame acceptance speeches—all without notes.

He opened with a prayer and began working his way through the list of people he wanted to thank. Typical of Irvin, he had the fans gathered in Canton riding right alongside him as he expressed heartfelt appreciation for those who had helped him along his journey.

As he neared his conclusion, Irvin had sons Michael (10) and Elijah (eight) stand. He told them how he had prayed, "'God, I have my struggles and I made some bad decisions. But whatever you do—whatever you do—don't let me mess this up.' I say, 'Please, help me raise them for some young lady so that they can be a better husband than I. Help me raise them for their kids so they can be a better father than I.'"

He addressed his boys directly: "And I tell you guys to always do the right thing so you can be a better role model than Dad."

Then Irvin recounted how he watched the previous year's class be enshrined and told his boys that those inductees, not him, were what hall of famers should be like.

That realization the year before had resonated with Irvin during a prayer time, and he had asked God why he must experience "so many peaks and valleys."

"At that moment," Irvin told an absorbed audience, "a voice came over me and said, 'Look up, get up, and don't ever get up. You tell everyone or anyone that has ever doubted, thought they did not measure up, or wanted to quit—you tell them to look up, get up, and don't ever give up. Thank you and may God bless you."

CAREER HIGHLIGHTS

Retired owning or sharing 20 Cowboys receiving records.

Selected to play in five Pro Bowls—two more than any other Cowboys receiver.

Recorded 1,000-yard seasons in seven of eight years, including five in a row from 1991 to 1995.

His eleven 100-yard games and seven consecutive during the 1995 season remain NFL records.

Holds the record for third-most 100-yard games in NFL history, with 47, behind Jerry Rice (65) and Don Maynard (50).

Caught at least 74 passes seven times in an eight-season stretch.

Led or tied for the team lead in receptions in 85 of his last 130 regular-season games.

Caught 87 passes for 1,315 yards and eight touchdowns, with six games of 100 yards or more, in his 16 career postseason games, the equivalent of a full regular season. His playoff receptions and yards rank second in the NFL all-time.

Played on three Super Bowl championship teams with the Cowboys and in four consecutive NFC Championship Games. During his career, Dallas won the NFC East six times.

Led the league with 1,523 receiving yards in 1991, on 93 receptions.

Named to the NFL's All-Decade Team of the 1990s.

Started a season opener as a rookie, catching a touchdown pass, the first Cowboys receiver in more than 20 years to do so.

Set school career records with 143 catches, 2,423 receiving yards, and 26 touchdown receptions, despite playing only three seasons at Miami.

FIVE COWBOYS MEMORIES

1. January 31, 1993

The Buffalo Bills started Super Bowl XXVII in a two-deep zone to try and keep the ball from getting into the hands of Michael Irvin and Alvin Harper. But when Troy Aikman kept finding tight end Jay Novacek underneath and

Emmitt Smith kept finding ample running room, the Bills defense had to adjust. Irvin took advantage of the single coverage. After a quiet first 28 minutes—only one catch—Irvin scored two touchdowns late in the first half and finished the game with 114 yards on six receptions. With the Cowboys ahead 14–10 in the second quarter and holding the ball on Buffalo's 19, Irvin beat the man coverage with a simple slant for a touchdown with 1:54 left before halftime. On the first play following a Thurman Thomas fumble, Aikman and Irvin hooked up for an 18-yard scoring strike. In a matter of 18 seconds, Irvin's two touchdowns gave the Cowboys a 28–10 lead, and they were off and running to an easy 52–17 win and their first Super Bowl championship in 14 years.

2. January 15, 1995

Less than eight minutes into the NFC Championship Game in a mucky Candlestick Park, three Cowboys turnovers—including a fumble by Irvin— had resulted in the San Francisco 49ers opening up a stunning 21–0 lead. "I was thinking we messed up," Irvin said after the game. "We spotted them 21. But I still thought we were in it." Thanks to Irvin, they were. He tied a NFC Championship Game record with 12 receptions, for a Championship Game–record 192 yards, and scored two touchdowns in what turned out to be a big comeback that came up short, with the 49ers holding on to win, 38–28, and preventing Dallas from playing in a third consecutive Super Bowl. Irvin scored the Cowboys' first touchdown on a 44-yard pass from Aikman. In the fourth quarter, he scored on a 10-yard pass that pulled the Cowboys to within 38–28. If pass interference had been called against Deion Sanders as he covered Irvin—Dallas coach Barry Switzer was penalized for unsportsmanlike conduct arguing the noncall—the Cowboys might have been able get to within a field goal of the 49ers with about five minutes to play. But no, there was no flag and no comeback in what was the biggest game, statistically, of Irvin's postseason career.

3. September 20, 1992

In his third game after returning from a contract holdout, Irvin answered criticism after three dropped passes in the previous two games by racking up a career-high 210 yards on eight catches and scoring three touchdowns for the second time in his career in a 31–20 defeat of the Phoenix Cardinals. Yardage-wise, it was the fifth-best game in franchise history to that point. "Before the game I felt like I needed a big game, I needed a 200-yard game," Irvin said. "The last couple of games I felt good. Today I felt great." It showed early, as one minute into the game, Irvin turned a 15-yard pass into an 87-yard scoring play—the longest of his career. After Phoenix had tied the score at 7–7, Irvin hauled in a 41-yard pass from Aikman for a 14–7 lead. His third touchdown, from the Phoenix four, gave Dallas a 28–10 lead. "Mike just kept getting open," Aikman said.

4. December 11, 1988

It was Irvin's rookie year, and with a 2–12 record entering the next-to-last game of the regular season, there had been little to celebrate. So when Irvin scored three touchdowns in a 24–17 win at the Washington Redskins, he celebrated each one. Irvin—playing with his high school coach, Frank Springer, in attendance—scored all three of the Cowboys' touchdowns on passes of 24, 61, and 12 yards from Steve Pelluer as Dallas ended a 10-game losing streak. Irvin celebrated his first touchdown with a bow and a spike. The second, he rejoiced by walking backward into the end zone, arms extended downward, and spiked the ball so hard that it bounced into the stands. After his final touchdown, Irvin danced with fans behind the corner of the end zone. "They are tough up there," Irvin said. "I wanted to give them a little show for their money."

5. January 14, 1996

In the four games leading up to the NFC Championship Game, Irvin had faced persistent double teams. The Green Bay Packers ended that trend, and Irvin and the Cowboys ended Green Bay's season with a 38–27 win at Texas Stadium. Irvin caught seven passes for 100 yards and two touchdowns, with both scores coming in the first quarter and propelling the Cowboys to a 14–3 lead. "I don't know what film they were watching, but they should have doubled him," Cowboys cornerback/wide receiver Deion Sanders said. With the victory, the Cowboys advanced to the Super Bowl for the third time in four years.

Statistics

Regular Season						
Season	*Team*	*G*	*Rec*	*Yds*	*Avg*	*TD*
1988	Dallas	14	32	654	20.4	5
1989	Dallas	6	26	378	14.5	2
1990	Dallas	12	20	413	20.7	5
1991	Dallas	16	93	1,523	16.4	8
1992	Dallas	16	78	1,396	17.9	7
1993	Dallas	16	88	1,330	15.1	7
1994	Dallas	16	79	1,241	15.7	6
1995	Dallas	16	111	1,603	14.4	10
1996	Dallas	11	64	962	15.0	2
1997	Dallas	16	75	1,180	15.7	9
1998	Dallas	16	74	1,057	14.3	1
1999	Dallas	4	10	167	16.7	3
Totals		159	750	11,904	15.9	65
Postseason						
Season	*Team*	*G*	*Rec*	*Yds*	*Avg*	*TD*
1991	Dallas	2	9	167	18.6	0
1992	Dallas	3	18	288	16.0	2
1993	Dallas	3	16	215	13.4	1
1994	Dallas	2	18	303	16.8	2
1995	Dallas	3	13	185	14.2	3
1996	Dallas	2	9	125	13.9	0
1998	Dallas	1	4	32	8.0	0
Totals		16	87	1,315	15.1	8

· 7 ·

Tom Landry

The Man behind the Image

Thomas Wade Landry
Class: 1990 (Junious "Buck" Buchanan, Bob Griese, Franco Harris,
 Ted Hendricks, Jack Lambert, Bob St. Clair)
Seasons with Cowboys: 1960–1988
Other NFL teams: None
Positions: Coach
College: Texas

$\mathcal{I}$t is difficult to think of Tom Landry without picturing the iconic image of his silhouette, topped by his famous fedora, standing majestically against the backdrop of Texas Stadium fans. And it is equally difficult to think of the glory days of the Cowboys franchise without picturing Landry.

"I think the whole Cowboys image came from him," quarterback Roger Staubach said following Landry's death in 2000. "I think Tom will always make the Dallas Cowboys more than a football team."

Indeed, Landry was the "only coach the Cowboys have ever had" for their first 29 years, winning 60.7 percent of games, claiming two Super Bowl championships, and ringing up a NFL-record 20 consecutive winning seasons.

In the process, Landry proved to be one of the most innovative coaches in NFL history, while carrying himself in a way that led players and rivals to praise his character and integrity.

"If there were a Mount Rushmore for the NFL," league commissioner Paul Tagliabue said at the time of Landry's death, "the profile of Tom Landry

71

would have to be there, wearing his trademark hat for all of us to marvel at. The truth is, Tom Landry was one of the greatest gifts ever given to the NFL. Coach Landry's presence on the Cowboys' sideline for three decades was the NFL at its best."

CHANGE OF CAREER PLANS

Landry's devotion to family came from his roots in the small Texas town of Mission, across the border from Mexico. His father, Ray, was an auto mechanic, volunteer fire department chief, and Sunday school superintendent at the Methodist church the Landrys attended. His mother, Ruth, was a homemaker.

Landry, the youngest of three children, had a speech impediment that made him so self-conscious that before he overcame it, he often chose to remain silent.

He played quarterback, fullback, defensive back, and punter for Mission High, leading the 1941 team to an unbeaten season in which the Eagles allowed only one touchdown. That all-around ability brought him the opportunity to play at the University of Texas.

During Landry's freshman year with the Longhorns, his brother, Robert, a pilot with the U.S. Army Air Forces, died when his plane exploded over the North Atlantic. After that semester, Landry decided to enlist in the army reserve and was soon called into active duty. He flew more than 30 combat missions in a B-17 during World War II, including one in which his plane ran out of fuel and he executed an emergency landing from which the entire crew walked away uninjured.

He returned to the Texas Longhorns in 1947 and was named an All-Southwest Conference fullback. The next season he was the Longhorns' captain; met his future wife, Alicia, on a blind date; and led the Longhorns to victory against Georgia in the Orange Bowl. As he walked off the field after his last game, he received a $6,000 contract offer from the New York Yankees of the All-America Football Conference.

He and Alicia married in January 1949. Four months later, he graduated with a business degree. Then he joined the Yankees, played in the AAFC's final season, and moved to the NFL's New York Giants, who had drafted him in 1947.

Despite his rather slow foot speed, Landry's intelligence and studious nature enabled him to become a star defensive back.

Giants teammate Frank Gifford once said Landry "probably was the best defensive back in the business" at the time.

"He always appeared to be looking beyond the game itself, searching for an unknown key," Gifford remembered. "While most of us played the game, he studied it. He was thorough in his preparation, leaving nothing to chance. There was no room for guesswork in his planning."

In 1954, Landry was made a player-coach, and he designed a new defensive alignment known as the 4–3, in which the two ends on the standard six-man line were dropped back into outside linebacker positions.

Before the 1956 season, Landry gave up the player part of his title, ending a six-year career, and became the Giants' full-time defensive coach. With Landry coaching his 4–3 scheme full-time and Vince Lombardi serving as offensive coordinator, the Giants routed the Chicago Bears, 47–7, in the 1956 championship game.

Two years later, when the Giants shut out the Cleveland Browns, 10–0, in the playoffs and held Jim Brown to eight yards rushing on seven carries, Giants coach Jim Lee Howell called Landry the "greatest coach in professional football."

The next year, 1959, two momentous events occurred. First, Landry became a born-again Christian. Second, at age 34, he was hired as head coach of the expansion Dallas Cowboys when team president and general manager Tex Schramm swooped in and offered him the job before he could accept the same offer from Bud Adams of the Houston Oilers and the upstart American Football League.

Landry did not keep those events exclusive of one another; his Christian character shined throughout his run as the Cowboys' coach.

"Tom was a very unique individual in that he had two very strong feelings; one was for football and the other about Christianity," Schramm said. "The manifestation of his great faith was his ability to coach one of the roughest sports on Earth and maintain his beliefs."

Landry went to the Cowboys not planning to make coaching a long-term career. He considered the profession too insecure and thought he would coach a few years and then put to use the engineering degree he had completed in 1959, at the University of Houston, by attending night school during off-seasons. The Cowboys' head job turned out to be the last one he ever held.

SHOW OF COMMITMENT

Bob Lilly was a rookie during the Cowboys' second season in 1961. In 1989, he recalled immediately noticing Landry's strong beliefs.

"He came from the New York Giants with high standards, ready to build the Cowboys from scratch with a long-range program for the '60s. But he had much more on his mind," Lilly said. "I never will forget our first team meeting in training camp. He said, 'Put God first, family second, and football third.' Afterward, I said, 'We'll never win because he has his priorities backward.' Now I believe he had them right."

It just took a while for the NFL's youngest coach's approach to show up positively in the won–lost record.

Dallas went 0–11–1 in its inaugural season, followed by records of 4–9–1, 5–8–1, 4–10, and 5–8–1. With the Cowboys 18–46–4 under Landry, common speculation expected him to be fired, if not at that time, then the following season, when his contract expired. That speculation only increased when owner Clint Murchison called a news conference.

Not only did Murchison *not* fire Landry, he gave him a 10-year contract extension. The Landry way would remain.

The breakthrough came two seasons later, in 1965, when the Cowboys won five of their final seven games to finish at 7–7. From there, Dallas improved to 10–3–1 the next season to begin a NFL-record 20 consecutive winning seasons.

During that span, the team won 13 division titles, five conference championships, and two Super Bowls, establishing and then cementing its legacy as "America's Team."

INCOMPARABLE INNOVATOR

Landry's teams did not just win; they won in new ways, although it took a few years for the new franchise to assemble the needed players.

Mike Ditka played and coached for Landry before becoming head coach of the Chicago Bears and then the New Orleans Saints.

"If he's not remembered as one of the greatest coaches who ever coached in the NFL, someone has made a terrible mistake," Ditka said. "He was an innovator. I honestly believe his contributions to the intellectual side of the game were greater than anyone who has ever coached."

In addition to developing the 4–3 defense, Landry did the following:

> Invented the "Flex" defense. Lining up one end and one tackle a few feet off the line of scrimmage gave the defensive line a picket-fence look and provided the deeper players better pursuit lanes. He created the defense while coaching for the Giants to counteract the "run to daylight" philosophy of Lombardi's offense. The Flex was designed to "take the daylight away."

Created the "multiple" offense. As opponents began copying his Flex defense, Landry knew that defensive players relied on reading offensive formations. He began shifting players and sending them in motion to create confusion. He also had his linemen stand up—or "hitch"—to temporarily block defenders' views of the shifting backs before the linemen settled into their stances

Popularized the shotgun. The San Francisco 49ers had used the shotgun in the 1950s to take advantage of their quarterbacks' running abilities. Landry, however, dropped his quarterback a few yards behind the center to allow him more time to read defensive alignments and identify developing holes.

Pioneered situational substitutions. By rotating players in and out according to situations, Landry was able to keep his players fresher and take advantage of their specific strengths against tiring opponents.

EMOTIONAL FAREWELL

As odd as it sounds, there became a time when it seemed as though the league had passed by the man who advanced both offenses and defenses perhaps more than any other coach in NFL history.

Landry's 1985 team finished 10–6 and won the NFC East. But the talent was thinning, and he could sense the Cowboys were beginning to fade. A 7–9 record in 1986 ended the streak of 20 winning seasons.

Landry believed the Cowboys needed three years to return to their accustomed success, and although he had been hinting at retirement throughout much of the 1980s, he signed a three-year contract during the summer of 1987, determined to turn the Cowboys around. That year, in a season that lost one game to a player's strike, a late four-game losing streak sunk Dallas to 7–8. The 1988 team went 3–13, for the franchise's fewest victories since its first season.

Landry did not get a chance to coach the third and final year of his plan. On February 25, 1989, while on the first tee of a golf course near his home in Austin, Texas, Landry received word that Schramm and an Arkansas oil and gas businessman named Jerry Jones were flying down to meet with him. Jones had just purchased the Dallas Cowboys, and after Landry completed his round, the new owner informed him that he was removing him as head coach.

"It was a very difficult meeting," Schramm remarked later that night. "Difficult and sad."

Just like that, the only head coach the Cowboys had ever known became the only head coach the Cowboys had ever fired.

"This is like [Vince] Lombardi's death," NFL commissioner Pete Rozelle said. "There are relatively few coaches whose careers compare with Tom. No question he's a hall of famer, in my opinion. He's not only been an outstanding coach, but a tremendous role model for kids and our fans. He has contributed a tremendous amount to the league."

Landry met with a group of about 50 players in the Valley Ranch meeting room two days after he was fired, on a Monday. He had cleaned out his office Sunday, while also dictating his farewell speech to Barbara Goodman, his longtime secretary.

He made it about halfway through that speech, telling the players that despite the 3–13 record that season, they had not quit on him and that the best thing they could do for him was to "work hard and turn the Cowboys around."

"There wasn't a dry eye in the place," linebacker Eugene Lockhart told reporters, admitting that he had shifted his eyes to the floor so he would not have to look at Landry as he spoke. "I couldn't stand it much more. It was more than anyone could take."

Landry walked out of the room to a standing ovation from his players, his head down and his hand over his own tear-filled eyes.

Landry would later look back on his firing with one regret.

"I just wish I would have been given the chance to finish the three years," he said.

STRAIGHT TO CANTON

With coaches not having a five-year waiting period before they can be elected into the Hall of Fame, Landry was voted in less than a year after he was fired. When his name came up during the selection meeting, his case was so easy that there was no need to discuss his credentials.

A couple of hours before his induction ceremony, Landry was asked how he hoped to be remembered.

"I never thought much about how to be remembered," he said. "I think the greatest reward for a coach is when players who have gone through your system and maybe didn't agree with you all the time, come back after they're out of football and tell you, 'Yeah, I understand what you were talking about.' Those are the special moments."

Some of those special moments included the five times former players from the Cowboys and Giants chose him to present them at their Hall of Fame inductions.

Former players have looked for opportunities to give insight into what the often-expressionless man under the fedora—"the man in the funny hat," Staubach once called him—was like outside of football.

"Because he stayed separate from the players, people said he didn't care," said Staubach, whom Landry selected to introduce him in Canton. "That wasn't true at all. He was very caring. He did so much for players that never was noticed. He's got a great sense of humor, which people also did not realize. But he was a little shy, and he decided to be distanced from the players. So a lot of people never got to see him."

Herschel Walker shared that during the difficult 1988 season, his brother was killed in an industrial accident, and Landry was the first member of the Cowboys organization to call him. Walker decided to play that Sunday to repay Landry for reaching out to him and rushed for 134 yards and scored a touchdown.

Tony Dorsett told how Landry helped him through a painful divorce. "He meant a lot to me," Dorsett said. "He helped me when I had hard times. I admire him and respect him to the utmost."

Landry helped Bob Hayes find jobs as he tried to overcome alcoholism. And Thomas "Hollywood" Henderson, who tested Landry's patience plenty and experienced more than his fair share of the coach's disciplinarian side, said, "Tom Landry is the greatest man I've ever known."

"He cared for us and wanted us to have a good life at home," Danny White said. "I don't even know how he shared that or how we knew that. But we just knew it. You could just feel it."

In May 1999, not quite 11 years after he last walked the Cowboys sideline, Landry was diagnosed with chronic myelogenous leukemia, a cancer of the white blood cells. He passed away February 12, 2000, in a Dallas hospital. He was 75.

"I called him 'Coach,' but he was like a second father to me," Lilly said at one of the multiple memorial services for Landry. "We are the legacy of Coach Landry, and we're going to spread that to our children."

That is just one of the ways in which Landry, as Staubach had said, made the Dallas Cowboys more than a football team.

CAREER HIGHLIGHTS

Holds the NFL record (tied) for longest coaching tenure with one team, at 29 seasons.

Coached five Super Bowl teams, with two winning the Lombardi Trophy.

Has the third-most career regular-season victories for a coach, with 250, behind Don Shula (328) and George Halas (318).

Holds the NFL record for most consecutive winning seasons, with 20 (1966–1985).

Led the Cowboys to 13 division titles.

Known for innovations that included either the introduction or revamping of the Flex defense, the multiple offense, the shotgun, and situational substitution.

Played as defensive back, punter, and kick returner with the New York Yankees and New York Giants.

Intercepted 32 passes as a player and averaged 40.9 yards per punt.

Served as player-coach with the Giants in 1954–1955.

Acted as full-time defensive coordinator from 1956–1959 with the Giants, with offensive coach Vince Lombardi.

Hired as the first head coach of the Dallas Cowboys.

Named an All-Southwest Conference player with the University of Texas.

FIVE COWBOYS MEMORIES

1. January 16, 1972

One year after reaching the Super Bowl and losing to the Baltimore Colts on a field goal with five seconds remaining, the Cowboys matched up against the Miami Dolphins and coach Don Shula in Super Bowl VI in New Orleans. With Roger Staubach passing for two touchdowns, temperamental Duane Thomas rushing for 95 yards and a score, and Walt Garrison rushing for 74 yards, Dallas won rather easily, 24–3, for its first Super Bowl championship. "There wasn't any doubt in my mind," Landry said. "I can't predict games, normally. I mean, I have no idea who's going to win. But this game, you knew what was going to come off. That's the year we put up with Duane Thomas the whole year, which was probably the greatest miracle that ever happened in sports."

2. January 15, 1978

In what Landry called the Cowboys' "greatest defensive performance," Dallas shut down the Denver Broncos to win Super Bowl XII, 27–10, in Louisiana. Landry's "Doomsday Defense" harassed former Cowboys quarterback Craig Morton into four interceptions, while forcing eight Bronco turnovers.

Morton, with 39 passing yards on 4-of-15 passing, barely had more passing yards than Cowboys fullback Robert Newhouse, who completed a 29-yard touchdown pass to Golden Richards. The Broncos were held to 156 yards of offense. Dallas defensive lineman Harvey Martin and Randy White were voted co-MVPs after combining for three sacks.

3. September 17, 1961

It took a full year longer than Landry had hoped, but he and the Cowboys picked up their first victory in the season opener of the franchise's second year, defeating the Pittsburgh Steelers, 27–24, in front of 23,500 onlookers at the Cotton Bowl in Dallas. After going 0–11–1 the season before, the Cowboys watched a 17–14 third-quarter lead turn into a 24–17 fourth-quarter deficit. But Dick Bielski tied the score on a 17-yard touchdown reception with 56 seconds remaining. Rookie kicker Allen Green, who had missed two of his three field goal attempts, booted a last-second 27-yarder for the victory. "It was exciting for us," Landry recalled. "You can't go through 12 games, not win a game, and then not be excited when you finally win one."

4. November 7, 1965

Landry had benched quarterback Don Meredith twice in the first six games in favor of rookies Jerry Rhome and Craig Morton. When Meredith struggled as the starter in a loss at the Pittsburgh Steelers, dropping the Cowboys to 2–5, pressure mounted to bench him again, perhaps for good. After two nights of barely sleeping, Landry called Meredith into his office and told him that he would be the starting quarterback for the rest of the season. Meredith responded by throwing two touchdown passes and leading Dallas to a 39–31 victory over the San Francisco 49ers. That started a stretch in which the Cowboys won five of their final seven games to finish 7–7 and record the franchise's first .500 season. The Cowboys did not have another losing season until 1986.

5. December 31, 1967

The 1967 NFL Championship Game is one of the most memorable football games ever played, at any level. At Lambeau Field in Green Bay, Bart Starr scored on a quarterback sneak in the final seconds to give the Packers a 21–17 victory and a berth in the Super Bowl. The game was good enough to become a classic on its own, but it was written into NFL lore as the "Ice Bowl" because of the game-time temperature of minus-13 degrees. With weather reports severely missing out on how cold that day would be, Landry was ill prepared and wore a borrowed heavy coat and heavy hat. Otherwise, he said, "I would have frozen to death, I guarantee you." The game resulted in the Cowboys being dubbed the "team that can't win the big one," until the victory in Super Bowl VI. "I didn't mind people saying we couldn't win the big one," Landry said, "because after the early years, it was nice to be winning at all."

Statistics

Season	Team	Regular Season			Postseason		Round Reached
		W	L	T	W	L	
1960	Dallas	0	11	1			
1961	Dallas	4	9	1			
1962	Dallas	5	8	1			
1963	Dallas	4	10	0			
1964	Dallas	5	8	1			
1965	Dallas	7	7	0			
1966 (A)	Dallas	10	3	1	0	1	NFL championship
1967 (A)	Dallas	9	5	0	1	1	NFL championship
1968 (A)	Dallas	12	2	0	0	1	Divisional
1969 (A)	Dallas	11	2	1	0	1	Divisional
1970 (A)	Dallas	10	4	0	2	1	Super Bowl (lost)
1971 (A)	Dallas	11	3	0	3	0	Super Bowl (won)
1972	Dallas	10	4	0	1	1	NFC championship
1973 (A)	Dallas	10	4	0	1	1	NFC championship
1974	Dallas	8	6	0			
1975	Dallas	10	4	0	2	1	Super Bowl (lost)
1976 (A)	Dallas	11	3	0	0	1	Divisional
1977 (A)	Dallas	12	2	0	3	0	Super Bowl (won)
1978 (A)	Dallas	12	4	0	2	1	Super Bowl (lost)
1979 (A)	Dallas	11	5	0	0	1	Divisional
1980 (B)	Dallas	12	4	0	2	1	NFC championship
1981 (A)	Dallas	12	4	0	1	1	NFC championship
1982	Dallas	6	3	0	2	1	NFC championship
1983	Dallas	12	4	0	0	1	Wild Card
1984	Dallas	9	7	0			
1985 (A)	Dallas	10	6	0	0	1	Divisional
1986	Dallas	7	9	0			
1987	Dallas	7	8	0			
1988	Dallas	3	13	0			
Totals		250	162	6	20	16	

Note: A indicates the team won its division; B indicates the team tied for first place.

· 8 ·

Bob Lilly

"Mr. Cowboy"

Robert Lewis Lilly
Class: 1980 (Herb Adderley, David "Deacon" Jones, Jim Otto)
Seasons with Cowboys: 1961–1974
Other NFL teams: None
Positions: Defensive tackle
College: Texas Christian

*B*ob Lilly remains "Mr. Cowboy." He was the franchise's first draft pick, the first member of the Ring of Honor, and the first Cowboy to be inducted into the Pro Football of Fame. He played on the team that appeared in the Cowboys' first Super Bowl and the team that won the first Super Bowl title for Dallas. Lilly spent his entire 14-year career with the Cowboys, earning seven All-Pro selections and 10 consecutive Pro Bowl berths. His 11 overall Pro Bowl selections remains the franchise record, and not until 2015 did another Cowboy match his record of playing in 196 consecutive regular-season games.

On and off the field, Lilly conducted himself in a manner that added shine to the Cowboys star.

"A man like that," Tom Landry once said of his defensive lineman, "comes along once in a lifetime."

The Dallas Cowboys and Bob Lilly might have been born for one another.

Lilly was born July 26, 1939, in Olney, Texas. Twenty-one years later, on September 24, 1960, about 130 miles to the southeast, the Cowboys made their debut in Dallas' Cotton Bowl stadium.

A half-hour drive to the west, in Fort Worth, the city that bookended Dallas in the area that would become known as the Metroplex, Lilly was en route to a consensus All-American season with the Texas Christian University Horned Frogs.

The following year, the Cowboys made Lilly the franchise's first pick in the NFL Draft. The pairing felt like destiny.

BACK TO TEXAS

John Ernest "Buster" Lilly introduced the young Lilly to football when he was eight years old. Buster scouted for the Throckmorton High School football team west of Fort Worth, and he took Lilly to one of the Greyhounds' Friday-night games.

Lilly immediately was hooked on the sport. When his dad gave him a football later that year, he was determined to become a football player. Despite being crippled by a motorcycle accident, Buster took Lilly out into the yard as often as he could to toss around the football.

Lilly played his first organized football game in sixth grade. As he grew, however, it became clear that his football future was not in throwing and catching a football, but in tackling those who did.

As a freshman, Lilly stood 6-foot-4 and weighed 180 pounds. The next year, he had grown to 210 pounds. The next year, he weighed 220. With his dad attending every game, Lilly developed into an All-Bi-District football player as a junior. His size also enabled him to earn All-State honorable mention as a junior.

Lilly was already making plans to enter the military after graduation. But in December of his junior year, he received a letter from Sammy Baugh.

Baugh had been his dad's hero as an All-American quarterback at TCU and then a versatile quarterback-defensive back-punter with the Washington Redskins. Baugh would later become a member of the Pro Football Hall of Fame's first class of 1963.

Baugh was coaching at Hardin-Simmons University, not far from Throckmorton, and he offered a football scholarship to Lilly based on game film he had watched. With "Slingin' Sammy" interested in him, college—and football—suddenly became a new option for Lilly.

Lilly's father was a farmer, and a severe drought forced the Lillys to move to Oregon, where family helped his father find work. The uprooted Lilly played his senior season at Pendleton High School. Lilly was 6-foot-5 and 225 to 230 pounds by then and ran a 10.6 100 in football cleats. He was All-State in football, second-team All-State in basketball, and qualified for the finals at the Oregon state track meet.

The move to the Pacific Northwest opened up new college football possibilities, and Lilly drew offers from Oregon, Oregon State, Washington, and Washington State. Idaho also was seriously interested, and back home in Texas, Bear Bryant offered him a scholarship at Texas A&M. When it came decision time, he chose to return closer to where he had grown up and play for Baugh's alma mater, TCU.

Lilly's sophomore year, the Horned Frogs finished 8–2–1, won the Southwest Conference, battled to a 0–0 tie against Air Force in a muddy Cotton Bowl game, and were ranked 10th in the final Associated Press poll. That was the fourth shutout of the season for TCU's defense. His junior year, TCU was 8–3 and shared the conference title with Arkansas and Texas. TCU's loss to Clemson in the Bluebonnet Bowl—Lilly was chosen Lineman of the Game—left the Horned Frogs seventh in the final AP poll. Lilly was named All-Conference.

Lilly's strengths of feat at TCU were not limited to the football field. In a prank that became known around campus as the "Lilly Test," he would pick out a foreign sports car parked in front of the student union building and, one end at a time, lift the car and move it onto the sidewalk.

Lilly entered his senior season of 1960 as a unanimous Preseason All-American. Said an unnamed teammate in TCU's 1960 football media guide, "If I was as big and strong as Lilly, I would charge people just to live."

Although the Horned Frogs slumped to 4–4–2, Lilly lived up to his preseason billing and not only picked up his second All-Conference honor, but he also was a consensus All-American.

In Lilly's three seasons, the TCU defense allowed an average of 7.7 points per game. Coach Abe Martin called Lilly the "best tackle I ever coached."

DOUBLE- AND TRIPLE-TEAMED

The Cowboys entered the NFL in 1960, but they did so too late to take part in the regular draft, held in late 1959. Instead, the team began filling its roster through a special expansion draft.

Dallas would have selected second in the 1961 draft—behind the expansion Minnesota Vikings—but it had traded its first pick to the Washington Redskins for quarterback Eddie LeBaron. The Cowboys, however, worked out a trade with the Cleveland Browns to get back into the first round and with the 13th pick—and the first in franchise history—selected Lilly. They also acquired the rights to linebacker Chuck Howley, who had retired from the Chicago Bears because of a knee injury. Adding Lilly and Howley to middle linebacker Jerry Tubbs provided the Cowboys a foundation for a good defense.

The Dallas Texans had drafted Lilly in the second round of the American Football League draft three weeks early, but the Cowboys were able to sign him to a rookie contract worth $11,500, with a $2,500 signing bonus, which he used to buy a Chevy Corvair. Lilly headed out from the dealership for Dallas and his first meeting with Landry. One block into his journey, the car broke down. The dealer upgraded Lilly to a new car, and he set out again for Dallas. Because of the car problems, he arrived late.

Landry stopped writing on the board at the front of the room when Lilly entered. Landry introduced the rookie to his players and then warned him that arriving late once training camp started would result in a fine.

Landry started Lilly at left defensive end. Lilly played there for two and a half years, and although he admittedly could not get comfortable in the position, he tied for the team lead in sacks as a rookie (three) and was named NFL Rookie of the Year. This was despite breaking five ribs, a wrist, and a thumb; spraining both ankles; and injuring a knee during the season. He also led the team the next two seasons, with 10 sacks in 1962 and five in 1963.

"I didn't contain reverses or quarterbacks very well as an end," he said. "I just didn't like sitting there and waiting around for a play to develop. At tackle, you just react and move."

The switch to tackle created those opportunities for Lilly to react and move. In 1980, when Lilly was on his way into the Hall of Fame, Landry said changing Lilly's position was the "best coaching decision I ever made."

That change came as Landry was developing the Flex defense, a scheme that further allowed Lilly to take advantage of his natural aggressiveness. A Pro Bowler in his second season—Lilly earned another invitation in 1964, starting his string of 10 consecutive Pro Bowl seasons. During those 10 years, he was more than opposing offenses could handle.

"I would never accept getting beat one on one," Lilly said. "You just never let it enter into your mind that the other guy can beat you. Some of them probably should have beaten me, but I wouldn't let them."

Opposing offenses attempted to limit Lilly's one-on-one opportunities. Still, Lilly continued to maintain a presence in the offensive backfield.

"I've never had anyone who was double- or triple-teamed so often," Landry said, "but he could move through the first man so fast then defeat the second."

COMPETITIVE NATURE

Lilly often was described as a fierce competitor.

"The competition is what I love," he once said. "That makes me a lot more intense. Personalities don't enter into it at all. My objective is to get the man with the ball. Nobody better get in my way."

The most public display of that competitiveness came at the end of Super Bowl V, in January 1971.

The Cowboys were playing in their first Super Bowl. Their previous four seasons had ended with playoff losses, with the first two against Vince Lombardi's Green Bay Packers and the most recent two to the Cleveland Browns. The label of the team that couldn't win the big game was hung on the Cowboys, and it cast a huge shadow over the players.

Playoff victories of 5–0 over the Detroit Lions and 17–10 over the San Francisco 49ers had Dallas confident entering the Super Bowl, especially the defense that had allowed only 25 points in its previous six games. The Cowboys were favored by two points over the Baltimore Colts.

Mike Clark gave the Cowboys a 6–0 lead with two field goals. The Colts tied the score in the second quarter when Johnny Unitas's pass was tipped by receiver Eddie Hinton and then Dallas defensive back Mel Renfro before settling into the arms of John Mackey at midfield. Mackey raced untouched into the end zone for a 75-yard scoring play.

The Cowboys regained the lead, at 13–6, before halftime. Craig Morton's intercepted pass in the fourth quarter set up a short Colt touchdown to tie the score again, at 13–13.

Another interception with less than two minutes remaining gave Baltimore the ball at the Dallas 28. With five seconds remaining, Jim O'Brien booted a 32-yard field goal to give the Colts a 16–13 victory.

Once again, the Cowboys had failed to win the big game. As Lilly writes in his autobiography, *Bob Lilly: A Cowboy's Life*,

> At that very moment, my frustration had reached its peak. I ripped off my helmet and hurled it 58 yards into the air. I was just so disgusted with the way we had played, and to lose in the final seconds was the straw that broke the camel's back. I just lost it. What made matters even worse is that a rookie from the Colts brought my helmet back to me and said, "Mr. Lilly, here's your helmet." I felt about an inch tall.

Years later, when Lilly looked back on that moment, he said, "In addition to feeling awful, I felt like an idiot."

Despite his regrets, the image of Lilly slinging his helmet remains the image that defines his competitive nature.

Then, of course, the Cowboys finally achieved the long-sought-after crowning moment by winning Super Bowl VI, 24–3, over Miami. The three points are the fewest ever allowed in a Super Bowl.

In that game, Lilly sacked Dolphin quarterback Bob Griese for a 29-yard loss.

"He is not enormous," Griese would later say of Lilly, "but he is strong enough so that there isn't any use arguing with him if he gets hold of your jersey. You just fall wherever Lilly wants."

Yet, Lilly did not rely on strength alone. He took pride in the time he spent studying game film.

"A man has to figure out what has to be done and how to do it," he said. "You have to be able to spin out of a block, recognize a play immediately, and then react accordingly. I figure I am as strong as anyone else, so getting the job done becomes a matter of pride and determination."

Lilly undeniably had plenty of that.

FIRST TO CANTON

Lilly did not miss a game—regular season or postseason—until the Cowboys' final game of his 13th and penultimate season. A severely pulled hamstring forced him out of the NFC Championship Game in 1973, a game Dallas lost to the Minnesota Vikings. That was the only game he missed during his career. His streak of 196 consecutive regular-season games played remained a franchise record until Jason Witten broke it in 2015.

Following the 1974 season, during which the Cowboys went 8–6 and saw their streak of eight consecutive playoff seasons end, an injury had Lilly ready to retire. Bone spurs in his neck had made it difficult for him to sleep at night, and he received pain-killing shots before games. But when Landry talked to him about playing one more year, Lilly delayed retirement.

However, the summer before the 1975 season, medical tests on Lilly's neck concerned doctors, who warned him that he risked permanent injury—perhaps paralysis—if he played until Jason Witten broke it in 2015.

Landry recommended that Lilly retire, and Lilly did not need convincing.

"It didn't take much time to make my decision after that," he said of the medical reports. "The chances are remote, but they do exist. There was no question that the pain would come back. I was prepared for that. The possibility of permanent damage—I wasn't prepared for that."

During the following season, Lilly became the first member of the Cowboys' Ring of Honor, Tex Schramm's brainchild as a way of honoring the franchise's great players instead of the typical retiring of a number. Although not officially retired, Lilly's number 74 was all but shelved. In the more than four decades since Lilly retired, no Cowboy has worn that number. In fact, "Mr. Cowboy" is the only Dallas player to wear 74.

In 1980, Lilly became the first Cowboy inducted into Canton. After being introduced by Landry on enshrinement day, Lilly told the crowd of the support he had received from his family. Neither of his parents could be there that day. His father had passed away, and his mother was in a Texas hospital.

"The fact that Tom Landry is introducing me means more than you know," Lilly said. "Basically, there have been three men in my life, my father, my college coach, and Tom Landry. This is the tough part. My father died 10 years ago, and my college coach died a year ago. These were the three men who influenced me the most in my life."

In turn, Lilly made his influence on the Cowboys, on and off the field.

"I don't think," Landry said, "Bob ever was aware of how good a player he was or how valuable he was."

CAREER HIGHLIGHTS

Picked as the Cowboys' first draft choice, first Cowboys Hall of Fame member, and first player inducted into the Ring of Honor.

Selected to play in the Pro Bowl 11 times, a Cowboys record, including 10 consecutive years (1964–1973).

Named All-Pro seven times.

Played in five NFL/NFC Championship Games and two Super Bowls.

Part of the Super Bowl VI championship team—the Cowboys' first Super Bowl–winning team.

Named to the NFL All-Decade Team for both the 1960s and 1970s.

Selected to the NFL 75th Anniversary All-Time Team and the AFL–NFL 25th Anniversary Team.

Played 14 seasons with the Cowboys. Only three players have played more, with 15 each.

Played in 196 consecutive games, a long-standing Cowboys record.

Started 194 of 196 games and 135 in a row from 1965–1974.

Shared the NFL career record with three touchdowns via fumble return at the time of his retirement.

Named NFL Rookie of the Year in 1961.

Holds the franchise record for sacks in a game, with five against the Pittsburgh Steelers in 1966.

Led the Cowboys in sacks his first three seasons.

Missed only one game in his 14 seasons.

Had the Bob Lilly Award—the Cowboys' annual award voted on by Cowboys fans and awarded to a player for sportsmanship, dedication, leadership, and achievement—named for him.

FIVE COWBOYS MEMORIES

1. January 16, 1972

Lilly's greatest moment as a Cowboy came in the franchise's first Super Bowl championship—a 24–3 defeat of the Miami Dolphins in Super Bowl VI—because "Next Year's Champions" had proved they could win a big game. Perhaps the signature play from Lilly's career came during that game, when he sacked Bob Griese for a 29-yard loss. That play remains the longest negative play in Super Bowl history. As Griese dropped back to pass, Lilly, from the right side of the Cowboys' defense and Larry Cole from the left, broke through the Dolphin front line, with Lilly beating a double team. Griese spun away from Cole and, upon seeing Lilly bearing down on him, reversed field. Griese set up to get a pass away, but Cole jumped and Griese tucked the ball away and made another spin move. Lilly grabbed Griese around the waist and drug him down from behind for the sack. "I got that sack because I could outrun Larry. That was probably the only reason," Lilly joked.

2. January 17, 1971

Lilly's memorable 58-yard helmet toss showed just how heartbreaking of a loss the Cowboys suffered to Baltimore in Super Bowl V. Lilly has cited two positives that came out of the game. The first was that teammate Chuck Howley was named the game's MVP—the first and only MVP from a losing team. The second was the experience from that first Super Bowl, which propelled the Cowboys to their Super Bowl victory the following year. Lilly said even though the Cowboys had a veteran team, the players "acted like kids" when they arrived in Miami for Super Bowl VI. "There seemed to be millions of people down there, running after us at all hours of the day and night, calling us on the phone and everything," he said. "I think we were awed by the whole thing when we went to our first Super Bowl. That's not an alibi, it's just a fact." But the following year, the Cowboys were prepared for the experience, and their opponents, the Miami Dolphins, were not. "I think losing the 1971 Super Bowl game helped us win in 1972," Lilly said.

3. *November 23, 1975*

At halftime of the Cowboys' game against the Philadelphia Eagles at Texas Stadium, Lilly became the first member of the Ring of Honor. In introducing Lilly to the "Bob Lilly Day" crowd, Coach Tom Landry said, "In my lifetime, there hasn't been a player as good as Bob Lilly. And I don't expect to ever see another one. He is the greatest player I've ever coached." In addition to having his name unveiled below the press box, Lilly received a Pontiac station wagon, a Browning shotgun, and a bird dog. And, for good measure, the Cowboys defeated the rival Eagles, 27–17.

4. *December 31, 1967*

Is the Ice Bowl not a treasured memory for any Cowboy who participated in the 1967 NFL Championship Game in Green Bay? Lilly woke up the morning of the game and looked out the hotel window to see a crisp, sunny morning. Soon thereafter, George Andrie, Lilly's roommate, returned from attending Mass looking colder and more serious than Lilly expected following a Sunday morning winter walk in Green Bay. "I just figured it was a solemn service when he walked in the room," Lilly said. "Then Andrie poured a glass of water, pulled back the curtain, and threw the water at the window. The water froze before it could reach the bottom of the window sill. It was 10 degrees below zero outside, and the wind was predicted to reach up to 35 miles an hour." Wanting to set a tone of toughness for the rest of the team, Andrie convinced Lilly that they should leave the hotel without their warmup jackets. "I practically froze to death before the game even started," Lilly said. "I ran back into the locker room, put on two pairs of long underwear, put Saran Wrap around my feet, and found a cover for my ears. I couldn't believe I was such a fool to leave my warmup jacket behind." Cowboys linemen were not allowed to wear gloves during the game because assistant coach Ernie Stautner had told them, "Men don't wear gloves in this league." After Bart Starr's quarterback sneak in the final seconds gave the Packers a 21–17 win—"It was a game of survival more than anything else," Lilly said—he took a shower in 60-degree water. It felt hot to him, however. "I was never more glad to leave a city," he said.

5. *November 20, 1966*

In the Cowboys' second meeting with the Pittsburgh Steelers during the 1966 season, Lilly established the Cowboys record for sacks, which has been matched only once. That day, the Cowboys recorded 12 sacks—which remains tied for the franchise record—with Lilly recording five in a 20–7 victory.

"Lilly's game was out of this world," Landry said afterward. "He seemed to be in their backfield on every play." Jim Jeffcoat tied Lilly's record in 1985, but no Cowboy has topped his mark.

Statistics

Season	Team	G	Interceptions			Fumble Returns		
			No.	Yds	TD	No.	Yds	TD
1961	Dallas	14	0	0	0	1	0	0
1962	Dallas	14	0	0	0	1	0	0
1963	Dallas	14	0	0	0	1	42	1
1964	Dallas	14	0	0	0	3	4	0
1965	Dallas	14	1	17	1	2	41	0
1966	Dallas	14	0	0	0	1	0	0
1967	Dallas	14	0	0	0	0	0	0
1968	Dallas	14	0	0	0	1	0	0
1969	Dallas	14	0	0	0	2	9	1
1970	Dallas	14	0	0	0	0	0	0
1971	Dallas	14	0	0	0	1	7	1
1972	Dallas	14	0	0	0	1	0	0
1973	Dallas	14	0	0	0	2	6	0
1974	Dallas	14	0	0	0	2	0	0
Totals		196	1	17	1	18	109	3

· 9 ·

Mel Renfro

Natural Athleticism

Melvin Lacy Renfro
Class: 1996 (Lou Creekmur, Dan Dierdorf, Joe Gibbs, Charlie Joiner)
Seasons with Cowboys: 1964–1977
Other NFL teams: None
Positions: Cornerback, safety
College: Oregon

Cowboys coach Tom Landry said Mel Renfro could play any skill position on the field and be a Pro Bowl player. That versatility could have cost Renfro a spot in the Pro Football Hall of Fame.

It was 1966, Renfro's third season in the NFL. He had made the Pro Bowl his first two seasons as a free safety and kick returner. He had intercepted seven passes his rookie year, showing how dangerous he was with the ball in his hands returning the pickoffs. He also had led the league in kickoff and punt-return yardage.

During his second year, he had averaged his career-high of 30.0 yards per kickoff return. He had taken one kick back 100 yards for a score, and he returned an interception 90 yards for a touchdown.

Although a defensive coach by nature, Landry spent the 1966 off-season pondering how dangerous Renfro could be if given more opportunities with the ball in his hands on offense. His preseason experiment of playing Renfro at halfback fared well, and the switch to offense was made.

Renfro, however, suffered an ankle injury in the season opener. Two weeks later, the experiment was over. Dan Reeves established himself at half-back, and after watching a hobbled Renfro, Landry decided defense was the best spot for him after all.

Playing defense, Renfro earned a spot in Canton.

"My career would have ended in the next four or five years," Renfro estimated, a few days before being inducted into the Hall of Fame, if he had remained on offense. "Eight years would have been the max unless they moved me to wide receiver."

Instead, Renfro played 14 seasons with Dallas, becoming one of the best defensive backs of all time, with 10 consecutive Pro Bowl berths and 52 career interceptions, which still ranks as the best in Cowboys history.

ALL-AROUND ATHLETE

Renfro's pure athleticism showed during his high school career at Jefferson High School in Portland, Oregon. In football, Jefferson boasted both Renfro and Terry Baker, who would win the Heisman Trophy as a quarterback at Oregon State. With that duo, Jefferson won 34 consecutive games and three state championships. Renfro was named a high school All-American in both football and track and field.

Renfro's coach, Tom DeSylvia, recalled Renfro as the best athlete he ever saw, citing two nonfootball examples. Renfro helped his team win a track meet by winning the pole vault the first time he had competed in the event. Then an All-City wrestler tried to put some of his best moves on Renfro, and Renfro pinned him.

The college football coaches recruiting Renfro came from far and wide, but he narrowed his choices to in-state schools Oregon and Oregon State.

"I was an introvert, a homeboy," he said, "and I didn't want to go far away."

Renfro chose Oregon, and he became a two-sport All-American for the Ducks. He lettered in track in 1962, and picked up two All-American designations by finishing second in the 120-yard high hurdles and third in the long jump at the NCAA championship meet. He also was part of the Ducks' 440-yard relay team that set the world record with a time of 40.0 seconds.

Football emerged as his main sport, however, with Renfro playing both offense and defense. He led the Ducks in rushing yards and points scored each season from 1961 through 1963. His junior year, he set school records for rushing yards (753), touchdowns (13), and points scored (78), and was named an All-American.

"I don't think you ever know in college that someone is going to be a hall of famer," said Baker, his high school teammate and college rival at Oregon State. "But we knew by the end of his junior year that he was going to the NFL."

Renfro was named an All-American again after his senior year.

Despite missing seven full games in his three seasons, he finished his college career with 1,540 yards rushing, 644 yards receiving, and 23 touchdowns. His career averages were impressive: 5.7 yards per rush, 15.7 yards per reception, 26.7 yards per kickoff return, and 12.9 yards per punt return. In his four 100-yard rushing games, he never had more than 13 carries. Twice, he had eight or fewer. Renfro ended his Oregon career as owner of six school records—four in football and two in track.

But his college football career ended two games early. Renfro missed the final regular-season game against Oregon State and the Sun Bowl because of a wrist injury suffered the night President Kennedy was assassinated in Dallas. Renfro was with friends in his dorm room on November 22, 1963. Upset and frustrated about the president's death, he drank a couple of beers. Suddenly, he rose from his seat and smashed his right fist into a mirror, severing a nerve.

"I felt touched and hurt by what happened," he said. "I was also despondent over the pressures of being married while I was in college and the pressure of performing on the football field and in the classroom."

Doctors told him that if the cut had been any deeper, he would have sliced a vein and could have bled to death. But the injury set up some sleight of hand by the Cowboys heading into the draft.

DRAFT DAY DEALING

The 1964 NFL Draft was held on December 2, 1963, a week and a half after Renfro's accident. Predraft physicals had yet to become standard, and teams were concerned about the severity of Renfro's injury and his pending recovery from the surgery.

In fact, at the AFL draft two days earlier, those fears had caused Renfro to fall all the way to the 10th round, where he was picked up by the Oakland Raiders.

With the Cowboys' love of fast, athletic players, it was no secret that they coveted him with the fourth pick overall.

"Renfro was by far the best player in the draft," Cowboys president and general manager Tex Schramm said.

The Cowboys, however, turned heads when they chose University of Texas defensive tackle Scott Appleton, whom they actually took for the Pittsburgh

Steelers as part of a trade for veteran receiver Buddy Dial, which helped Dallas fill an immediate need. Leaving Renfro on the board heightened other teams' concerns about the injury.

Cowboys vice president of player personnel Gil Brandt called not selecting Renfro a "calculated risk."

"In those days people didn't have the technology they have now," he said. "The league knew my feelings about Mel, and when we didn't draft him in the first round, we probably could have gotten him in the third round."

Waiting until the third round, however, was a risk the Cowboys were not willing to take.

When their turn came in the second round, the Cowboys took advantage of the fact that there was no time limit for making picks. They called an orthopedic surgeon from Portland and had him drive to Eugene to take a look at Renfro's wrist. After a six-hour wait, the Cowboys received a good report from the surgeon and chose Renfro.

"A devious little ploy with small risk," a chuckling Landry claimed.

Renfro has said that he believes the Cowboys, at the least, created an impression for other teams that the injury put his career in some jeopardy.

Then for the Cowboys, it became a matter of signing Renfro before the AFL's Raiders could.

Brandt had met Renfro at the Portland airport after Renfro's junior season at Oregon when both of their flights were cancelled. They wound up sharing a ride to Seattle. Renfro also had talked with Brandt about his wrist injury after it occurred.

"Because the NFL was often bidding with the American Football League for the same players, predraft relationships were vitally important," Brandt said. "Mel and I had become pretty good friends."

Brandt called Renfro after the draft and informed him that he was flying into Portland to meet with him. Renfro picked him up at the airport at 5 a.m., and while the two drove back to Eugene, they negotiated a contract. But a witness was required for the signing of a contract. They stopped a little over halfway to Eugene and secured their witness in the form of a secretary on, of all places, the Oregon State campus.

FINDING A HOME ON DEFENSE

Renfro's impact was immediate, as he earned the right to start as a rookie based on his performance during training camp.

The year before he arrived, the Cowboys ranked next-to-last among the league's 14 teams in yards allowed and yielded 27.0 points per game. During

Renfro's rookie season, Dallas was second in yards allowed and improved its scoring defense by 6.4 points per game.

He was fourth in the league in interceptions, with seven, and led the league in return yardage on kickoffs (1,017) and punts (418). He was fifth in all-purpose yards, with 1,435. The four players ahead of him were all offensive players: Cleveland running back Jim Brown, Minnesota running back Bill Brown, Washington receiver/running back Charley Taylor, and Green Bay running back Jim Taylor.

Renfro was Deion Sanders before there was a Deion Sanders.

After Renfro had been voted into the Hall of Fame in 1996, Brandt said, "He had no weakness. He could do everything. People say Deion Sanders is a great player. Well, Mel could do everything Deion does."

Renfro was selected to the Pro Bowl after his rookie season, beginning a string of 10 consecutive such honors. That certainly was not what he expected coming out of Oregon.

"I had no idea what pro football had in store for me," Renfro said. "My first year, though, I realized I had great football ability. I never thought I'd be a hall of famer or All-Pro. But after my first year, I said, 'Hey, I can do this.'"

It was in his third season that Landry gave in to the temptation of switching Renfro to offense, back to the position he had loved most in college.

"He had more ability and skills than any player we had," Landry said. "He could do anything and play anywhere. He had a great feel for the game."

Because of the ankle injury, however, the offensive experiment was short-lived.

"I was always getting hit from the blind side because I had a dancing style [of running]," Renfro said. "I didn't have the strength and power to be a running back."

"Mel didn't have the body strength to take the pounding that a running back takes," Brandt said. "His body would have never stood up, and he probably would have been a five-year player and out."

But Renfro was able to carry that offensive mentality to the defensive side of the ball. His long arms, keen instincts, and ability to anticipate routes allowed him to shut down opposing receivers in the Cowboys' man-to-man scheme.

In 1970, after being moved from free safety to cornerback, he intercepted a pass in all three of the Cowboys' playoff games. Of his four postseason interceptions, none proved more significant for the franchise than his first, in the Divisional round of the playoffs that year.

The Cowboys led the Detroit Lions, 5–0, late at the Cotton Bowl. The Lions had struggled against the Dallas defense, gaining only 156 yards late into the fourth quarter. But they were driving, reaching the Dallas 29-yard line, and Renfro was thinking on the field of how his team had lost four of its five playoff games.

With their tendency for coming up short in the postseason, the Cowboys had been branded "Next Year's Champions." Although their team led, the Cowboys fans among the 73,167 in attendance feared the Lions would finish their drive in the end zone and send their team into "next year" early again.

But Renfro picked off a tipped Bill Munson pass with less than a minute to play, and the Cowboys advanced to the conference championship. They won that game, against the San Francisco 49ers, before losing to the Baltimore Colts. But that "next year" label was on its way out, erased for good one year later, when Dallas swept through the playoffs en route to their first Super Bowl championship.

"Those games [in the 1970 playoffs] catapulted us into winning the big one," Renfro said more than two decades later. "The dominoes started to fall."

OUT OF THE DESERT

Respect for Renfro as a player and competitor existed league wide. Gene Washington, a receiver with the 49ers in the 1970s, said there were some cornerbacks, like Willie Brown and Emmitt Thomas, who were as good as Renfro, "but no one was better."

"He was phenomenal," Washington said, "because he was so quick, and he could play you tough or with finesse."

Charley Taylor of Washington said he never saw Renfro getting mixed up in any trash-talking or altercations during a game.

"Mel just quietly went about his business," he said.

But still, Renfro had to wait 19 years from when he retired until he received the ultimate recognition for his abilities with his induction into the Hall of Fame.

Some, including Renfro, believed that off-the-field issues, mostly after his career had ended, were held against him.

In 1969, while still playing, he filed a racial discrimination lawsuit, and won a settlement the following year, against an all-white duplex in North Dallas. He believed that suit was held against him.

After his playing days, he claimed the Cowboys would not hire him as an assistant coach, even though they had given similar jobs to other former players. Failed restaurant ventures forced him to file for bankruptcy. In 1981, he was sentenced to six months in jail for failure to pay child support.

Landry thought Renfro may have been caught up in a numbers game when it came to Cowboys players who were voted in, like Roger Staubach, Bob Lilly, Tony Dorsett, and Randy White.

"We're all prejudiced about our players when it comes to something like that," he said. "There are lots of deserving players that don't ever make it."

Landry, Schramm, and former teammates all lobbied for Renfro's inclusion. Len Casanova, Renfro's football coach at Oregon, wrote letters to the Hall of Fame supporting his former player.

Renfro admitted that the feeling of rejection left him bitter. A life change adjusted his attitude.

"I had to give up a lot of hatred and anger," he said. "I had to give up a lot of things I was comfortable with. The last thing was alcohol. I loved to drink beer, but I gave it up in 1994. That was the key. That was when I finally turned my whole life over to God."

Renfro began working with troubled youths in his hometown of Portland, particularly in the poor neighborhood in which he grew up, in the northeast part of the city.

"I looked back at where I had been and all of the things I had accomplished," he said, "and none of it seemed to mean a whole lot."

Then, in 1996, in his 14th year of eligibility—one year shy of when his candidacy would have been transferred to consideration by the Hall's Seniors Committee—Renfro was voted in.

Disappointed by coming up short before and not wanting to relive the stress of sitting by the phone waiting for a phone call, Renfro went to work on selection day. He hoped working would remove the tension he knew from experience he would feel throughout the day. When work failed to help, he returned home. Moments after walking in the door, a radio station called to tell him he was a hall of famer.

Renfro could look back and see how the years of waiting had been a time in which the "Lord also humbled me."

"I really think that's why I hadn't gotten into the Hall of Fame before, because my life wasn't together," he said. "I had too much sin and too much baggage that I was carrying, and I had to get rid of that. When I did, I realized what my life was all about."

As a result, Renfro's induction came at a time when he said he was truly happy for the first time.

"I struggled with identity all of my life," he said. "I was a great athlete and I scored touchdowns and won games, but there was no fulfillment. We're here to do the Lord's work, and if you're not following His lead, you can wander around the desert for a long time. That's what I did."

CAREER HIGHLIGHTS

Named to the Pro Bowl his first 10 years in the league.

Tied with Larry Allen and Jason Witten for second-most Pro Bowl selections by a Cowboy, behind Bob Lilly (11).

Selected All-Pro five times and All-Conference seven times.

Chosen Defensive MVP of the Pro Bowl a week after playing in Super Bowl V.

Led the NFL in interceptions (10) in 1969.

Leads the Cowboys in career interceptions (52) and is second in average yards per kickoff return (26.4).

Intercepted a pass in all three playoff games during the 1970 season.

One of nine players to participate in at least 14 seasons with the Cowboys.

Named a two-sport All-American at the University of Oregon, in football and track.

Named All-American halfback at Oregon in 1962 and 1963.

Selected as a three-time member of the All-Coast team (1961–1963), when Oregon was not affiliated with a conference.

Played on two Super Bowl-winning teams, in four Super Bowls, and in eight NFL/NFC Championship Games.

FIVE COWBOYS MEMORIES

1. *January 16, 1972*

Paul Warfield of the Miami Dolphins led the NFL in touchdown receptions in 1971, with 11. In the Dolphins' two playoff games, he had accounted for 265 yards on nine receptions, with a touchdown. Warfield was such an obvious strength of the Miami offense that before Super Bowl VI, President Richard Nixon suggested to Dolphin coach Don Shula that even with Renfro expected to cover Warfield, the Dolphins should feature the down-and-in pattern with Warfield. But Renfro won that matchup, holding Warfield to 39 yards on four catches and keeping him out of the end zone. With Miami's downfield weapon stymied, Dallas' defense led the way to the Cowboys' first Super Bowl championship, by a score of 24–3.

2. *1970 playoffs*

Renfro picked off a pass in each of the Cowboys' three postseason games. His late interception sealed a first-round, 5–0 defeat of the Detroit Lions. In the conference championship game, the Cowboys led the San Francisco 49ers, 10–3, in the third quarter, but the 49ers were driving. Renfro intercepted a John Brodie pass at the Dallas 19. The Cowboys promptly marched for another touchdown and a 17–3 lead in what turned out to be a 17–10 win that put them in their first Super Bowl. Then, in Super Bowl V—which the Cowboys lost, 16–13, to Baltimore—Renfro ended a Colt scoring threat with a second-quarter interception at the Dallas 15.

3. January 24, 1971

A week after the disappointment of the last-second loss to the Baltimore Colts in Super Bowl V, Renfro enjoyed the reward for his performance during the 1970 season. Playing in his seventh consecutive Pro Bowl, he was named the game's defensive MVP for displaying his all-around skills. Renfro returned two punts for touchdowns and also helped the NFC defense control AFC receivers Paul Warfield (Green Bay) and Warren Wells (Oakland). The NFC won, 27–6.

4. January 15, 1978

Renfro's career was winding down. After playing a reduced role much of his 14th season in the league, a knee injury prevented him from playing in the final four games and continued to bother him in the playoffs. When the Cowboys took on the Denver Broncos in Super Bowl XII, Renfro suited up but was not expected to play. That changed when cornerback Bennie Barnes got injured in the first half. The Cowboys' 27–10 win was the last game of Renfro's career. "That was exciting, and a great way to go out," he said. "Not many players go out with a Super Bowl victory."

5. November 29, 1964

Renfro led the league in kickoff-return yards and punt-return yards during his rookie season, and his special teams skills were on full display in a 45–21 loss to the Green Bay Packers. He accounted for 273 total return yards and a touchdown in the game, returning eight kickoffs for 156 yards and bringing back four punts for a total of 117 yards. His touchdown came on a 69-yard punt return in the second quarter. His 273 return yards remain the franchise's single-game record—by 49 yards over the next-best return day by a Cowboy.

Statistics

Defense

Regular Season			*Interceptions*				*Fumble Recoveries*		
Season	*Team*	*G*	*No.*	*Yds*	*Avg*	*TD*	*No.*	*Yds*	*TD*
1964	Dallas	14	7	110	15.7	1	2	0	0
1965	Dallas	14	2	92	46.0	1	2	1	0
1966	Dallas	11	2	57	28.5	0	0	0	0
1967	Dallas	9	7	38	5.4	0	2	28	0
1968	Dallas	14	3	5	1.7	0	1	6	0
1969	Dallas	14	10	118	11.8	0	0	0	0
1970	Dallas	14	4	3	0.8	0	2	0	0
1971	Dallas	14	4	11	2.8	0	0	0	0
1972	Dallas	14	1	0	0.0	0	1	3	0
1973	Dallas	14	2	65	32.5	1	2	0	0
1974	Dallas	11	1	6	6.0	0	1	6	0
1975	Dallas	11	4	70	17.5	0	0	0	0
1976	Dallas	9	3	23	7.7	0	0	0	0
1977	Dallas	11	2	28	14.0	0	0	0	0
Totals		174	52	626	12.0	3	13	44	0

Postseason			*Interceptions*				*Fumble Recoveries*		
Season	*Team*	*G*	*No.*	*Yds*	*Avg*	*TD*	*No.*	*Yds*	*TD*
1966	Dallas	1	0	0	0.0	0	0	0	0
1967	Dallas	2	0	0	0.0	0	0	0	0
1968	Dallas	1	0	0	0.0	0	0	0	0
1969	Dallas	1	0	0	0.0	0	0	0	0
1970	Dallas	3	3	32	10.7	0	0	0	0
1971	Dallas	3	0	0	0.0	0	0	0	0
1972	Dallas	2	0	0	0.0	0	0	0	0
1973	Dallas	2	0	0	0.0	0	1	2	0
1975	Dallas	3	1	0	0.0	0	0	0	0
1977	Dallas	3	0	0	0.0	0	0	0	0
Totals		21	4	32	10.7	0	1	2	0

Special Teams

Regular Season		*Punt Returns*				*Kickoff Returns*			
Season	*Team*	*No.*	*Yds*	*Avg*	*TD*	*No.*	*Yds*	*Avg*	*TD*
1964	Dallas	32	418	13.1	1	40	1,017	25.4	0
1965	Dallas	24	145	6.0	0	21	630	30.0	1
1966	Dallas	21	123	5.9	0	19	487	25.6	1
1967	Dallas	3	−1	−0.3	0	5	112	22.4	0
1969	Dallas	15	80	5.3	0	0	0	0.0	0
1970	Dallas	13	77	5.9	0	0	0	0.0	0
1974	Dallas	1	0	0.0	0	0	0	0.0	0
Totals		109	842	7.7	1	85	2,246	26.4	2

Postseason		Punt Returns				Kickoff Returns			
Season	Team	No.	Yds	Avg	TD	No.	Yds	Avg	TD
1966	Dallas	0	0	0.0	0	5	124	24.8	0
1970	Dallas	4	23	5.8	0	0	0	0.0	0
Totals		4	23	5.8	1	5	124	24.8	0

Others—Rushing: 8–52; receiving: 4–65.

• _10_ •

Deion Sanders

Created for Primetime

Deion Luwynn Sanders
Class: 2011 (Richard Dent, Marshall Faulk, Chris Hanburger, Les
  Richter, Ed Sabol, Shannon Sharpe)
Seasons with Cowboys: 1995–1999
Other NFL teams: Atlanta Falcons (1989–1993), San Francisco 49ers
  (1994), Washington Redskins (2000), Baltimore Ravens (2004–2005)
Positions: Cornerback, wide receiver, kick returner, punt returner
College: Florida State

$\mathcal{I}$t was difficult to determine which part of Deion Sanders's Hall of Fame induction ceremony seemed most fitting.

First, there was the moment when he concluded his speech, pointed toward his bust on the stage, said "I like him, but something's missing," pulled a black bandana from his jacket pocket, and added to his likeness a black do-rag like he had worn underneath his helmet.

Or perhaps it was when among the more than one hundred people he thanked during his acceptance speech were guests/recording artists Snoop Dogg, Nelly, and Ice Cube.

It might have been the fact that the person Sanders chose to introduce him was his agent. After all, the biggest hit during Sanders's mostly underwhelming rap career was titled "Must Be the Money."

Actually, the most fitting moment for the man who gave himself the nickname—and developed the persona—of "Prime Time" could have come six months earlier, when Sanders learned he had been voted into the Hall during his first year of eligibility.

"I was an original," Sanders said.

He was that, especially on the field, regardless of the type of field.

Playing in the NFL and in Major League Baseball, Sanders's athletic ability and work ethic allowed him to become the most successful two-sport star of the modern era. In football, he made eight Pro Bowls during his 14-year career. A triple threat on defense, offense, and special teams, he set a NFL record with 19 return touchdowns. On defense alone, he was so good at shutting down opposing receivers that despite a reputation for shying away from tackles, Sanders still belongs in every conversation for determining the best cover corner in the game's history.

"If 'shutdown corner' didn't start with him," his agent, Eugene Parker, said, "he gave it credence."

A PROMISING ATHLETE

Sanders never denied the appeal of the money he earned playing football. And baseball. And rapping. And appearing in commercials as a two-sport star. The money was important to him because of a promise he had made to his mother when he was seven years old.

His mother, Connie Knight, was cleaning dishes in their apartment in the projects of Fort Myers, Florida. She worked as a janitor at a hospital to support him, and he promised her, "I'm going to make a lot of money, and you will never have to work another day of your life."

It was big talk from a small boy, but as he did throughout his sports career, Sanders backed up that talk.

To fulfill that promise, Sanders felt he needed a persona that would make him more marketable and earn him more money. Thus, "Prime Time" was born.

The nickname—along with another, "Neon Deion"—came when he was starring in multiple sports at North Fort Myers High School. The stories of how Sanders picked up that nickname from a teammate vary depending on which former teammate or coach is being asked. But they all center on Sanders's phenomenal athletic ability, which showed as early as his youth football days with the Fort Myers Rebels.

His coach, Dave Capel, recalled his team's game in Georgia for the national championship. Capel's offensive philosophy was simple: get the ball to Deion. A stunned opponent that had had its way with outmanned teams all season could not tackle the fast and elusive little kid from Florida.

"They couldn't figure out how he could zigzag so fast," Capel said. "He lived across the street from a cemetery. When he got off the bus from school, he had to run through the cemetery to get to his house. He was scared to go through it, so he zigzagged as fast as he could."

That youth football team was far from the last befuddled by Sanders.

At North Fort Myers High, he was chosen All-State in three sports: football, basketball, and baseball. His senior year in football, he passed for 839 yards and rushed for 499 yards in an option offense. On defense, he picked off four passes. For the basketball team, he averaged 24 points per game.

The Kansas City Royals drafted him in the sixth round in 1985, but he turned down the Royals' $75,000 offer because he wanted to see how good he could be in football.

Ron Hoover, his football coach at North Fort Myers, called Sanders a "coach's dream."

"He had everything you wanted—hard worker, smart, a great leader," Hoover said. "If he wanted, he would have been a great receiver."

But Prime Time was still just a nickname then. It became a persona at Florida State.

Football was the sport in which Sanders became one of the nation's most sought-after recruits. He had also visited Georgia and Florida before choosing the Seminoles. At Florida State, Sanders researched NFL salaries and didn't like what he saw for his position.

"The defensive backs weren't making any money," he said. "They weren't even making a million. It upset me. I needed to take care of Momma. I just upped my personality and began to market myself. It was a character I had in me. I just blew him up. I knew I had the goods, and I had the product."

That, he did.

Sanders gave up basketball, but he did take part in three sports at Florida State. He played two seasons of baseball, hitting .333 in 60 at-bats, with 11 stolen bases in his first season. His sophomore year, he played in 60 games, hitting .267, with 15 extra-base hits, 21 runs batted in, and 27 steals.

Sanders also competed in track, winning Metro Conference titles in the 100 and 200 meters as a freshman. One day, he played in the first game of a doubleheader for the baseball team, went to the track and ran a leg of the 4x100 relay in his baseball pants, and returned to the baseball field in time to deliver the game-winning hit in the second game of the doubleheader.

His junior year, Sanders qualified for the Olympic trials in the 100 with a time of 10.26 seconds.

"I'm convinced," longtime Florida State track coach Dick Roberts said, "that if Deion devoted his energies to track exclusively, that he would be in the mold of America's great sprinters: Jessie Owens, Bob Hayes, and Carl Lewis."

But, again, football provided the prime time stage Sanders sought.

He started at cornerback as a true freshman for the Seminoles and was named All-American his sophomore and junior years. The New York Yankees drafted him in June 1988, and he signed and played in 28 games before returning to Florida State for his senior season of football. He won the Jim Thorpe Award, given to the nation's top defensive back, and ranked in the top 10 in the country with five interceptions in nine games and led the nation by averaging 15.2 yards per punt return. The Seminoles finished 11–1 and ranked third in the Associated Press poll after defeating Auburn in the Sugar Bowl. Florida State went 4–0 in bowl games in Sanders's four years.

For his career, he intercepted 17 passes—including three in bowl games—and scored seven touchdowns on returns (four interceptions, three punts.)

"I think the best athlete I ever coached was Deion Sanders," said Bobby Bowden, his football coach at Florida State. "We had other players who were good in their own way. But I don't think we ever had anyone with as much natural talent."

Yet, Sanders did not rely on talent alone.

"I tell people this and they don't believe me," Bowden said. "He was one of the hardest working players I ever coached. He had a work ethic second to no one."

STRIKING GOLD WITH THE 49ERS

The Atlanta Falcons selected Sanders fifth overall in the 1989 NFL Draft and handed him the largest contract ever for a rookie defensive back: Signing bonus included, the deal was for $4.41 million over four years or, including the option year, $5.16 million over five years.

In the first quarter of his first NFL game, Sanders returned a punt 68 yards for a touchdown. It was a sign of things to come, not only with the Falcons, but also in the league.

Sanders played five years for Atlanta, scoring 10 touchdowns. Three came on interception returns, three came on kickoff returns, two came on punt returns, and two were on offense as a receiver.

In Sanders's first three seasons, the Falcons transformed from a 3–13 team his rookie year to a 10–6 NFC West runner-up that earned the franchise's first playoff victory in 13 years.

All the while, he continued his side job as a professional baseball player. Sanders played 103 minor-league games in the Yankees' system in 1989, making his major-league debut on May 31, and 13 more games in June and as a September call-up. The next year, he split time between the Yankees (hitting .158) and class AAA Columbus (.321), until leaving New York in July after some contract hassling. The Yankees eventually waived him. That allowed him to sign with the Atlanta Braves as he played out his contract with the Falcons.

When Sanders hit the free-agent market, he and the San Francisco 49ers had a mutual need: one another.

The 49ers had lost to the Dallas Cowboys in the NFC Championship Game the previous two seasons. They were loaded on offense, with quarterback Steve Young, running back Ricky Watters, and receivers Jerry Rice and John Taylor. They needed to upgrade their defense, however, to combat the Cowboys' offensive firepower.

They signed linebackers Ken Norton Jr. (from the Cowboys) and Gary Plummer, defensive end Rickey Jackson, and pass rusher Richard Dent. The one other needed piece was a defensive back to line up across from Michael Irvin. In Sanders, San Francisco found that final piece.

Sanders, for his part, wanted a piece of jewelry, and he believed the 49ers would provide him the opportunity to win a Super Bowl ring. The match was made when Sanders signed a one-year contract worth $1.2 million, below his market value. Both the 49ers and Sanders got what they wanted.

Sanders intercepted six passes in 1994 and racked up league highs with 303 return yards and three touchdowns during the regular season, earning him the NFL Defensive Player of the Year award and his fourth consecutive Pro Bowl selection.

During the postseason, San Francisco routed the Chicago Bears to set up a third consecutive NFC Championship Game showdown with the Cowboys.

San Francisco forced three Dallas early turnovers in jumping out to a 21–0 first-quarter lead that propelled them to a 38–28 win. Sanders also picked off a Troy Aikman pass, and it was his defensive stop against Irvin that thwarted Dallas' late rally and led Cowboys coach Barry Switzer to draw an unsportsmanlike conduct penalty while arguing for a pass interference call.

With the Cowboys dispatched, the 49ers went on to defeat the San Diego Chargers, 49–26, in Super Bowl XXIX. That game, paired with Sanders's playing in the 1992 World Series with the Atlanta Braves, made him the first athlete to play in both a Super Bowl and a World Series.

Sanders's one-year contract paid off for both him and San Francisco. And his next contract was far from below market value.

PAYDAY IN DALLAS

Sanders beat the Cowboys *and* joined them. He again broke a record with his contract. Dallas owner Jerry Jones signed Sanders to a seven-year, $35 million contract, with the final two years voidable. That made him the league's highest-paid cornerback, and the $12,999,999 signing bonus was the largest ever given out in the NFL.

In as flamboyant of a manner as he high-stepped into end zones, Sanders showed up for the news conference announcing his signing wearing a pin-striped blue suit and white dress shirt with "Prime Time" embossed on the left collar. Gold bracelets were on each wrist; he sported diamond earrings; and, as writer Rick Cantu of the *Austin American-Statesman* described it, "enough gold around his neck to open a jewelry store."

"Deion was going to get his money," Jones said. "Now the question was: 'Who is going to have Deion help them to the Super Bowl?' I wanted him to be with the Dallas Cowboys. Someday, people are going to learn that I'm not in this for the money. I didn't buy the Dallas Cowboys to make money. I'm here to win."

Sanders said "the biggest decision of my life" was based on that same desire to win, not the money.

"Looking at the financial part of it, I admit there were other teams out there that were going to do better," he said. "But I really wanted to be a Dallas Cowboy. Being with the 49ers last season was wonderful. . . . But here in Dallas, I plan on a three-, four-, five-year run at the Super Bowl."

Sanders didn't make his Cowboys debut until the eighth game of the season because of his baseball commitment with the San Francisco Giants and surgery for an ankle injury. The late start cost him a chance at his fifth straight Pro Bowl, but he did return in time to help Dallas finish off another NFC East championship and a run to the franchise's fifth Super Bowl title.

The Cowboys did not make it back to the Super Bowl, but Sanders did return to his form. For three of his five years in Dallas—1996, 1998, and 1999—he didn't play baseball. With Sanders a one-sport player in 1996, the Cowboys made him a true two-way player for the only time in his career and the NFL's first such player in 34 years. Sanders was second on the team in receiving yards. The following year, however, he returned to spot roles on offense.

Sanders made the Pro Bowl from 1996 to 1999 with the Cowboys and then was released for salary-cap purposes. He played in 2000, with the Washington Redskins; retired; and then, at the age of 36, returned to play with the Baltimore Ravens in 2004 and 2005.

AN ORIGINAL

Sanders was considered a shoo-in for the Hall of Fame in 2011, his first year of eligibility.

"He's as good as I've ever seen," said Aikman, who played and practiced against him.

Sanders drew similar praise at every stop during his 14 seasons in the NFL.

"You couldn't throw at Deion without risking a substantial turn of events," said Merton Hanks, a teammate with the 49ers.

Scott Case, who played with Sanders for his five years in Atlanta, called Sanders "fearless."

"He was never scared of getting beat," Case said.

Case added that Sanders would bait opposing receivers and quarterbacks into believing he had been beaten on a route, intentionally missing a jam at the line of scrimmage or hanging back and giving a receiver a cushion to attract a throw that he could swoop in and pick off.

"I've never seen a guy like Deion who would just mess with receivers," Case said. "And I'm talking about great receivers. You can do that with some young guy, but when you start talking about the Jerry Rices and Henry Ellards—when you can do that to those guys, you're pretty special."

Cowboys safety Darren Woodson cited Sanders's work ethic.

"No one saw the work he put in leading up to the game," he said. "I got a window of that his first year with us. I started to see what made him special."

Woodson told of how Sanders would watch video of receivers he would face and kept notes and films on them.

"He'd watch those tapes over and over again," Woodson said. "He put in so much time. He didn't show it. He didn't want everyone to see it. But the guy did so much work."

That may have been the Sanders that football fans did not see, but his freakish natural ability and that desire to be the best is what made him the NFL's first true shutdown corner. All that other stuff—the flash, the dash, the jewelry, the talk—is what made him "Prime Time." No doubt, Sanders excelled at both.

"Deion had the ability to not only focus on his craft and play football at the highest level, he could also entertain," said Parker, his agent. "He always used to say, 'I do what I love and I love what I do.' He wanted to express that exuberance for what he was doing."

He did, all the way to the steps of Canton. And that is what made Deion Sanders an original.

CAREER HIGHLIGHTS

Selected to play in eight Pro Bowls, including four with Dallas.

Played in both a World Series and a Super Bowl, the only athlete to do so.

Named to the NFL All-Decade Team for the 1990s as a cornerback and a punt returner.

Selected All-Pro nine times.

Set an NFL record with 19 career touchdowns by any type of return.

Holds Cowboys career records for average yards per punt return (13.3) and punt returns for touchdowns (four).

Returned a punt 68 yards for a touchdown in his NFL debut with the Atlanta Falcons.

Intercepted 53 passes during his career.

Led the NFL in punt returns in 1998, with a 15.6 average.

Led the NFC in interceptions twice, with six in 1991 and seven in 1993.

Ranked second all-time in the NFL in interception return yardage (1,331) and tied for second for touchdowns via interception returns (nine) at the time of his retirement.

Became the first player with two interception returns for touchdowns of at least 90 yards in the same season in 1994, playing for San Francisco.

Named NFL Defensive Player of the Year in 1994.

Played on two Super Bowl championship teams in successive years: San Francisco (XXIX) and Dallas (XXX).

Started 16 games at cornerback and eight games at wide receiver for the Cowboys in 1996, becoming the NFL's first two-way starter since the Philadelphia Eagles' Chuck Bednarik, who retired in 1962.

Played 11 seasons of professional baseball between 1988 and 2001, including nine seasons in the major leagues (Yankees, Braves, Reds, Giants), and had a .263 career batting average.

Batted .533 with the Atlanta Braves in the 1992 World Series.

FIVE COWBOYS MEMORIES

1. January 28, 1996

By Deion Sanders's standards, Super Bowl XXX was a relatively quiet night. The Cowboys defeated the Pittsburgh Steelers, 27–17, and Larry Brown—the cornerback on the opposite side of Sanders—was voted MVP after intercepting two passes. Sanders contributed to that. Pittsburgh avoided throwing Sanders's way most of the game, even when he lined up against its leading receiver, Yancey Thigpen, who was held to three receptions for 19 yards. "Deion forced some balls over to Larry's side," defensive coordinator Dave Campo said, "and [Brown] came through." In fact, Sanders's flashiest play came on offense, midway through the first quarter, when he hauled in a 47-

yard pass from Troy Aikman to the Pittsburgh 14. That was the game's only pass play longer than 22 yards, and it set up a short touchdown pass to Jay Novacek that gave Dallas a 10–0 lead.

2. September 21, 1998

Aikman did not play because of injury. Emmitt Smith left in the second quarter with a pulled groin. But the Cowboys still had Deion Sanders, and he stepped up to lead Dallas past the New York Giants, 31–7, at Giants Stadium. Despite missing most of the second quarter due to dehydration, Sanders accounted for 226 total yards on offense, defense, and special teams. He opened the scoring with a 59-yard punt return in the second quarter, part of his 100 yards on five punt returns. He closed the scoring with a 71-yard interception return in the fourth quarter, which made him the first Cowboy ever to score two touchdowns on returns in the same game. He also caught a 55-yard pass that set up a touchdown.

3. January 7, 1996

Sanders scored one touchdown in 12 career postseason games, and he made it count. His 21-yard touchdown run on a reverse broke a 3–3 tie in the second quarter and started a run of 27 unanswered points by the Cowboys in a 30–11 defeat of the Philadelphia Eagles that advanced them to their fourth consecutive NFC Championship Game. Sanders also had a reception for 13 yards, one interception return of 12 yards, and two punt returns for 21 yards against the Eagles. His run with 4:35 left in the second quarter was the biggest of those. He had to reverse field after receiving the handoff. The play impressed Aikman. "I've never seen anything like it," the quarterback said. "It was absolutely unbelievable. I started to try to throw a block but decided, Naw, I'll just get out of the way." That play also was the only rushing touchdown of Sanders's career, both regular season and postseason.

4. October 29, 1995

For a player who loved the limelight, Sanders could not have handpicked a better place and opponent for his Cowboys debut: in the Georgia Dome and against the Atlanta Falcons, the team that had drafted him out of Florida State and for whom he had played his first five seasons. The Cowboys' 28–13 victory was a rather nondescript game for Sanders, but that fact served notice to Dallas fans that he indeed would make a difference with the Cowboys. For most of the game, the Falcons avoided throwing toward Sanders, who started at right cornerback but played both corner positions. In fact, in the five downs he played on offense, he caught as many passes as he allowed Falcon receivers to catch against him: one. Falcon receiver Bert Emanuel caught an 11-yard pass from Jeff George on Atlanta's second possession for the only completion against Prime Time. On Atlanta's next series, on third down from the Dallas three, George went Emanuel's way again, but Sanders broke in front of the receiver and batted down the pass. The Falcons had to settle for a field goal when a touchdown would have given them a 14–0 second-quarter lead. Sanders's catch on offense went for six yards on a quick screen. But playing offense helped make up for the lack of action that came his way on defense. "I wasn't frustrated that they wouldn't throw at me because I was involved in the offense," he said after the game. "If I wasn't, I might have gotten bored."

5. November 2, 1998

The Philadelphia Eagles had elected to kick away from Sanders on their first three punts. On the fourth, punter Tommy Hutton mistakenly kicked where Sanders could field the ball. "He made us pay," Hutton said. Sanders's 69-yard punt return for a touchdown staked the Cowboys to a 17–0 second-quarter lead and set the tone for an easy 34–0 victory at Texas Stadium. The return was Sanders's second for a touchdown on the season and his fifth return of at least 30 yards. His success had caused teams to play keep-away with punts. In his first three games, Sanders had run up 247 punt return yards and a touchdown. In the next three games, he'd had only four returns for a total of minus-three yards, with three fair catches. But given a chance on Hutton's fourth punt of the game, he electrified the Monday night crowd. He also intercepted a pass early in the fourth quarter and returned it 21 yards. On offense, he had one reception for 11 yards, giving him 106 total yards for the game.

Statistics

Defense/Offense

Regular Season			Interceptions				Receiving			
Season	*Team*	*G*	*No.*	*Yds*	*Avg*	*TD*	*No*	*Yds*	*Avg*	*TD*
1989	Atlanta	15	5	52	10.4	0	1	−8	−8.0	0
1990	Atlanta	16	3	153	51.0	2	0	0	0	0
1991	Atlanta	15	6	119	19.8	1	1	17	17.0	0
1992	Atlanta	13	3	105	35.0	0	3	45	15.0	1
1993	Atlanta	11	7	91	13.0	0	6	106	17.7	1
1994	San Francisco	14	6	303	50.5	3	0	0	0.0	0
1995	Dallas	9	2	34	17.0	0	2	25	12.5	0
1996	Dallas	16	2	3	1.5	0	36	475	13.2	1
1997	Dallas	13	2	81	40.5	1	0	0	0.0	0
1998	Dallas	11	5	153	30.6	1	7	100	14.3	0
1999	Dallas	14	3	2	0.7	0	4	24	6.0	0
2000	Washington	16	4	91	22.8	0	0	0	0.0	0
2004	Baltimore	9	3	87	29.0	1	0	0	0.0	0
2005	Baltimore	16	2	57	28.5	0	0	0	0.0	0
Totals		188	53	1,331	25.1	9	60	784	13.1	3

Postseason			Interceptions				Receiving			
Season	*Team*	*G*	*No.*	*Yds*	*Avg*	*TD*	*No*	*Yds*	*Avg*	*TD*
1991	Atlanta	2	1	31	31.0	0	0	0	0.0	0
1994	San Francisco	3	2	15	7.5	0	0	0	0.0	0
1995	Dallas	3	1	12	12.0	0	3	95	31.7	0
1996	Dallas	2	1	22	22.0	0	0	0	0.0	0
1998	Dallas	1	0	0	0.0	0	0	0	0.0	0
1999	Dallas	1	0	0	0.0	0	0	0	0.0	0
Totals		12	5	80	16.0	0	3	95	31.7	0

Regular Season		Punt Returns				Kickoff Returns			
Season	*Team*	*No.*	*Yds*	*Avg*	*TD*	*No*	*Yds*	*Avg*	*TD*
1989	Atlanta	28	307	11.0	1	35	725	20.7	0
1990	Atlanta	29	250	8.6	1	39	851	21.8	0
1991	Atlanta	21	170	8.1	0	26	576	22.2	1
1992	Atlanta	13	41	3.2	0	40	1,067	26.7	2
1993	Atlanta	2	21	10.5	0	7	169	24.1	0
1994	San Francisco	0	0	0.0	0	0	0	0.0	0
1995	Dallas	1	54	54.0	0	1	15	15.0	0
1996	Dallas	1	4	4.0	0	0	0	0.0	0
1997	Dallas	33	407	12.3	1	1	18	18.0	0
1998	Dallas	24	375	15.6	2	1	16	16.0	0
1999	Dallas	30	344	11.5	1	4	87	21.8	0
2000	Washington	25	185	7.4	0	1	−1	−1.0	0
2004	Baltimore	5	41	8.2	0	0	0	0.0	0
2005	Baltimore	0	0	0.0	0	0	0	0.0	0
Totals		212	2,199	10.4	6	155	3,523	22.7	3

Regular Season		Punt Returns				Kickoff Returns			
Season	Team	No.	Yds	Avg	TD	No	Yds	Avg	TD
1991	Atlanta	3	33	11.0	0	6	124	20.7	0
1994	San Francisco	0	0	0.0	0	1	25	25.0	0
1995	Dallas	4	38	9.5	0	0	0	0.0	0
1996	Dallas	0	0	0.0	0	1	28	28.0	0
1998	Dallas	2	411	20.5	0	0	0	0.0	0
1999	Dallas	2	6	3.0	0	0	0	0.0	0
Totals		11	118	10.7	0	8	177	22.1	0

Others—Rushing: 9-minus 14 (postseason 4–39, 1 TD); passing: 0–2.

Tex Schramm

Master Innovator

> **Texas Earnest Schramm Jr.**
> **Class:** 1991 (Earl Campbell, John Hannah, Stan Jones, Jan Stenerud)
> **Seasons with Cowboys:** 1960–1989
> **Other NFL teams:** Los Angeles Rams (1947–1956)
> **Positions:** Contributor
> **College:** Texas

*W*hen Tex Schramm took his first job in the NFL, there was no Pro Football Hall of Fame. It was fitting when, in 1991, he became the first enshrined executive who had not owned or coached a team, because Schramm introduced more than his fair share of "firsts" to the league.

"I truly believe," Hall of Fame coach Don Shula once said of Schramm, "he had as much, or more, to do with the success of professional football as anyone who has ever been connected with the league."

Innovator. Genius. Icon. Visionary. All have been used to describe the man who was the first Cowboy and ran the franchise for 29 years.

"Tex Schramm was one of the visionary leaders in sports history—a thinker, doer, innovator, and winner with few equals," Commissioner Paul Tagliabue said at the time of Schramm's death in 2003. "He played a major role in building the NFL into America's passion by developing a glamour franchise with national appeal and by his leadership on so many league issues."

Indeed, Schramm's impact went far beyond building the Cowboys into one of sports' preeminent franchises; he also ascended into a position of great influence within the league and introduced numerous changes that today's fans still enjoy.

To provide a sample: instant replay, the play clock, referees' microphones, extra-wide sideline borders, multicolor striping on 20- and 50-yard lines, and cheerleaders; even the very makeup of the league itself, because it was Schramm who met with AFL principal founder Lamar Hunt to forge the merging of the rival leagues into what became today's NFL.

"He was a remarkable person, a remarkable figure in the history of pro football," Hunt said. "He made so many contributions. You would run out of ink if you tried to write them all down."

WORKING HIS WAY UP

Perhaps there was no one born more to start up the Cowboys franchise than a man named Texas.

Texas Earnest Schramm Jr. was a Californian by birth and did not step foot in the Lone Star State until enrolling at the University of Texas, his father's alma mater. Schramm left the university in 1941, to enter the U.S. Air Force, and then returned to Texas. While completing his journalism degree, he began working as sports editor of the *Austin American-Statesman* newspaper, a position he held for two years.

In 1947, Schramm parlayed his degree and newspaper experience into a job as publicity director of the Los Angeles Rams, writing stories for newspapers as part of his unenviable duty of trying to get media coverage alongside the more popular sports of baseball, boxing, and college football. He once recalled how Los Angeles had five newspapers at the time, and he would try to get the sports sections to give him two or three paragraphs for the Rams.

As he gained experience with the Rams, he was able to move into the areas of scouting and the draft as an assistant to the president. When his replacement as publicity director left in 1952, he hired a bright young man named Pete Rozelle, who would later become NFL commissioner.

Even in hiring a publicity director, Schramm displayed the tough negotiating skills that would create frustration with players that, later, would produce humorous stories.

"He said they were offering $5,500," Rozelle recalled of his interview with Schramm. "And I said I had in mind $6,000. He said no, that he had $5,500 in mind. So I said fine. I didn't have any more success negotiating with Tex than some of his players."

After practically running the day-to-day operations of the Rams, Schramm was named general manager and held that position through the 1956 season. During his 10 years with the team, Los Angeles turned in nine winning seasons and won the 1951 world championship.

After repeated squabbles with team management, Schramm became an assistant director of sports broadcasting for CBS, where he worked on football broadcasts and hired Pat Summerall to announce New York Giants games. He also proposed and orchestrated the first network broadcast of a Winter Olympics in 1960, with Walter Cronkite anchoring coverage in Squaw Valley, California.

His success in television led to job offers from competitors, but he declined all of them.

"I guess, subconsciously, I was wanting back in football," he said. "That must have been in the back of my mind when I turned down two or three opportunities when I was at CBS."

In his third year at CBS, he received a football opportunity he could not turn down.

FOOTBALL'S YANKEES

The NFL awarded deep-pocketed Texas businessman Clint Murchison Jr. an expansion franchise in Dallas to go head-to-head with the upstart AFL, which included the Dallas Texans. Chicago Bears owner George Halas recommended Schramm to Murchison, and the 39-year-old was charged with starting the Cowboys.

"I had always wanted to take a team from scratch and build it," Schramm said. "This was the opportunity."

The Cowboys were a team that had to be built from scratch—and from a one-room rented office. His goal was simple: make the Cowboys into an organization that would be football's version of baseball's New York Yankees.

The Yankees "were tops, first class," Schramm said. "That's the way we wanted to be. Football is such a great and emotional business, and I wanted to look back and say I was part of greatness."

Two of his most important hires would come to reflect the management structure Schramm believed a team needed to succeed after watching jealousy and in-fighting cripple the Rams.

Gil Brandt, from whom Schramm had received scouting reports on Big Ten players while Schramm was with the Rams, was hired as head scout. Tom Landry, a well-reputed defensive assistant coach with the New York Giants, was hired as head coach.

The three men's roles were clear: Brandt determined which players to bring in, Landry determined how to use them, and Schramm determined how much to pay them. Murchison's contentment with being "only" the owner of a successful franchise allowed the trio to thrive in those roles for 29 years—to the tune of a 270–178–6 record.

The Cowboys' inaugural team lost its first 10 games and finished the season 0–11–1.

"Failure never entered my thinking," Schramm said. "We were just so excited and exhilarated. We knew we were on the right track."

The 1961 team won three of its first four games but staggered the rest of the way to a 4–9–1 record. In their first five years, the Cowboys did not win more than five games in a season.

"Those were the great years," Schramm said, looking back fondly more than three decades after being hired by Murchison. "You couldn't wait to wake up, there was so much to accomplish. It was just so exciting—a hell of a lot more exciting than the successful years."

Of course, that was said in hindsight. At the time, Cowboys fans and the local media were growing restless with the losing team, and the head coach bore much of the criticism. Schramm believed in Landry so much that he recommended that Murchison make a public show of support for Landry. The owner handed the coach a 10-year contract extension. With uncertainty about the head coach removed, the Cowboys took off.

They went 7–7 in 1965, and followed the next year with a 10–3–1 season for their first winning record and first playoff berth. That started a streak of 20 consecutive winning seasons—a mark that no other NFL franchise has achieved. Included were 13 divisional titles, five conference championships, five Super Bowl appearances, and two Super Bowl victories.

"They won because of Tom, but Tex gave them aura that made them feel they were better than everybody else," said Charley Casserly, general manager of the rival Washington Redskins from 1989 to 1999. "That gave everyone in the league, especially us, more inspiration to play and beat them."

Under Schramm's leadership, the Cowboys did become the Yankees of the NFL. In the process, they became "America's Team."

In the late 1970s, Cowboys games were broadcast on 225 radio stations, including 16 in Spanish. The *Dallas Cowboys Weekly* newspaper, which Schramm created, boasted a circulation of 95,000—more than the national publication *Pro Football Weekly's* subscription base. Cowboys merchandise accounted for 30 percent of the league's apparel market, and the famed Dallas Cowboys Cheerleaders—which Schramm also created—sold more than 1 million posters and were featured in two made-for-television movies.

NFL Films proposed the title of "Champions Die Hard" for the highlight film of the 1978 defending world championship team that had lost to the Pittsburgh Steelers, 35–31, in Super Bowl XIII. The Cowboys' public relations director said he did not like the title, however. Bob Ryan, editor in chief at NFL Films, considered the national popularity of the Cowboys and came back with the title "America's Team."

Never one to miss an opportunity, as soon as the highlight film came out, Schramm distributed one hundred thousand "America's Team" calendars.

"Once our popularity got started, we wanted to keep it going," he said. "I think we were probably more image-conscious than other teams. We tried to do everything first class, from top to bottom."

IMPROVING THE GAME

Pete Rozelle ascended to the NFL commissioner's position two days before the Cowboys officially became a franchise. His working relationship with Schramm from their Rams days led to Schramm assuming a trusted role in Rozelle's NFL.

That treatment was no more evident than when Rozelle asked Schramm to take on a key role in discussions with the AFL about the rival leagues merging. It was Schramm who called Hunt—whose Texans had moved to Kansas City to become the Chiefs in 1963—and asked to meet with him. Their first meeting, in the parking lot of the Love Field airport in Dallas, kicked off months of secret negotiations.

Schramm would have preferred to put the AFL out of business, but when the younger league signed a television deal with NBC, it became obvious that both leagues were going to stick around. It also was clear that the leagues' battles over players would be detrimental to the health of each.

"Both leagues were being hurt," Schramm said. "The whole structure was in trouble."

Schramm and Hunt continued to discuss bringing the leagues together until, on June 7, 1966, a merger was announced. For the 1970 season, the leagues would become one. Until then, the champions of each league would meet in the AFL–NFL World Championship Game. The first game was played in January 1967. By the third such meeting, in 1969, the game had become known as the Super Bowl.

The appeal of the revamped 26-team league attracted a deal with ABC to begin broadcasting *Monday Night Football* in the new-look league's first season, 1970, and the NFL was on its way to becoming the nation's most popular sport on television.

Schramm's role in the merger might have been enough on its own to earn him a spot in Canton. But, of course, his contributions to the league went far beyond the union. Schramm served more than two decades as chairman of the Competition Committee, which recommends rules changes. Among the changes Schramm came up with or had a hand in developing and implementing, whether through the Competition Committee or his innovations with the Cowboys, were the following:

Instituting instant replay for reviewing game officials' calls. Schramm's influence in bringing the controversial measure to fruition prompted Rozelle to call him the "godfather of instant replay."

Installing microphones on referees so they could announce penalties and other information to fans and television viewers.

Implementing the 30-second play clock.

Creating the six-division alignment with the AFL–NFL merger, allowing for two wild-card teams to make the playoffs, along with the division winners.

Beginning the tradition of the Cowboys playing on Thanksgiving Day by volunteering to help fulfill Pete Rozelle's desire to play a second game on the holiday. Schramm remembered the Texas–Texas A&M games he had watched on Thanksgiving and thought Dallas could be part of such a tradition.

Developing the Dallas Cowboys Cheerleaders. When Schramm introduced his team's cheerleaders in 1972, the idea was not novel. But none of the other teams' cheerleaders had dressed liked the Cowboys'. The ultraconservative, devoutly religious Landry was not a fan of their "revealing attire." Schramm's wife Marty thought the idea would run its course after a couple of years. One look at today's NFL sidelines, however, shows Schramm's idea became widely popular.

Employing wider sideline striping to assist officials in making out-of-bounds calls and multicolored striping of the 20- and 50-yard lines to help television viewers better gauge where teams were on the field.

Installing luxury suites at Texas Stadium to provide extra income.

Using computers to help with drafts. The idea came from when the CBS anchor studio for the 1960 Olympics was set up in a building IBM had leased for its Olympic computer operation, which led to Schramm becoming friends with IBM engineers.

Founding the Cowboys' state-of-the-art headquarters known as Valley Ranch.

Creating the team's groundbreaking *Dallas Cowboys Weekly* newspaper.

"Ideas poured out of him—big ideas, small ideas," Tagliabue said. "He was such a thinker, a doer. . . . It was like there were a dozen Tex Schramms."

END OF THE RUN

Schramm's run with the Cowboys ended in 1989, when Jerry Jones bought the franchise from Bum Bright. Unlike Landry's, Schramm's exit was not immediate.

After accompanying Jones to Austin, Texas, to inform Landry that he had been fired, Schramm remained with the Cowboys during the process of the ownership change being approved by the league's owners. His role, however, greatly diminished.

"Right after the sale, I was prepared to see if I could help [Jones] make the transition," Schramm said. "But from the very first day, it became obvious that wasn't going to be the case. I just wasn't involved in anything."

It was an inglorious end to a glorious run atop the Cowboys alongside Landry and Brandt.

"I don't hide the fact that I'm history conscious," Schramm had said. "I want the organization to be remembered in such a way that everyone who was a part of it—the players, coach, and people working in the front office—will look back and know they were part of something special, something great."

As the sale process progressed, Schramm began working on his next job.

A little less than two months after Jones took over the Cowboys, the sale was approved, and Schramm left to lead the development of an international league that became known as the World League of American Football—and, later, NFL Europe. He held that job for 16 months before being forced out because of philosophical differences with board members.

His election to the Pro Football Hall of Fame came in January 1991.

"Deep down, I didn't think I was going to get in," he said after learning the news. "I didn't think it would come true. I don't know if that was a defense mechanism or not. But when I heard it, it was probably one of the most emotional moments of my life."

The day before his enshrinement, Schramm still carried a pinch-me feeling.

"I keep thinking," he joked, "that somebody is going to call and say, 'Wait a minute. There's been a recount. We really meant to elect Hank Stram, not Tex Schramm.'"

During his enshrinement speech, Schramm said he regretted that the Cowboys of the 1980s, when their string of consecutive winning records ended, did not enjoy the success of the 1970s.

"Nonetheless," he continued, "I'm proud of the 20-year run of winning seasons, the five Super Bowls. I'm very comfortable with that. I don't have any bitterness as far as the new [Cowboys] are concerned. They have their opportunity for their own era. We'll look back in 25 years and see how they did."

Schramm was 71 years old when he entered the Hall. There was one last, great honor for him to receive. But he was unable to soak in the full experience.

In the spring of 2003, Jones announced that Schramm would be inducted into the Cowboys' Ring of Honor the following season. He would be the 12th Cowboy so commended since the Ring of Honor had been established in 1975.

That July, however, Schramm passed away from natural causes. He was 83.

"Once he was told he was going to be in the Ring of Honor, it was the pinnacle, the last thing he wanted," his daughter, Christi Wilkinson, recalled upon his passing. "It was his beloved Cowboys, and they were recognizing him. He felt like he had come full circle."

Naturally. Schramm had created the Ring of Honor, too.

CAREER HIGHLIGHTS

Served as president and general manager of the Cowboys for 29 years, during which time Dallas had a 270–178–6 record, reaching the playoffs 18 times, playing in five Super Bowls, and winning two Super Bowls. Dallas recorded 20 consecutive winning seasons from 1966 to 1985.

Acted as the NFL's chief negotiator in talks that led to the merger of the NFL and the AFL.

Headed the NFL's Competition Committee for more than two decades.

Created numerous innovations adopted by the NFL, including instant replay for officials, wild-card teams, the 30-second play clock, wireless microphones on referees, wider-painted sidelines, and multicolored striping of the 20- and 50-yard lines.

Created the Cowboys Ring of Honor, introduced the Dallas Cowboys Cheerleaders, made Cowboys home games a Thanksgiving Day tradition, came up with the idea to include revenue-producing luxury suites at Texas Stadium, started the *Dallas Cowboys Weekly* newspaper, and made computer data part of the team's drafting setup.

FIVE COWBOYS MEMORIES

1. 1960 Offseason

Upon being hired to start up the Cowboys franchise, Schramm made two hires that developed into longstanding relationships: chief scout Gil Brandt and head coach Tom Landry. Brandt had provided scouting reports to Schramm on a part-time basis for the Los Angeles Rams. "I remember that first fall," said Schramm. "I had given him and a couple others some free agents to go find and sign. I gave Gil eight or nine, and about two days later he called and said, 'They're all signed, where do I go now?'" Landry had built his name as defensive coordinator for the New York Giants, serving alongside Vince Lombardi under Coach Jim Lee Howell, who called Landry the "greatest coach in professional football." The Schramm–Brandt–Landry triumvirate led the Cowboys for 29 years. "You knew if you worked for Tex," Brandt said, "you weren't going to be an errand boy or have somebody looking over your shoulder. He gave you a job and allowed you to do it."

2. 1966–1985

Twenty consecutive winning seasons. No other NFL team has done that. In fact, no other team has put together a string of more than 16 straight years with a winning record. The Cowboys did not just eke by during the streak. They qualified for the playoffs 18 times during those 20 campaigns, and their regular-season record was 208–79–2, for a .723 winning percentage. They won at least 10 games in 16 seasons—one of the exceptions was the strike-shortened season of 1982—and for the first 12 years of that streak, the regular season consisted of 14 games. "Twenty winning seasons, 18 playoffs, and doing it with an organization that was looked upon as having style and class," Schramm said. "The Cowboys personified what winning and what the National Football League is all about."

3. January 16, 1972

Twelve seasons after the Cowboys took the field for the first time, they reached the NFL summit with a 24–3 victory against the Miami Dolphins in Super Bowl VI. The victory not only brought the Cowboys their first championship, but it also ended the "Next Year's Champions" talk that had encircled the team following big playoff losses the previous five years. Instead of continuing to look back, the Super Bowl championship allowed the franchise to look ahead. Heading into the following season, Schramm told reporters, "This team has the potential to become a dynasty."

4. January 15, 1978

Six years after winning their first Super Bowl, the Cowboys won their second, dispatching the Denver Broncos, 27–10, in New Orleans. That was a revamped team from the one that had won the NFC East and lost in the division round of the playoffs the season before. Lee Roy Jordan had retired after the 1976 season, offensive lineman Rayfield Wright played only two games because of injury, and cornerback Mel Renfro took on a reduced role in his final season. All three men were eventually inducted into the Ring of Honor. Among those giving the Cowboys a new look, however, were two future hall of famers: rookie running back Tony Dorsett and defensive tackle Randy White, who became a full-time starter for the first time in his career. Linebacker Thomas "Hollywood" Henderson and offensive linemen Tom Rafferty and Pat Donovan also stepped into starting roles that season. "The satisfaction this time," Schramm said after the Super Bowl win, "is that we won with an almost completely new team."

5. December 2, 1963

Schramm's preferred method for building the Cowboys was through the draft. He liked speedy athletes, and he did not hesitate to draft with the big picture in mind. The 1964 draft exemplifies Schramm's philosophy. That was the year the Cowboys selected three future hall of famers. The Cowboys had made no secret of their strong desire to draft Oregon running back Mel Renfro. But with the fourth pick, they instead chose Texas defensive tackle Scott Appleton to trade his rights to the Pittsburgh Steelers for veteran receiver Buddy Dial. (Appleton wound up signing with the AFL's Houston Oilers instead.) Renfro had undergone surgery for a hand injury, and when the Cowboys did not select him, teams backed off. That left Renfro available for the Cowboys to grab in the second round. In the seventh round, Dallas took Bob Hayes of Florida A&M as a future pick because Schramm wanted the fastest player available. The next year, Hayes won two gold medals as a sprinter in the Olympics and then joined the Cowboys for the 1965 season. In the tenth round, the Cowboys selected 1963 Heisman Trophy-winning quarterback Roger Staubach of the U.S. Naval Academy, although he would have to fulfill his military obligations before coming to the Cowboys in 1969. Renfro, Hayes, and Staubach wound up playing a combined 35 seasons with the Cowboys and appeared in 19 Pro Bowls.

Emmitt Smith

Rushing Champion

Emmitt James Smith III
Class: 2010 (Russ Grimm, Rickey Jackson, Dick LeBeau, Floyd Little, John Randle, Jerry Rice)
Seasons with Cowboys: 1990–2002
Other NFL teams: Arizona (2003–2004)
Positions: Running back
College: Florida

*B*efore Emmitt Smith had played in his first game with the Cowboys, he told teammate Michael Irvin that he would become the NFL's all-time leading rusher. Irvin, as he recalled the moment, looked at Smith "like he was crazy for even thinking that."

"But I've learned," Irvin said as Smith neared the end of his career, "not to doubt Emmitt if he's determined."

Told more times than he wanted to hear what he would not be able to do on a football field, Smith determined to make a career out of proving what he could do. When he left the Cowboys after 13 seasons to finish his playing days in Arizona, he already had accomplished what he had told Irvin he would before his rookie season The numbers 18,355, 164, 78 are Smith's legacy. No NFL running back has rushed for as many—in order—yards, touchdowns, and 100-yard games as Smith.

When Smith signed a ceremonial contract with Dallas in 2005 so he could retire as a Cowboy, when his statistics had been totaled for good, Jim Brown was asked where Smith ranked among the league's all-time great running backs.

Said Brown, "I think that Emmitt is right there. . . . I think there are 10 or 12 guys who are pretty much in the same category, and he ranks right up there."

EARLY DOUBTERS

Well-known high school recruiting expert Max Emfinger famously said of Smith at the end of his high school playing days, "Emmitt isn't a franchise player. He's a lugger, not a runner."

Not fast enough. The label chased Smith from high school into college and then from college into the pros. Like many would-be tacklers, however, the label could not bring him down.

"Everybody said he couldn't do it," said Mark Manela, the fullback who lined up with Smith in the backfield of Escambia High School in Pensacola, Florida. "We knew he could. He was always one step ahead of everybody. You ask him how fast he was, he said it depended on who was chasing him."

Smith learned early how to succeed against bigger and faster players. As a 10-year-old, he played up against opponents who were a year or two older. He admitted there were times when he felt intimidated.

"What I learned was to overcome my fears and not worry about how big they were because I had my own talent," he said. "I gained more confidence in myself."

Norm Ross, then–deputy superintendent of Escambia County Schools, used a Smith story to teach about perseverance. Smith was 14 and became ill running a hill during a hot, humid summer workout. Older players mockingly called him "rookie." Other players asked Ross, the basketball coach at the time, to come check on Smith's condition. When Ross arrived, Smith was already back on his feet, finishing the drills.

"A lot of kids that age would have been apprehensive," Ross said. "But Emmitt was determined to do it. He was not going to quit. He gained a lot of respect that day."

Determined would be the hallmark description for Smith's career.

In another sign of things to come, Smith helped Escambia become a championship team. The Gators had been a down-on-their-luck program until Coach Dwight Thomas made Smith a starter as a freshman in 1985. Smith rushed for 1,525 yards and 19 touchdowns that season, leading Escambia into the division playoffs.

As a sophomore, Smith gained 2,424 yards rushing and scored 26 touchdowns. Escambia won its first state championship. The Gators successfully defended their title the following season, despite moving up a classification, with Smith rushing for 2,818 and 33 touchdowns.

The Gators missed out on the playoffs Smith's senior season because of a loss to rival Pensacola High. Smith had a long touchdown run wiped out on what Escambia fans still consider a controversial call.

Smith ended his Escambia career with 8,804 yards rushing—second-most by a prep schoolboy at the time—and 106 touchdowns. He topped 100 yards rushing in 45 of his 49 games, including the final 28 of his high school career.

There was no trickery involved in running up those numbers.

"We did three things at Escambia," Thomas said. "We handed it to Emmitt, we pitched it to him, and we threw it to him. Everybody knew he was going to get the ball. They just couldn't stop him."

Despite that, there remained doubters—like Emfinger—about Smith's ability to carry the load at the next level.

HIGH-IMPACT COLLEGE CAREER

Smith remained a Gator, committing to the University of Florida, and it did not take him long to answer questions about whether he could have the success in college that he had enjoyed in high school.

Smith was given his first start in the third game of the 1987 season. The week before, as a backup, he had rushed for 109 yards on only 10 carries in the Gators' easy win against Tulsa. His first start came at 11th-ranked Alabama. The freshman broke the school's single-game rushing record, gaining 224 yards on 39 carries and leading Florida to an upset win.

He rushed for 1,341 yards and scored 13 touchdowns that season, reaching the 1,000-yard mark in his seventh game—faster than any college player had ever reached that milestone. Smith was named the Southeastern Conference's Freshman of the Year, finished ninth in voting for the Heisman Trophy, and was MVP of the Aloha Bowl.

As a sophomore, Smith missed two games and came 12 yards shy of reaching 1,000 for the season. In the All-American Bowl, he ran for 159 yards and scored both of Florida's touchdowns in a 14–10 victory against Illinois, earning his second-consecutive bowl MVP honor.

As a junior, he ran for a school-record 1,599 yards and 14 touchdowns, and broke school records with a 316-yard day against New Mexico and a 96-yard touchdown run against Mississippi State. He was named a consensus All-American, received the SEC's Player of the Year award, and finished seventh in Heisman voting.

A change in NFL policies left Smith with a big decision to make. Following the 1989 season, Commissioner Paul Tagliabue announced that for the first time, juniors would be eligible to enter the draft. Smith chose to leave the Gators a year early, citing the risk of injury and uncertainty over his role with pass-happy Steve Spurrier taking over Florida's head position.

"Every guy has a dream of being in the NFL," Smith said, adding,

> I'm not going to stand here and give you a sob story about my family needing money, because I feel like they don't really need money. It's a personal goal of mine, and I want to achieve it in the best way possible. I feel like this past season helped me increase my stock [in the draft], and I don't want to risk the chance of decreasing it.

Smith departed Florida having established 58 school records, including 3,928 career rushing yards. He accounted for 4,391 yards from scrimmage, scored 37 touchdowns, and rushed for at least 100 yards in 23 games. During his three years playing at the collegiate level, he averaged 126.7 rushing yards per game and still holds the Gator records for most rushing yards by a freshman, a sophomore, and a junior.

FALLING FOR DALLAS

In a draft considered deep at running back, Smith generally rated as the second-best at the position, behind Penn State's Blair Thomas. The biggest question about Smith remained his speed, even though his time of 4.56 in the 40 at the scouting combine was an improvement on the 4.6 times he had been clocking.

Still, Smith's instinctive running style had him as a sure first-round pick. Where he would go in that round, however, was up for speculation.

"The only thing about him is his speed," Buffalo Bill scouting director John Butler said. "You'd like to see the home-run speed, but if he was to be there when we draft [16th], we'd sure have to stop and think. He's tremendously productive."

As expected on draft day, Thomas was the first running back selected, second overall to the New York Jets. Some draft boards had Smith going as high as the fourth pick. But through the 10th pick, Smith's name had not been called.

That did not help alleviate Smith's concerns from a dream he'd had the previous week in which he went completely undrafted. He thought because of the large number of teams with defensive needs, he might not be picked in the first round.

The Cowboys were one of those teams coveting a frontline defensive player, even though they had a need at running back. They had forfeited their first pick—the top pick, as it turned out—for taking quarterback Steve Walsh in the previous year's supplemental draft. Their first pick would be at 21, a pick they had received from Minnesota in the Herschel Walker trade.

When defensive end Ray Agnew of North Carolina State and linebackers James Francis of Baylor and Lamar Lathon of Houston did not go in the first eight slots, the Cowboys began working the phones in an attempt to trade up. But as Dallas busily worked to position itself to fill its defensive need, Agnew was chosen with the 10th pick, and Francis went off the board at number 12. The Houston Oilers grabbed Lathon at 15, and the Cowboys turned their attention to landing a top-flight running back. They targeted Smith.

The Bills, who'd had interest in Smith, instead went for defense with the 16th pick. Dallas had reached an agreement with Pittsburgh for the Steelers' pick at number 17—for the Cowboys' pick at 21 and a third-round pick—and Smith had found his NFL home.

It just so happened that when Emmitt was a youngster, he was watching Tony Dorsett and the Cowboys play with his father, Emmit (with one "t")—himself a former talented football player—and told his dad that one day he would be playing for the Cowboys.

"That would be a good goal for you to have," father told son.

SURPASSING PAYTON

In Dallas, Smith joined a team that had spent its first pick the previous two years on building-block offensive players: Irvin and quarterback Troy Aikman. Smith quickly proved he belonged with those two.

"You could see the vision, the balance, and you knew he had God-given abilities," fullback Daryl Johnston said of Smith's first workout with the team.

Smith did not expect to play much his rookie season. Coach Jimmy Johnson had different plans. Smith had only eight carries through his first two games, but the next week, at the Washington Redskins, he was given the ball 17 times. He responded by rushing for 63 yards and scoring a touchdown. He scored again the following week, and in week 5, he turned in his first big game, rushing for 121 yards on 23 carries and scoring once as the Cowboys ended a three-game losing streak with a 14–10 win against Tampa Bay.

Dallas finished that season 7–9, but the offensive foundation was in place. Smith rushed for 937 yards and 11 touchdowns. That was the last season the Cowboys failed to make the playoffs until 1997, and the last season Smith did not reach 1,000 yards until 2002.

Smith led the NFL in rushing yards his second, third, and fourth seasons. That fourth campaign, he had held out the first two games of the season because of a contract dispute. After the Cowboys started 0–2, owner Jerry Jones made Smith the highest-paid running back in NFL history.

The final game of that regular season went a long way in cementing Smith's reputation as a tough running back. The Cowboys were playing the New York Giants and needed a win to clinch a first-round bye and home-field advantage in the playoffs. Smith separated his right shoulder near the end of the first half but gutted his way through the second half. His 229 all-purpose yards and one touchdown enabled the Cowboys to win in overtime and set up their run to their second consecutive Super Bowl victory.

That game also wrapped up Smith's third-straight rushing title. He was voted the league MVP and, after rushing for 132 yards and scoring two touchdowns in Super Bowl XXVIII, named that game's MVP.

In 1995, his sixth season, he led the league in rushing attempts (377), rushing yards (1,773), and rushing touchdowns (25). That season, he earned his sixth consecutive Pro Bowl selection, and the Cowboys won their third Super Bowl in four years.

Although the Cowboys would not return to the Super Bowl after that year, Smith remained a reliable, durable threat. He ran for more than 1,000 yards the next six seasons. Only twice during that span did he gain fewer than 1,200 yards. Following his holdout year, he played in 15 or 16 games all but once, when he appeared in 14 games in 2001.

Smith's string of 1,000-yard seasons ended at 11 in 2002, but that campaign provided the crowning moment of his career.

In the eighth game of the season—his 193rd game as a Cowboy—Smith broke Walter Payton's all-time record of 16,726 yards against the Seattle Seahawks at Texas Stadium. Naturally, he did so on a day in which he ran for more than 100 yards and scored a rushing touchdown—two things he did more than anyone else in league history.

Irvin, to whom Smith had made that prediction before he had gained a yard in the NFL, was standing on the Cowboys sideline to watch it come true.

UNTOUCHABLE NUMBERS?

The 2002 season turned out to be Smith's last wearing a star on his helmet. Bill Parcells was hired to replace Dave Campo after that season, and although it was reported that Smith and Jones agreed that it would be best for Smith to leave the only team he had ever played for, there was plenty of speculation that Parcells was behind the decision.

The reason? At 34, following his 13th season, Smith just did not have the speed needed to be a feature back in the NFL.

Smith headed west to join the Arizona Cardinals on a two-year contract. Injuries limited him to five games in 2003, when he rushed for 256 yards. He returned in 2004, played in all but one game, and rushed for 937 yards—the exact same total as his rookie season. Smith called it a career after that campaign.

"The game of football has lost one of its classiest men to ever put on a uniform," ESPN analyst Joe Theismann said. "Emmitt proved everybody wrong until he got to the Cowboys and started setting records and winning championships. And then when he gained 900 yards this year, he shoved it back in everyone's face one more time."

Smith's final rushing total is staggering: 18,355 yards.

"You can always argue about who was the greatest," Cowboys Hall of Fame running back Tony Dorsett said. "But I don't think you can argue that he has put the record out of sight."

With numbers like his career rushing total, along with the 164 rushing touchdowns and 78 games of at least 100 yards rushing, Smith was an easy inclusion in the Hall of Fame.

"Historians would say he's in the top three or four running backs ever to play the game," said Johnson, his former coach. "He could do things no other running back could do."

Jason Garrett, a teammate of Smith's, called him a "rare, rare football player."

"Think about what he did over the course of time and the position he played," Garrett said. "Week in and week out, defensive coaches since he was 14 years old told everybody, 'That's Emmitt Smith. We've got to stop that guy,' whether it was in high school, certainly at Florida, and in the NFL."

Few could stop Smith, however.

"When you look at it," said Thomas, his high school coach, "of all the boys who put a football under their arms and ran with it—he ran for more yards and more touchdowns."

Just as Emmitt predicted.

CAREER HIGHLIGHTS

Holds the NFL record as all-time leading rusher, with 18,355 yards.
Holds the Cowboy record as all-time leading rusher, with 17,162 yards.
Won four NFL rushing titles (1991–1993, 1995).
Played on three Super Bowl-winning teams (XXVII, XXVIII, XXX).

Named MVP in Super Bowl XXVIII and NFL MVP in 1993, the first player to win those honors in the same season.

Holds the NFL record as all-time leader in career rushing touchdowns (164) and second all-time in total touchdowns (175).

Selected to play in eight Pro Bowls.

Gained 21,579 total yards from scrimmage, second all-time in league history.

Set an NFL record with 25 rushing touchdowns in 1995.

Holds the NFL record with eleven 1,000-yard rushing seasons.

Named NFL Rookie of the Year in 1990.

First player in NFL history with five consecutive seasons of at least 1,400 yards rushing (1991–1995).

One of three players to score at least 10 touchdowns in each of his first seven seasons in the league, along with Jim Brown and LaDainian Tomlinson.

Holds the NFL record for most career rushing attempts, with 4,409.

Scored 100 touchdowns in the first 93 games of his career.

Scored a record five rushing touchdowns in Super Bowls.

Rushed for at least 100 yards with the Cowboys standing at 64–19, including a 7–0 record in the playoffs.

Set a NFL record with seventy-eight 100-yard rushing games, with his 76 as a Cowboys franchise record.

Started 216 of 218 career games with the Cowboys, including the postseason.

Retired as number one in NFL postseason history with 1,586 rushing yards, 19 rushing touchdowns, seven 100-yard rushing games, and eight consecutive games with a rushing touchdown.

FIVE COWBOYS MEMORIES

1. January 2, 1994

One game in Smith's career rises above the rest, as it, more so than any other, symbolizes the running back's toughness. In the last game of the 1993 regular season, with a first-round bye and home-field advantage with the NFC playoffs at stake, Smith not only played against the New York Giants with a painful separated right shoulder, but he also accounted for 229 all-purpose yards, scored a touchdown, and carried the Cowboys to a 16–13 overtime victory. He injured the shoulder late in the first half and went to the locker room for treatment. At halftime, coach Jimmy Johnson was considering using Smith as a decoy in the second half. A determined Smith—"[I]it was the first time I saw him get in Jimmy's face," offensive lineman Nate Newton said—told Johnson to scrap the decoy idea. "Give me the ball," Smith said. Then he asked the offensive linemen to run downfield and pick him up after he was tackled. "My shoulder is killing me," he told them. Wearing a thigh pad taped to the injured shoulder as additional cushioning, Smith played the entire second half. In the Cowboys' only possession of overtime, Smith touched the ball on nine of 11 plays and gained 41 of Dallas's 52 yards, and Eddie Murray's field goal won the game. With home-field advantage, the Cowboys won both playoff games at Texas Stadium en route to winning Super Bowl XXVIII. "Great men do great things," teammate Charles Haley said of Smith's performance against the Giants. "To strive to be the best, you have to put yourself in danger, and that's what he did today."

2. October 27, 2002

Fitting for a player who turned in seventy-eight 100-yard rushing games during his career, Smith needed to near that mark if he was to break Walter Payton's all-time rushing record at Texas Stadium. Smith got the needed 93 yards and more. On an 11-yard run early in the fourth quarter, he surpassed Payton's record of 16,726 yards and, for good measure, the 100-yard mark in a game against the Seattle Seahawks. A 55-yard first quarter set Smith up to break the record at home before the Cowboys hit the road for back-to-back games. On his second carry of the fourth quarter, needing 10 yards to break the record, he slipped through a crease in the left side of the line and surged through an arm tackle that tripped him up—and possibly prevented a 70-yard touchdown run. He then lunged forward for an 11-yard gain and a new place in the NFL record book. In addition to his family and members of the late Payton's family being in attendance, Daryl Johnston—his lead blocker for so many of his yards—was on the sideline as an announcer for Fox Sports. Irvin, his former "Triplets" partner, also was on the Cowboys sideline. "I was very aware of how much I needed," Smith said of the run. "The crowd was jumping up and yelling. Trust me. I knew. Once I broke the line of scrimmage, I knew it had to be the one."

3. January 30, 1994

At halftime of Super Bowl XXVIII, with Dallas trailing the Buffalo Bills, 13–6, Smith held out his hands to offensive coordinator Norv Turner and told him to place the ball there in the second half. "I do what Emmitt says," Turner later said with a laugh. On that night, Turner followed Smith's advice, and it worked. Smith rushed for 132 yards on 30 carries and scored two touchdowns in leading the Cowboys to a 30–13 win and earning the Super Bowl MVP award. The Cowboys had tied the score at 13–13 in the third quarter when Smith and his offensive line took over. On an eight-play, 64-yard scoring drive, Smith carried seven times for 61 yards. His 15-yard run to cap the possession put the Cowboys ahead, 20–13. An interception on Buffalo's ensuing possession gave Dallas the ball at the Bills' 34-yard line. Smith gained 25 yards on that drive—16 rushing and nine receiving—and his one-yard touchdown plunge gave the Cowboys a 27–13 advantage with less than 11 minutes remaining in the game. The MVP trophy went along nicely with the third consecutive NFL rushing title and Associated Press MVP award Smith had picked up during the regular season.

4. October 31, 1993

On a game played in driving rain, Smith broke the Cowboys' single-game rushing record, gaining 237 yards on 30 carries as Dallas won at the Philadelphia Eagles, 23–10. "I don't know if this was his best performance since I've seen him have so many great games," quarterback Troy Aikman said. "But I don't know if I've seen him run any harder than he did today. He was phenomenal." Smith gained 65 yards in the first quarter and had 129 yards by halftime. But he saved his best for last, exploding for 94 yards on eight carries in the fourth quarter. He broke Tony Dorsett's franchise record of 206 rushing yards, which had also come against Philadelphia. Smith's total was the sixth-best in NFL history at that point. Smith, who averaged 7.9 yards per carry, clinched the victory with a 62-yard scoring run in the final four minutes. The win was the fifth in a row for Dallas after Smith returned from a two-game holdout to start the season.

5. November 28, 1996

On Thanksgiving Day, facing the arch-rival Washington Redskins, Smith rushed for a season-high 155 yards, scored three touchdowns, and passed the 1,000-yard mark for the season and the 10,000-yard mark for his career. He became the 12th running back in NFL history to reach 10,000 yards. Smith accounted for all three Cowboys touchdowns in the 21–10 victory. It was one of nine times during his career that he scored at least three touchdowns in a game. He had gained only 18 yards and been benched the previous week against the New York Giants. He also had not practiced all week because of a sore ankle. Still, Washington coach Norv Turner, familiar with Smith from his days as Cowboys offensive coordinator, was not surprised by the running back's performance. "He's one of the greatest competitors you're going to be around," Turner said. "When somebody told me Emmitt had a problem, I expected to see a special effort out of him."

Statistics

Regular Season			Rushing				Receiving			
Season	Team	G	No.	Yds	Avg	TD	No.	Yds	Avg	TD
1990	Dallas	16	241	937	3.9	11	24	228	9.5	0
1991	Dallas	16	365	1,563	4.3	12	49	258	5.3	1
1992	Dallas	16	373	1,713	4.6	18	59	335	5.7	1
1993	Dallas	14	283	1,486	5.3	9	57	414	7.3	1
1994	Dallas	15	368	1,484	4.0	21	50	341	6.8	1
1995	Dallas	16	377	1,773	4.7	25	62	375	6.0	0
1996	Dallas	15	327	1,204	3.7	12	47	249	5.3	3
1997	Dallas	16	261	1,074	4.1	4	40	234	5.9	0
1998	Dallas	16	319	1,332	4.2	13	27	175	6.5	2
1999	Dallas	15	329	1,397	4.2	11	27	119	4.4	2
2000	Dallas	16	294	1,203	4.1	9	11	79	7.2	0
2001	Dallas	14	261	1,021	3.9	3	17	116	6.8	0
2002	Dallas	16	254	975	3.8	5	16	89	5.6	0
2003	Arizona	10	90	256	2.8	2	14	107	7.6	0
2004	Arizona	15	267	937	3.5	9	15	105	7.0	0
Totals		226	4,409	18,355	4.2	164	515	3,224	6.3	11

Postseason			Rushing				Receiving			
Season	Team	G	No.	Yds	Avg	TD	No.	Yds	Avg	TD
1991	Dallas	2	41	185	4.5	1	1	2	2.0	0
1992	Dallas	3	71	336	4.7	3	13	86	6.6	1
1993	Dallas	3	66	280	4.2	3	13	138	10.6	1
1994	Dallas	2	27	118	4.4	3	4	8	2.0	0
1995	Dallas	3	74	298	4.0	6	6	60	10.0	0
1996	Dallas	2	39	196	5.0	2	7	24	3.4	0
1998	Dallas	1	16	74	4.6	0	1	10	10.0	0
1999	Dallas	1	15	99	6.6	1	1	14	14.0	0
Totals		17	349	1,586	4.5	19	46	342	7.4	2

• 13 •

Roger Staubach

Hall of Fame Person

Roger Thomas Staubach
Class: 1985 (Frank Gatski, Joe Namath, Pete Rozelle, O. J. Simpson)
Seasons with Cowboys: 1969–1979
Other NFL teams: None
Positions: Quarterback
Colleges: New Mexico Military Institute, U.S. Naval Academy

> There wasn't a player on the Cowboys, offense or defense, who didn't look to him and think, "As long as we've got Roger in the game we have a chance to win this thing. . . ." The opposition thought that way, too. — Jim Hanifan, head coach, St. Louis Cardinals (1980–1985)

*R*oger Staubach led the Dallas Cowboys to 23 fourth-quarter, come-from-behind victories. Fourteen times with Staubach at quarterback, the Cowboys rallied to win in the final two minutes of regulation or in overtime.

"Captain Comeback"—Staubach earned that nickname.

"I will never forget staring into his eyes in a huddle," said Tom Rafferty, a center with the Cowboys for the final four years of Staubach's career. "When he'd want something, his eyes would get this incredible, intense look. I couldn't believe it, that someone could be that competitive."

Staubach led Dallas to a .743 winning percentage during the regular season (84–29) and an 11–6 record in the playoffs. The Cowboys won two Super Bowls with him as signal-caller. But more than that, throughout the course of his 11-year career, he earned the respect of teammates and opponents alike, not just because he won, but because of *how* he won.

"The Cowboys have been perceived as 'America's Team,'" said safety Cliff Harris, whose entire 10-year career overlapped with Staubach's tenure in Dallas. "They were the clean-cut team. It's because of Roger. They developed his image. That's what he is: Captain America."

The Cowboys drafted Staubach as a "future pick" in 1964, and waited for him to fulfill his military obligations with the U.S. Navy. He did not make his NFL debut until 1969, as a 27-year-old rookie. He was worth the wait.

GUIDED BY FAITH

One of the most clutch quarterbacks in NFL history did not even start at the position until his senior year in high school.

Baseball was the sport a young Staubach dreamed of playing. In those dreams, he would envision himself in the uniform of his hometown Cincinnati Reds, not the Dallas Cowboys. He would be a center fielder, not a quarterback. And in his wildest dreams, it was Cooperstown, New York—not Canton, Ohio—where he would be inducted into his sport's Hall of Fame.

His athletic career began as a six-year-old baseball player, but he played whatever sport was closest to him growing up in Cincinnati. In neighborhood basketball games, he would go toe-to-toe with bigger kids for rebounds. In tackle-the-man-with-the-football games, "I always had to be the man with the ball," he said.

Staubach began playing organized football as an end on the St. John's Catholic Youth Organization team. Bernie Sinchek, who would watch Staubach play then and later was his freshman coach at Purcell High School, remembered Staubach having a "funny little gait" that "you see maybe only once in a hundred athletes."

"He could shift directions and give you eight cents' change after stopping on a dime," Sinchek said.

Purcell was a big high school, and Staubach played defensive back as a junior, while the seniors played offense. His senior year, he became the starting quarterback.

The Cavaliers did not pass much, and Staubach's ability to scramble led to friends calling him "Roger the Dodger." He received more than 40 football scholarship offers, including from all the major Ohio college programs. Staubach and his father patiently considered not only what each school offered athletically, but also academically and morally.

"I came from a strong religious family with parents who loved me and who not only preached good things, but practiced them," Staubach once said.

That faith remained important to him and guided him, including his decision-making on where he would attend college.

Staubach was intrigued by one Big Ten university in particular, but when he visited the school, he took note of the time several varsity players spent out on the town at night and the classes they missed during the day. "I'm not criticizing those things, mind you," Staubach said in recalling that visit. "I'm only saying they are not for me."

Staubach wound up choosing the U.S. Naval Academy because he believed that was where he could receive the best education. "I don't want to goof off," he cited at the time in explaining his decision. "I need to go to a school that will teach me some discipline."

Navy, however, wanted Staubach to attend a junior college or military prep school for one year to improve his English grades.

Although a move made for academic reasons, Staubach's one year at New Mexico Military Institute provided a boost to his football career. His coach there, Bob Shaw, had played in the NFL and in the Canadian Football League, and he had been an assistant coach with the Baltimore Colts and San Francisco 49ers before taking the job in New Mexico. Shaw helped develop Staubach's quarterback skills, from throwing to ball-handling and faking handoffs.

RUNAWAY HEISMAN WINNER

In his first year with Navy, Staubach quarterbacked the freshman team so well that varsity coach Wayne Hardin thought he was ready to start as a sophomore. But the Midshipmen had two experienced quarterbacks, including a senior whom Hardin made the starter at the beginning of the 1962 season.

In the first three games, Staubach played six minutes, failed to complete any of his four passes, and lost 14 yards rushing. Navy was 1–2 in those games. Looking to jump-start the offense, Hardin gave Staubach more playing time in the next game, against Cornell. Staubach completed nine of 11 passes for 99 yards and one touchdown, plus ran for two touchdowns. Navy won easily, 41–0, and Staubach was the Midshipmen's quarterback.

"I guess that was the beginning," he said. "I played a pretty good game."

Staubach capped his first varsity season by completing 11 of 13 passes for 188 yards and rushing for 34 yards, as the Middies routed rival Army, 34–14.

Hardin got to work during the off-season designing a new offense around Staubach's running ability—it was at Navy that his "Roger the Dodger" nickname gained prominence—and his team benefited.

The Midshipmen went 9–1 during the 1963 regular season, with a four-point loss at Southern Methodist University the only blemish. Staubach passed for 1,474 yards—completing 66.5 percent of his passes—and rushed for 418 yards. Passing and rushing combined, he accounted for 14 touchdowns.

After the regular season, Staubach was runaway winner of the Heisman Trophy, garnering 517 first-place votes and 1,860 total points. Billy Lothridge, a quarterback at Georgia Tech, was a distant runner-up, with 504 points and 65 first-place votes.

"He is far away the finest I have ever seen—as good as anybody who ever played the game, and I have seen Johnny Unitas and Y. A. Tittle," Hardin said when Staubach received the Heisman.

Navy's season had earned the Midshipmen the number-two ranking in the Associated Press's final poll and a matchup with number one-ranked Texas in the Cotton Bowl. Texas upended Navy, 28–6, with Staubach rushing for his team's only touchdown.

As only the third junior to win the Heisman, Staubach entered his senior season as a heavy favorite to become the first to win the award twice. Injuries limited his effectiveness in 1964, however, and Navy, which entered the season ranked 10th in the nation, limped to a 3–6–1 record.

Still, Staubach—who earned seven varsity letters at Navy in football, basketball, and baseball—received an invitation to play in the College All-Star Game.

"I think that's the first time people realized I could play, that I had a good arm and wasn't just a scrambling quarterback," Staubach said. "I had thought that was going to be the last game I ever played, so I really prepared for it."

In addition to his physical skills, Staubach's leadership ability shined at that game.

"I coached the College All-Star game for 10 years," said Pro Football Hall of Fame quarterback Otto Graham. "Of all the quarterbacks in that game, Roger was the best I ever had. He was a great leader—that's the most important thing for a quarterback."

Ralph Neely was a lineman from the University of Oklahoma who played in that same game. Neely, who would later be Staubach's teammate with the Cowboys, recalled how the quarterback's leadership stood out among all the other players as they practiced for the All-Star Game.

"The first time we were on the field, nobody knew anybody," Neely said. "But after half an hour you could have taken a vote on captain, and it would have been no contest. We would have voted for Roger then, same as we did later."

SERVING HIS COUNTRY

The only drawback with Staubach as far as pro teams were concerned was the four years of military he was obligated to serve.

The year he had spent at military prep school made him eligible for the draft following his junior season. The Cowboys drafted him in the 10th round—with the 129th overall pick—as a "future" pick. In the AFL Draft, the Kansas City Chiefs chose him 122nd overall, in the 16th round.

Cowboys personnel director Gil Brandt visited with Staubach's parents to see if he would consider leaving the Naval Academy for pro football.

"But they almost threw me out of the house for suggesting that their son not live up to his obligations at Navy," Brandt recalled.

"I had an obligation," Staubach would later say of his four years of active, full-time duty. "If I had gotten out of that, I would have regretted it the rest of my life."

At the time, however, Staubach believed his football career would probably come to an end when he left the Naval Academy. Brandt sent a football to Staubach, and Staubach kept his throwing arm in shape by working out with others in his unit.

"The desire never left me," he said. "I just knew I was going to pay the price to try to be the very best at what I did."

Included in his four years of service was one year in Vietnam as a supply officer and a port commander.

"From a pro football standpoint, the service definitely set me back," he said. "From a personal standpoint, nothing better could have happened to me than spending four years in the Navy."

His noted work ethic had much to do with his time in service.

"I really feel, first of all, that you have to work hard in life," he has said. Staubach continued,

> It takes a lot of unspectacular preparation to get spectacular results. There's that old saying, "There are no traffic jams on the extra mile." I learned that in sports and business, it's important. You have to control the idea of, What's in it for me? You have to think, How does that affect somebody else? Some people don't think that way. When everything's going well, they're great. Something goes wrong, they're going to jump ship first.
>
> The real team players you can trust give a darn about someone other than themselves. Adversity reveals genius and prosperity conceals it. You kind of find out the best in people when times are tough. The best people just hang in there and fight the fight.

"CAPTAIN COMEBACK"

Staubach joined the Cowboys in 1969, as a 27-year-old rookie. Craig Morton, a first-round draft choice in 1965, had been the full-time quarterback for one year, leading Dallas to a 12–2 record and the NFL Capitol Division title. Staubach appeared in six games that season as Morton's backup. Morton remained the starter through 1970, as the Cowboys reached their first Super Bowl and lost to the Baltimore Colts.

The day after the Cowboys returned home from Super Bowl V, Staubach was on the practice field, alone, throwing passes to a target. Two days later, he was asking if someone could film his workouts so he could study them. An assistant told Staubach he had six months to prepare for the next season.

"I don't have six months, and I'm ready now," Staubach replied. "If I don't start or play this season, it will be my last with the Cowboys."

When the Cowboys struggled to a 4–3 start, Coach Tom Landry turned to Staubach. In what would become the trademark of Captain Comeback's career, in his first start, he led the Cowboys to a 16–13 win at the St. Louis Cardinals, throwing a fourth-quarter touchdown pass to erase a four-point deficit and then, after the Cardinals had tied the score, marching the Cowboys downfield to set up Toni Fritsch's game-winning field goal in the final two minutes.

That started a seven-game winning streak to end the regular season, followed by playoff victories against Minnesota and San Francisco—in one of the most dramatic comebacks of his career—and then the franchise's first Super Bowl championship, with a 24–3 defeat of the Miami Dolphins.

A severely separated throwing shoulder caused Staubach to miss most of the following season, but he regained his starting job in 1973 and held onto it until his retirement after the 1979 season. Beginning with his return from injury in 1973, the Cowboys made the playoffs in all those seasons except 1974, and they won the division title five times. They also won their second Super Bowl title, defeating the Denver Broncos—quarterbacked by Morton—in Super Bowl XII.

The comeback became his signature, most notably the playoff win against San Francisco in December 1972 and the "Hail Mary" divisional-round game against the Vikings in December 1975.

Said defensive back Charlie Waters,

> If there was a chance we knew we were going to win. We knew he could do it. Whatever it took for us to get the ball back to the offensive team, we were going to do it. If we could just get the ball back to Roger, we knew he would make the other players play harder. Everyone believed Roger could pull off a miracle. And he did.

Time after time after time.

FORCED OUT BY CONCUSSIONS

Staubach retired at age 37. Considering he had entered the league at 27, he was a young 37 in football terms.

In Staubach's last game, a 21–19 playoff loss to the Los Angeles Rams, he had his head strike hard against the Texas Stadium turf on a hit by Ram linebacker Jack "Hacksaw" Reynolds. It was his fifth concussion of that season, and in light of the mounting total from his career, doctors recommended that he retire. He did so with the best career passer rating (83.4) in NFL history.

"There is no question in my mind," Cowboys president and general manager Tex Schramm said when Staubach retired, "that Roger Staubach is this country's greatest sports hero, maybe of our time.

The league-wide respect for Staubach was clear as reaction poured in following his decision. Not surprisingly, most praised him for more than his quarterbacking abilities.

"He has all his priorities set up, which is very important," Dallas linebacker Bob Breunig said. "More than anything, he has a sensitivity to people, and he gives so much to people. No one will ever know how much."

Said Philadelphia Eagles coach Dick Vermeil, "As an athlete, he was as courageous as you'll see. He gives everything to the job at hand. I think he's the same kind of person in life. He does everything to do it right. We just can't have enough of those kinds of people representing the NFL."

Then there was the praise for Staubach from former Green Bay quarterback Bart Starr, who had entered the Hall of Fame two years earlier and led his teams to five NFL championships and two Super Bowl championships.

"He is one of the finest ever to play the game," Starr said. "If you look back on your career, you see some things you would want to change. And looking back at mine, I think if I had some of that Staubach competitiveness, I'd have been much better."

New Orleans Saints quarterback Archie Manning predicted that Staubach would "walk right into the Hall of Fame five years from now."

Manning was correct, as Staubach was voted in during his first year of eligibility. He was joined in the Class of 1985 by O. J. Simpson, with him and Simpson becoming the first Heisman Trophy winners voted into the Hall.

Staubach chose Landry as his presenter.

"In any profession, there are two ways to measure a winner: how he performs his job and how he performs as a person," Landry said in introducing Staubach, "Roger is All-Pro in both categories. If they have a Hall of Fame for people, they better save a spot for him, too."

CAREER HIGHLIGHTS

Started at quarterback in six NFC Championship Games (winning four) and four Super Bowls (winning two).

Nicknamed "Captain Comeback" for his 23 fourth-quarter come-from-behind victories in the regular season and postseason, including 14 that came within the final two minutes or in overtime.

Named MVP of Super Bowl VI.

Awarded the Heisman Trophy in 1963, as a junior at the U.S. Naval Academy.

Held the NFL record for highest passer rating (83.4) at the time of his retirement.

Led the NFL in passing four times.

Named to the NFL All-Decade Team for the 1970s.

Rushed for 2,264 yards in his career, averaging 5.5 yards per carry and scoring 20 touchdowns.

Selected to play in six Pro Bowls, including five in a row from 1975–1979.

Won the NFL Players Association's MVP Award in 1971.

Nominated for NFL Man of the Year five times, winning the award in 1978.

Holds the Cowboys record for best quarterback rating (104.8 in 1971).

First Cowboys offensive player inducted into the Hall of Fame.

FIVE COWBOYS MEMORIES

1. January 16, 1972

Roger Staubach's 10th game after becoming starting quarterback during the 1971 season was Super Bowl VI, and he led the Cowboys to their first Super Bowl victory with a 24–3 defeat of the Miami Dolphins. His 18-yard pass to Bob Hayes set up a field goal for a 3–0 lead in the first quarter. Another 21-yard completion to Hayes led to a short touchdown pass to Lance Alworth in the second quarter and a 10–0 lead. Duane Thomas's three-yard touchdown run in the third quarter put the Cowboys up, 17–3, and Dallas put the game away when Staubach hooked up with tight end Mike Ditka for a seven-yard touchdown pass in the final quarter. Staubach completed 12 of 19 passes for 119 yards and the pair of scores in being selected the game's MVP. That championship marked the beginning of the Cowboys' glory days. "A big weight was taken off, and that moment in the locker room afterwards was probably the highlight for me," he said. "Once you win a Super Bowl, it's a feeling that is never repeated. I think the second one can never be as good."

2. January 15, 1978

For Staubach, a second Super Bowl win came six years later. The Super Bowl XII championship, however, was not quite as artistic as the first. In the Cowboys' 27–10 victory over the Denver Broncos, the teams combined for 10 turnovers. The Cowboys defense forced seven turnovers in the first half, but the offense struggled to take advantage and Dallas held a 13–0 lead at the half. "We had a very worried offense at halftime," Staubach said after the game. "When they told us how many turnovers the defense had gotten for us and we had got only 13 points out of them, we felt we had a very inept offensive team at that time." But that changed in the second half. Staubach threw a 45-yard touchdown pass to Butch Johnson in the third quarter, and fullback Robert Newhouse completed a 29-yard touchdown pass to Golden Richards in the fourth quarter on a trick play.

3. December 16, 1979

In what turned out to be his final regular-season game, Staubach twice led the Cowboys back from deficits to beat the Washington Redskins, 35–34, at Texas Stadium. The win gave Dallas the NFC East championship and ended Washington's playoff hopes. Staubach completed 24 of 42 passes for 336 yards and three touchdowns, giving him a franchise-record 27 for the season. He also wrapped up the league passing title. After falling behind 17–0 in the second quarter, the Cowboys scored 21 unanswered points, including Staubach's 26-yard touchdown pass to Preston Pearson. The Redskins scored 17 unanswered points of their own in the fourth quarter for a 34–21 lead, which looked safe with 3:49 to play and the Cowboys on their own 41. Staubach then completed three straight passes, capped by a 26-yard scoring pass to Ron Springs with 2:20 left. Larry Cole's tackle for a loss on John Riggins forced the Redskins to punt, and Dallas gained possession at its 25 with 1:46 to go. A completion to Tony Hill and two to Pearson put the Cowboys at the Washington eight with 45 seconds on the clock. Following an incompletion, Staubach lofted a pass to Hill, who caught the pass behind cornerback Lemar Parrish in the end zone for the winning touchdown. Considering that the Cowboys had rallied from behind twice, Tex Schramm called the game the "greatest comeback ever." Said Staubach, "We were out of it . . . then we were in it . . . then we were out of it . . . then in it. I've never played in a game like this before. I can't remember when I've ever been so excited about a game. This beats them all."

4. December 23, 1972

A shoulder injury had limited Staubach to only four games and 20 passes during the 1972 regular season, and Craig Morton started the Cowboys' opening-round playoff game at the San Francisco 49ers. Staubach replaced Morton in the third quarter, with the Cowboys trailing, 28–13. A Toni Fritsch field goal pulled Dallas to within 28–16, but they still had that 12-point deficit with 1:53 remaining and the offense at its own 45-yard line. No problem for Captain Comeback. Although his arm was not at full strength, Staubach passed for two touchdowns in that span and a 30–28 Dallas win. The first score came on a 20-yard pass to Billy Parks with 1:20 to play. Mel Renfro then recovered an onside kick, and three plays later, with 52 seconds left, Staubach hit Ron Sellers for a 10-yard score and what some, considering the ramifications, call the greatest among Staubach's 23 come-from-behind victories.

5. December 28, 1975

One of football's most famous plays—the "Hail Mary"—began with a Staubach pass in the opening round of the 1975 postseason, at the Minnesota Vikings' Metropolitan Stadium. The play also received its name from Staubach. After trailing 7–0 at halftime, the Cowboys had taken a 10–7 lead in the fourth quarter. But the favored Vikings drove for a touchdown and a 14–10 lead with 1:51 remaining. On their ensuing possession, the Cowboys faced a fourth-and-15 in their own territory. A pass to Drew Pearson gave Dallas a first down at midfield. After an incomplete pass on first down, with 32 seconds to play, Staubach asked Pearson in the huddle if he remembered a play they had run on Thanksgiving Day the season before, a "turn-in and take-off." Pearson did remember.

Staubach dropped back into the shotgun formation that Landry had installed that season, fielded the snap, and pump-faked left to freeze the free safety. He then pivoted back to his right and launched a pass for Pearson along the right sideline. Staubach's pass was underthrown, and Pearson turned back to the ball. He pulled the ball in just inside the five-yard line and stepped into the end zone as an orange flew past him, representing Viking fans' hopes of playing in that season's Super Bowl in Miami's Orange Bowl stadium. Staubach was knocked to the ground as soon as he released the pass and did not see Pearson's catch. The stadium's sudden silence, however, revealed the outcome. In postgame interviews, Staubach told the media that he had released the ball and said a "Hail Mary." The name stuck. When Pearson first heard Staubach's account, he did not know what a Hail Mary was. "It was a great play, but there are a lot of great plays," Pearson has said. "It's the name that has kept it alive."

Statistics

Regular Season			Passing						Rushing			
Season	Team	G	Cmp	Att	Int	Yds	TD	Pct	No.	Yds	Avg	TD
1969	Dallas	6	23	47	2	421	1	48.9	15	60	4.0	1
1970	Dallas	8	44	82	8	542	2	53.7	27	221	8.2	0
1971	Dallas	13	126	211	4	1,882	15	59.7	41	343	8.4	2
1972	Dallas	4	9	20	2	98	0	45.0	6	45	7.5	0
1973	Dallas	14	179	286	15	2,428	23	62.6	46	250	5.4	3
1974	Dallas	14	190	360	15	2,552	11	52.8	47	320	6.8	3
1975	Dallas	13	198	348	16	2,666	17	56.9	55	316	5.7	4
1976	Dallas	14	208	369	11	2,715	14	56.4	43	184	4.3	3
1977	Dallas	14	210	361	9	2,620	18	58.2	51	171	3.4	3
1978	Dallas	15	231	413	16	3,190	25	55.9	42	182	4.3	1
1979	Dallas	16	267	461	11	3,586	27	57.9	37	172	4.6	0
Totals		131	1,685	2,958	109	22,700	153	57.0	410	2,264	5.5	20

Regular Season			Passing						Rushing			
Season	Team	G	Cmp	Att	Int	Yds	TD	Pct	No.	Yds	Avg	TD
1969	Dallas	1	4	5	0	44	1	80.0	3	22	7.3	0
1970	Dallas	1	0	0	0	0	0	0.0	0	0	0.0	0
1971	Dallas	3	31	51	0	321	3	60.8	15	75	5.0	0
1972	Dallas	2	21	40	0	272	2	52.5	8	82	10.3	0
1973	Dallas	2	18	37	6	269	2	48.6	9	60	6.7	0
1975	Dallas	3	48	79	4	670	7	60.8	19	100	5.3	0
1976	Dallas	1	15	37	3	150	0	40.5	2	8	4.0	0
1977	Dallas	3	37	61	2	482	3	60.7	11	35	3.2	0
1978	Dallas	3	37	72	3	459	5	51.4	8	47	5.9	0
1979	Dallas	1	12	28	1	124	1	42.9	1	3	3.0	0
Totals		20	223	410	19	2,791	24	54.4	76	432	5.7	0

Others—Receiving: 1-minus 13.

• *14* •

Randy White

Complete Dominance

Randy Lee White
Class: 1994 (Tony Dorsett, Bud Grant, Jimmy Johnson, Leroy Kelly, Jackie Smith)
Seasons with Cowboys: 1975–1988
Other NFL teams: None
Positions: Defensive tackle
College: Maryland

Charlie Waters tagged the nickname "Manster" on his Cowboys teammate Randy White. "Half man, half monster," Waters explained. That might have been the only time White was called half anything on a football field.

Throughout his 14-year career, all with the Cowboys, White was a *complete* handful for opposing linemen and offensive coordinators.

A nine-time Pro Bowler, a NFL Defensive Lineman of the Year, and a Super Bowl co-MVP, White was one of the most dominating defensive tackles to ever play the game—often compared to Mr. Cowboy himself, Bob Lilly.

And to think, when Dallas selected him in the 1975 draft, the Cowboys envisioned him as the franchise's next great linebacker, in the line of Lee Roy Jordan.

President and general manager Tex Schramm reflected on the day the Cowboys turned down a chance to draft running back Willie Payton with the second pick overall so they could grab White.

"We thought we had the next Dick Butkus or Tommy Nobis," Schramm said.

Instead, White became a lineman, and the results are reflected in Canton.

"He had a hunger to play this game," said Cowboys defensive coordinator Ernie Stautner. "Then you add his amazing strength and quickness to that, and you had an extra special player. He's one of the greatest to play this game."

THRIVING ON DEFENSE

The man who would play in six NFC Championship Games and three Super Bowls had to endure some less-than-stellar times playing at Thomas McKean High School in Wilmington, Delaware. His high school football team never reached the playoffs.

However, his basketball team, for which White started at forward, qualified for three state finals. He also pitched and played first base at McKean, and a scout from his favorite team—the Philadelphia Phillies—expressed interest in drafting him and offered him a $30,000 bonus. But White had already decided to play football at the University of Maryland, and his father told the scout there was no need to draft him.

White was recruited by Maryland coach Roy Lester as a 6-foot-4, 225-pound fullback, the position he had played at McKean in addition to linebacker. Jerry Claiborne came in as Maryland head coach before White's sophomore season and moved him to defensive end to take advantage of his strength and quickness. The move to defense, plus the presence of Claiborne, taught White the importance of hard work and paying attention to details.

"Coach Claiborne was a disciplinarian to the nth degree," White said. "He was a tough coach. He'd check our rooms, and if the bed wasn't made or if there was one piece of paper on the floor, he'd say, 'If I can't count on you to get the little things right, how can I trust you on the big things?'"

In 1973, White's junior season, the Terrapins earned their first national ranking in 12 seasons and their first bowl berth since 1956. White became the Terps' first consensus All-American in 13 years.

His senior season was even better. He led Maryland with a school-record 12 sacks and had a team-high 24 tackles for loss. The Terps went undefeated in the Atlantic Coast Conference for their first conference championship in 18 years, and the team was ranked 10th in the Associate Press poll when it received an invitation to the Liberty Bowl.

Tennessee defeated Maryland, 7–3, on a late touchdown set up by Maryland's botched punt snap. Despite his team's loss, White was chosen the Liberty Bowl MVP. He also received his second All-American award, was voted the ACC's Player of the Year, and won both the Outland Trophy and the Lombardi Award as the nation's best lineman.

He turned the heads of NFL scouts when he ran the 40 in 4.6 seconds.

SWITCHED TO TACKLE

White did not expect to play pro ball far from his college home. The Baltimore Colts possessed the number-one pick and told him they wanted to draft him. Five days before the draft, however, the Colts traded the top pick to the Atlanta Falcons, who chose quarterback Steve Bartkowski.

The Cowboys owned the second pick from a trade the previous season that sent quarterback Craig Morton to the New York Giants in exchange for a first-round pick in 1975 and a second-round pick in 1976.

Dallas narrowed its options to White and running back Walter Payton, the Black College Player of the Year out of Jackson State. The Cowboys' brain trust of Schramm, vice president of player personnel Gil Brandt, and head coach Tom Landry agreed on selecting White.

"I had researched the [injury] rate on running backs," Brandt recalled, continuing,

> At the time, only two backs who were in the league longer than five years were starting. One was O. J. [Simpson], the other was Rocky Bleier. Most backs couldn't take the pounding. We liked Walter a lot, but we were afraid he might last only three or four years. With Randy being a defensive player, we felt he could play a long time. With a number-one pick, the longevity factor is huge.

Payton, of course, did have staying power in the league, as he became the league's all-time leading rusher. But throughout the years, Schramm, Brandt, and Landry consistently stated that White had proved to be the correct choice for their team at that time.

"Both were great players, but I'd take White again if I had the chance," Landry said in 1989, the year White retired. "He helped take us to a world championship."

That championship came following the 1977 season, in Super Bowl XII. But to get there, the Cowboys had to find the best position for White.

At draft time, Jordan had just completed his 12th season as the Cowboys' middle linebacker. Brandt envisioned White eventually replacing him. As an assistant with the Giants, Landry had successfully transformed Sam Huff from a college defensive lineman into one of the best linebackers of the late 1950s and 1960s.

White, however, struggled with the position switch. He would later say that he never felt comfortable at linebacker, that he thought too much and reacted too little there. Although fast for a college lineman, pass coverage in the NFL was not his thing.

"I knew I was in trouble that first camp at Thousand Oaks when I was covering Tony Dorsett one-on-one," White said. "All I'd ever see was the back of his jersey running down the field after he caught the ball."

"Randy White was not put on this earth to backpedal," Waters said. "You want to put him near the ball and turn him loose."

After playing part-time his first two seasons, White moved to right defensive tackle during the 1977 preseason.

"It was like somebody took the handcuffs off me and said, 'Randy, go do what you can do,'" he said.

He promptly became a star in Landry's Flex defense. The comparisons to Jordan gave way to comparisons to another Cowboys legend.

"They started mentioning my name with Bob Lilly and I said, 'Whoa, wait a minute,'" White once remembered. "I said, 'If I can do this for 14 years like Bob did, then go ahead and mention my name with him. But Bob Lilly is Mr. Cowboy, and as far as I'm concerned he's the greatest Cowboy who ever played.'"

Still, White played up to the comparisons.

A TRUE THROWBACK

In his first season at defensive tackle, White had 118 tackles and 13 sacks. Dallas won the NFC championship, and in a 27–10 defeat of the Denver Broncos in Super Bowl XII, White was named co-MVP with fellow defensive lineman Harvey Martin—the only time the award has been shared by two players.

Eight months later, White's father Guy passed away. It was his father who had told him to do things right, not halfway. The following season, 1978, was the best of White's career, statistically: 123 tackles and 16 sacks. He was named the NFC Defensive Player of the Year. Those two years were the start of a stretch during which White earned nine consecutive Pro Bowl invitations.

From 1977 to 1986, excepting the strike-shortened season of 1982, White averaged 102 tackles per season for what for most of those years was known as the Cowboys' Doomsday II defense. It could be argued that White was the heart and soul of those defenses.

"Randy was a blue-collar worker on a country club team," Stautner said. "He didn't read the *Wall Street Journal*. All he wanted to do was play football and be the best at what he was doing. Randy was the toughest, most intense player I ever coached."

White was not one to rest on his accomplishments.

"You start counting your trophies and reading about how good you are," he once said, "and pretty soon somebody's going to come along and knock you on your tail."

"I don't think I've ever coached a player who brought everything to the field on every play like Randy White," Landry said. "Whether he was playing a lowly rookie or an All-Pro, he gave his opponent the same treatment. He could have played in any era in this league."

Stautner called White a "throwback to another era."

"He's one of those guys who is extremely tough-minded," Stautner said. "Losses always bothered him. Nothing interfered with him playing well."

That attitude played out in a work ethic that made White a player who could be counted on not only to play at full speed but also to play every game. He played in 209 regular-season games, missing just one game in 14 seasons. That came on Thanksgiving Day 1979, and White claimed that he would have been able to play if the game had been played on Sunday rather than Thursday.

In the first decade of his career, off-field matters came closer than injuries to keeping White off the field.

In 1982, the players called for a strike after the second week of games. When replacement players took the field two months later, White cited personal reasons for being one of the most prominent veterans to join them.

"The longer the strike went on," White said, "the more I felt that this wasn't the players' strike, but [players union executive director] Ed Garvey's strike. All we did was waste eight weeks of football."

White's decision to cross the picket line placed him at odds with teammates, including Dorsett, who referred to White as "Captain Scab." One day as White drove up to the Cowboys' Valley Ranch headquarters, someone from among the picketing players yelled out "Scab!" Others joined in. Dorsett shouted, "I hope he's a better captain for the scabs than he was for us."

White stopped his truck, ready to take on anyone who tried to stop him from reporting to practice. The veteran players moved out of White's way. Two days later, Dorsett dropped his picket sign and joined the team. White and Dorsett would wind up being inducted together into both the College Hall of Fame and Pro Football Hall of Fame, as well as the Cowboys' Ring of Honor.

In 1984, White ended a lengthy preseason holdout the week before the season opener. His return came abruptly, with Landry already having told reporters that he was preparing to start the season without his star defensive tackle.

"There's only one Randy White," said John Dutton, the Cowboys' other starting defensive tackle, upon White's return. "It's a totally different game with him in there. He does so many things the average fan doesn't see. He's the stopper in the middle. He makes the rest of us better."

Injuries did, however, begin to catch up with him near the end of his career. He had shoulder surgery after the 1986 season, to take care of an injury he had played through. White played in every game in 1987, but he did miss one start. He also developed a problem with a bulging disc in his neck. The shoulder and neck problems held his tackle total to 64, although he did register six sacks.

The neck injury severely hampered him in 1988, when he assumed a part-time role, primarily as a standup defensive end or outside linebacker. He made a career-low 16 tackles, with 1.5 sacks.

That would be his final season in the NFL.

INTO RETIREMENT

Less than two months after Jerry Jones bought the Cowboys in February 1989, fired Landry, and replaced him with Jimmy Johnson, White called it quits. The neck injury had limited his mobility too much.

"Physically, I felt I wasn't able to perform at the level I wanted to," he told one reporter. "It was just time for me to retire. Last year I was in a backup-type role. It wasn't something I enjoyed."

And although at the time of his retirement he avoided citing Landry's firing as a factor, he later admitted that if Landry had remained, he probably would have played one more year.

"I feel sorry for Randy," Landry said. "He couldn't finish his career the way he would have liked to. He was such a great player."

"Fourteen years of pounding caught up to me," White admitted.

The comparisons to Lilly never stopped for White, even as he prepared to enter the Hall of Fame in 1994.

"They were different in ability," Landry said. "But they were both as good as any coach could ever expect to have. Randy wasn't nearly as big as Bob, but he was much faster. He could run people down easier and had great quickness off the ball."

Waters—the man responsible for the "Manster" label—was Lilly's teammate for five years, White's for seven.

"Lilly was a puff of smoke, and the guard would look to see where he went," Waters said. "He had great body control. Randy developed his style from the martial arts that influenced us all in the 1970s under [strength coach]

Bob Ward. He incorporated force and finesse at the same time. Lilly wasn't a real mean guy. Randy was mean."

At least on the field, White could be mean. Off the field, he was a quiet, lead-by-example type who loved fishing almost as much as football.

"Any man who can be as destructive on the field as Arnold Schwarzenegger in the movies and as gentle, compassionate, and down-to-earth off the field as Mother Teresa, that's a hell of a man," Stautner said the day of White's induction. "That's why he is here today."

During his acceptance speech, White revealed what had propelled him through his 14 seasons.

"I was always motivated by fear," White said. He added,

> Not the kind of fear where you were going to run away. The fear of not succeeding. That always pushed me and motivated me. I never wanted to embarrass myself on the football field.
>
> I always wanted to be prepared mentally and physically to do the best job I could, so when it was all over, I could look at myself and say, "I did the best I could."

The Manster did just that. Completely.

CAREER HIGHLIGHTS

Played in 209 regular-season games, missing one game in 14 seasons.

Named co-MVP of Super Bowl XII.

Played in three Super Bowls and six NFC Championship Games.

Played in nine Pro Bowls, all consecutively (1977–1985).

Named first-team All-Pro in seven seasons.

Selected as NFC Defensive Player of the Year in 1978.

Named NFL Defensive Lineman of the Year in 1982.

Totaled 35.5 sacks from 1983–1985.

Totaled four sacks in his three Super Bowl appearances (although sacks did not become an official statistic until 1982).

Recorded 1,104 tackles, 701 solo tackles, and 111 sacks in his career.

Named a consensus All-American and ACC Player of the Year at the University of Maryland.

Won the Outland Trophy and the Lombardi Award.

FIVE COWBOYS MEMORIES

1. January 15, 1978

For the only time in Super Bowl history, co-MVPs were selected for Super Bowl XII, and White was one of them. He and Harvey Martin led Dooms-day II's dominance of the Denver Broncos in a 27–10 victory. On his 25th birthday, White made five tackles in the game and had an 11-yard, third-down sack of Bronco quarterback Craig Morton that forced a punt on Denver's first possession. The Cowboys' defensive game plan centered on pressuring Morton, and Dallas had Morton and his replacement, Norris Weese, on the run throughout the game. White, along with blitzing safety Charlie Waters, pressured Morton into one of his four interceptions. "We knew we'd get to them eventually," White said. "We had two weeks to prepare. We knew it was on our shoulders if we were going to win the game." One of the big questions with White and Martin sharing the award was whether they would also share the new Thunderbird given to the game's MVP. They each received their own car, but there was one surprise for White. "I thought if they give you the car, it was yours," he said. "Well, I found out at the end of the year, you had use of the car for a year and then you had the option to buy it at the end of the year or you could turn it back in. That was a little disappointing."

2. December 4, 1983

White's single-game career high of 3.5 sacks came in a regular-season contest in Seattle, when the Cowboys' defense sacked Dave Krieg eight times and forced four turnovers in an impressive 35–10 victory. White and the Cowboys also shut down rookie running back Curt Warner, who entered the game as the AFC's leading rusher, and a Seahawk offense that had averaged 33 points per game in the previous five games. Warner was limited to only 22 yards on 12 carries, and Seattle did not reach the end zone until the Cowboys had built up a 28–3 lead in the fourth quarter. White could have had more sacks—he shared one with John Dutton and had another wiped out by penalty. "In our Flex defense, if we're playing it right, we can control a good running back," White said after the game. "Anytime you can control the running back and put them in passing situations, you can pin your ears back more and go after the quarterback."

3. November 22, 1984

On Thanksgiving Day, the Cowboys recorded more sacks than any opponent in New England Patriot history, and White led the way with three of Dallas'

10 sacks. The Cowboys defeated New England, 20–17, at Texas Stadium, on Rafael Septien's 23-yard field goal with four seconds left, moving Dallas into the NFC East lead. An in-game adjustment by Cowboys defensive coordinator Ernie Stautner moved White to a stand-up position like a linebacker, from where he could launch an outside rush, wreaking havoc on Patriot quarterback Tony Eason. Two of White's sacks came in the first half, as the Cowboys took a 10–3 lead going into halftime.

4. *December 21, 1980*

Defensive tackles use strength and quickness to make tackles. In the last game of the 1980 regular season, at Texas Stadium, White raced 49 yards downfield to tackle an opposing receiver. Scott Fitzkee of the Philadelphia Eagles caught a pass from Ron Jaworski at the Eagles' 48-yard line on a simple five-yard slant pattern. But with the Cowboys blitzing, Fitzkee broke a tackle at midfield and saw half a field of open, green turf in front of him. White had started to rush Jaworski but turned around when the throw was made. When Fitzkee cleared the would-be tackler, White was four yards behind, over Fitzkee's left shoulder, and in full pursuit. Fitzkee veered right, away from White. Cowboys defenders began to verge on Fitzkee at the Dallas 10, and when Fitzkee cut back in White's direction, the Cowboys lineman grabbed Fitzkee from behind and dragged him down at the Cowboys' six. When the played ended, CBS analyst Tom Brookshier began to tell play-by-play announcer Pat Summerall how Fitzkee had run the 100-yard dash in 9.6 seconds in high school. As the replay rolled, Brookshier took note that White had made the tackle. "I don't believe I just saw that," Brookshier said. "You said Fitzkee ran a 9.6 in high school?" Summerall asked.

5. *November 11, 1984*

The 1984 Cowboys, riding a streak of nine consecutive playoff seasons, were 6–4 and losers of three of their past five games when they visited the St. Louis Cardinals. Badly needing a win, the Cowboys defense rose to the occasion in a 24–17 victory that moved Dallas into a share of the division lead with Washington. White led the way, pressuring St. Louis quarterback Neil Lomax all day. He had one of the five sacks by the Cowboys, who forced six turnovers and blocked a field-goal attempt. "We had our backs to the wall," White said. "We don't need anything to motivate us more than that."

Statistics

Regular Season			Tackles					
Season	*Team*	*G*	*Solo*	*Ast*	*Total*	*Sacks*	*Int*	*Fum*
1975	Dallas	14	13	6	19	7.0	0	2
1976	Dallas	14	25	17	42	6.0	0	1
1977	Dallas	14	70	48	118	13.0	0	2
1978	Dallas	16	75	48	123	16.0	0	0
1979	Dallas	15	50	41	91	5.0	0	1
1980	Dallas	16	56	32	88	6.5	0	0
1981	Dallas	16	61	33	94	8.5	0	0
1982	Dallas	9	11	21	43	2.5	0	1
1983	Dallas	16	67	33	100	12.5	0	1
1984	Dallas	16	81	27	108	12.5	0	0
1985	Dallas	16	61	34	95	10.5	0	0
1986	Dallas	16	73	30	103	6.5	0	2
1987	Dallas	15	39	25	64	6.0	1	0
1988	Dallas	16	8	8	16	1.5	0	0
Totals		209	701	403	1,104	114.0	1	10

Postseason

Season	*Team*	*G*	*Sacks*	*Int*	*Fum*
1975	Dallas	3	4.0	0	0
1976	Dallas	1	0.0	0	0
1977	Dallas	3	2.0	0	0
1978	Dallas	3	1.0	0	1
1979	Dallas	1	1.0	0	0
1980	Dallas	3	0.5	0	0
1981	Dallas	2	1.0	1	0
1982	Dallas	3	2.0	0	0
1983	Dallas	1	0.0	0	0
1985	Dallas	1	0.0	0	0
Totals		21	11.5	1	1

Others—Kickoff returns: 1–15 (playoffs 1–0).

· 15 ·

Rayfield Wright

Long Road to Canton

Larry Rayfield Wright
Class: 2006 (Troy Aikman, Harry Carson, John Madden, Warren Moon, Reggie White)
Seasons with Cowboys: 1967–1979
Other NFL teams: None
Positions: Tight end, offensive tackle
College: Fort Valley State

Twenty-two years. Twenty-two *long* years.

Roger Staubach and Rayfield Wright played their last game in the NFL on the same date in 1979. Yet, when Wright gained entrance into the Pro Football Hall of Fame in 2006—22 years after becoming eligible—his former teammate's bust had already held residence in Canton for more than two decades.

In 13 seasons, Wright earned six Pro Bowl selections, was voted first-team All-Pro three times, played in five Super Bowls, and started with six NFC Championship Games.

If anyone knew of Wright's value as the Cowboys' right tackle, it was Staubach.

"Rayfield protected me," Staubach once said, "in the same manner in which the Secret Service protects our nation's president—with vigilance."

That was one reason why, long after his entry into Canton, Staubach had continued to lobby electors to vote Wright in.

"He's been a hall of famer for a long time," Staubach said when Wright did receive that honor, "and finally we're going to go celebrate."

Wright addressed his wait during his acceptance speech.

"Some say that patience is a virtue," he said. "After 22 years of eligibility, God knows that I'm not a saint. But I am a Dallas Cowboy."

DEVOTED TO FAMILY

Wright, who was 6-foot-6 and 255 pounds during his playing days with the Cowboys, was big from day one—he weighed 12½ pounds at birth. Perhaps he was born to be an offensive lineman in the NFL. It took a while for that to become clear, however, because the future hall of famer could barely earn a spot on his high school football team.

Wright grew up in Griffin, Georgia, going by his first name, Larry. In fact, not until after he had begun playing for the Cowboys would he go by his middle name.

His father Sam—who stood seven feet tall—left his family when Rayfield was three. His maternal grandfather and the family's spiritual leader, Judge Williams, died when Wright was five.

He found father figures in a local scoutmaster, a Baptist minister, and a deacon in his church, but, without doubt, the two biggest influences in his life came from his mother, Opel, and his grandmother, Prentice Williams. His grandmother, who was six feet tall, was known as "Big Mama."

On cold mornings, Wright would get up early with his grandmother to light the fireplace so the four-room clapboard house the family rented for five dollars per week would be warm when his two brothers and his sister woke up. After the fire began to burn, Big Mama and Wright would say their morning prayer together. One day, when Wright was 10, he asked if he could say that morning's prayer. In his prayer, he asked God for the ability to do something that would help his mother, his grandmother, his family, and other people.

"Son, do you believe what you prayed?" Big Mama asked at his conclusion.

"Yes, ma'am."

"You keep that in front of you," she instructed him, "and don't you ever let it go."

Wright did as Big Mama said, and that prayer became a defining moment for his life.

Wright was raised on the power of prayer and responsibility to family. A job loading tubs of firewood paid him 25 cents a day when he worked after school and 50 cents per day on weekends. On weekdays, Wright kept 10 cents for himself and gave 15 cents to his mother. On weekends, he chose to give up 30 of his 50 cents as his way of helping the family.

COWBOYS OVER THE NBA

Wright's mother had not allowed him to play football growing up because she feared he would get injured. Because of that and his tall, lanky build, he was not able to make his team at Fairmont High School until his senior year of 1962–1963.

But he had excelled in basketball, averaging 28 points and 20 rebounds per game at Fairmont. Loyola University in Chicago offered him a scholarship, but his family did not have the finances to send him there.

With no options for attending college, Wright decided to enlist in the military with friends. A few months before his departure for basic training, his cousin, John Willis—a captain on the football team at Fort Valley State, a historically black college in the central Georgia town of Fort Valley—decided to take up Wright's cause. The university had a new football and basketball coach named L. J. "Stan" Lomax, and Willis told the coach about his 6-foot-3, 200-pound cousin who was good at basketball.

"Quite frankly, I was pretty skeptical," Lomax recalled. "I had no idea why someone like that would still be available. A lot of the guys we'd hear about turned out to be five or six inches shorter than advertised."

But once Wright visited the campus and Lomax could put his own eye-balls on the big kid, Lomax wanted Wright. Bringing Wright to his teams would require a trip to Griffin and a meeting with Wright's mother, Big Mama, his pastor, his scoutmaster, and his air force recruiting officer.

After a three-hour meeting, held mostly without Wright, his mother and grandmother stepped out onto the porch where Wright was waiting. Tears were in their eyes. The air force recruiting officer followed them outside and informed Wright that he could attend Fort Valley.

Wright began to cry.

"If you drop out or flunk out," the officer warned him, "you'll be drafted immediately."

That sequence of events was not lost on Wright as he prepared to enter the Hall of Fame.

"Had Bubba not told Coach Lomax of my athletic ability, I wouldn't be sitting here," he said. "And if God had not blessed me with this athletic ability, then Bubba wouldn't have had anything to say to Coach Lomax."

Wright missed the first quarter of his freshman year while his exit from his military obligation was worked out. He reported to the basketball team midway through the season. Two weeks later, he owned a starting position.

After the school year ended, Wright returned to Griffin, took a job in a mill, and did not report to the beginning of football practice. That angered Lomax, a World War II veteran whom Wright said "commanded respect." Lomax called Wright to ask why he was not at practice.

"Coach, I didn't know I was supposed to play football," Wright explained. "I thought I was on a basketball scholarship."

"No, you have an *athletic* scholarship," Lomax said, "so get your fanny back down here."

Lomax initially placed Wright at free safety. Due to his lack of football experience, his football skills were raw.

"Son, you're just as green as grass," an assistant coach told him. "You see those cows over there in that pasture?"

"Yes sir," Wright responded.

"I'll put you over there," the coach said, "and they'll eat you up."

Wright's work ethic helped him improve quickly, however, and he was named All-Conference in basketball and football.

During his junior year, the NBA's Cincinnati Royals—the forerunner of today's Sacramento Kings—called him with an offer: the chance to attend their camp as a free agent and play alongside all-everything guard Oscar Robertson, one of the basketball players he had admired and wanted to pattern himself after as a player.

Basketball had been Wright's favorite sport, and the offer tempted him. But he declined the invitation for two reasons. First, he wanted to complete his college degree. Second, he remembered the air force recruiter's warning about what would happen if he left school, and he feared the recruiter had not forgotten, either.

Wright asked the Royals to call him during his senior year, and they said they would. By that season, he had grown to 6-foot-5 and 230 pounds, and added the tight end, defensive end, and punter positions to his resume. Before the Royals could follow up with Wright, he received a call from the Dallas Cowboys.

"We're thinking about drafting you," Gil Brandt told him.

Wright's immediate response: "For what?"

Dallas chose Wright in the seventh round of the 1967 draft.

"When I saw films of Wright," Coach Tom Landry told reporters, "and saw this hulk of a man playing safety, I almost flipped. He's a good prospect, and we're looking for great things from him."

Wright asked Lomax to travel to Dallas with him to help him negotiate his first contract. The flight was Wright's first.

"The highest I had ever been up in the air was on top of a house," he said.

It did not help that the plane took off during a thunderstorm.

"I was scared to death," Wright said. "I was trying to inch over onto Coach Lomax for security, and he was almost in my lap."

Wright signed a three-year, $65,000 contract with the Cowboys. His signing bonus consisted of $10,000 and a new Pontiac Bonneville. The first $5,000 went to pay off the family home in Griffin. He also deposited $4,800 into a bank account for his mother and grandmother and kept the remaining $200 for himself.

NAME AND POSITION CHANGE

Wright began his Cowboys tenure as "tight end Larry Wright."

The position and the name did not stick for long. Defensive lineman Larry Stephens was with Dallas during Wright's rookie season, and the Cowboys drafted another defensive lineman named Larry—Larry Cole—in 1968. Wright began going by his middle name, Rayfield.

And backing up veteran Pettis Norman, Wright was finding difficulty making a name for himself at tight end, catching one pass for 15 yards in his first two seasons.

In 1969, Wright's third season, Landry called him into his office and told him he was moving to tackle. Wright informed his coach that he had never played that position.

"Coach, are you sure?" he asked.

Landry said he was.

Wright replied, "If you believe in me, Coach, I'll give it everything I have."

"I believe," Landry said.

The two shook hands, and Wright played right tackle—the most important spot in the offensive line during that era of the NFL—for the next 11 seasons.

"His move to offensive tackle was one of the best things to happen to the Cowboys in the '70s," Staubach said. "He became the best offensive lineman in the '70s."

Wright watched heavyweight boxer George Foreman and picked up from his fights how to use a quick punch to stun defensive linemen and prevent them from penetrating the line of scrimmage.

He also watched game films of some of whom he considered the league's best tackles, including Forrest Gregg, Bob Brown, Bob Reynolds, and Ernie McMillan. He studied each intently and tried to adopt their strengths as a part of his technique, but that did not work in practice. So instead, he decided to lean on his basketball experience.

"If am guarding a guy playing basketball, I'm going to stay between him and the (basket)," he once explained. "You do that by quickly shuffling your feet, whether you go left or right. If you cross your feet, you get beat and the guy will drive by you. So what I said was the quarterback was the basket and the defensive end is the guy dribbling the ball. I have got to stay between these two guys."

Wright's unique combination of size, strength, and speed led receiver Bob Hayes to nickname him "Big Cat."

Big Cat earned a big reputation as a feared and respected offensive lineman.

Jack Youngblood, who received seven Pro Bowl invitations as a defensive end with the Los Angeles Rams and was inducted into the Hall of Fame in 2001, said more than two decades after his career had ended that he still had nightmares about facing Wright.

"He was definitely one of my nemeses in my career," Youngblood said. "There's no question that he was a dominant offensive right tackle at that point in time."

Youngblood said Wright had the "whole package" as a tackle.

"He had finesse and he had size and quickness and great feet," he said. "I'm sure it broke his heart to go from a tight end. He went from being a pretty boy to one of those grunts, but he turned into a wonderful player."

Defensive end Carl Eller, who played 15 of his 16 seasons with the Minnesota Vikings and made six Pro Bowls, said Wright's size, strength, and quickness posed matchup problems for even the NFL's best defensive ends.

"An all-day fight with Rayfield Wright definitely is not my idea of a pleasant Sunday afternoon," Eller quipped.

"Mean" Joe Greene called Wright the best offensive linemen he ever played against.

Wright appeared in six Pro Bowls, all successively from 1971 to 1976. With him on the line, the Cowboys won 10 division titles and 74 percent of their games. Wright was a part of two Super Bowl championship teams, and he played in five Super Bowls overall. At the time of his Hall of Fame induction, he was the only offensive lineman to have accomplished that.

The Cowboys led the NFL rushing five times with Wright at right tackle.

Running back Calvin Hill made the Pro Bowl four times. Wright was blocking for him all four seasons.

"In the 1970s, he was the standard," Hill said. "When you thought about offensive linemen, he was the guy that you automatically thought of."

"THE ROAD LESS TRAVELED"

The Cowboys placed Wright on waivers on March 31, 1980—the same day that Staubach announced his retirement. A knee surgery and leg injuries had taken their toll on him, and Landry asked him to retire. Wright, who had one year remaining in his contract, still believed he could play and declined to retire. The Philadelphia Eagles signed him, but he retired during training camp.

Then the long wait began.

Not until 2004 did he even make the list of 15 finalists to be considered by the Hall of Fame's voting committee. He was not among the five voted in, however.

In 2006, the Seniors Committee submitted his name to the voters. That year, he became the Cowboys' first offensive lineman voted in

Wright was with Brandt when told of the news. When he entered a holding room before a news conference introducing the newest members, he was greeted by Staubach, Troy Aikman (who also was voted in that day), Emmitt Smith, and the Jerry Jones family.

"I'm so happy for you, Rayfield," said a teary-eyed Staubach, who had worked for years to rally support for his old teammate's cause.

Wright shared with reporters the tremendous sense of relief that had overcome him.

"I wanted it to happen, but I didn't know if it would," he said. "It's overwhelming."

He was so unsure that he would be voted in that he had yet to think about whom he would ask to present him on enshrinement day.

That turned out to be Lomax, his college coach who had previously presented him at Hall of Fame ceremonies for Fort Valley State and the state of Georgia.

"In just a few moments, Rayfield Wright will come to this position," Lomax told the Canton crowd of 19,078 dotted heavily with Cowboys jerseys. "He will come here and he will speak to you. You will soon find that any continuance of the belief that nice guys finish last can be forever dispelled."

Wright told the crowd about learning the poem *The Road Not Taken* in eighth grade.

"It's about two roads," Wright explained. "One was well traveled, the other was grassy and wanted wear. Through this poem, I discovered that life would give me choices. It was recognizing those choices that proved to be the greatest challenge. Looking back, my instinct was to always take the easy road. But the easy road never came my way."

Wright then began sharing his life story, thanking the family, friends, coaches, and teammates who had helped him along the road he had traveled to Canton.

He concluded with a message for young athletes, telling them that it takes courage to dream.

He told them,

Take a leap of faith. Listen to your parents and respect your elders. Learn from your successes and your losses. Defeat is possible and [is] a challenge to do better next time. Be satisfied you gave the game everything that you had and remember this: And don't be afraid to travel the road less traveled, because Larry Rayfield Wright did, and you can, too.

CAREER HIGHLIGHTS

Selected to play in six Pro Bowls in consecutive seasons (1971–1976).

Named first- or second-team All-NFL in six consecutive seasons (1971–1976).

Won two Super Bowl championships with the Cowboys.

Played in five Super Bowls, the first offensive lineman to do so.

Named NFL Offensive Lineman of the Year in 1972 and 1974.

Part of 10 NFL Capitol/NFC East East Division championships.

Named to the NFL All-Decade Team for the 1970s.

Started in six NFC Championship Games.

Helped Dallas qualify for the postseason in 12 of his 13 seasons.

Contributed to the Cowboys leading the league in offense five times and ranking among the top six in the league for total offense in all 13 of his seasons.

Blocked for the Cowboys' first five 1,000-yard rushers.

Helped the Cowboys post a .741 regular-season winning percentage (137–48–1) and win 60 percent of their postseason games (15–10).

Started his professional career as a tight end before becoming starting right tackle in his third year.

Inducted into both the Pro Football Hall of Fame and the Cowboys' Ring of Honor, the first offensive lineman to be so recognized.

FIVE COWBOYS MEMORIES

1. November 23, 1969

Rayfield Wright spent the first two months of the 1969 season—his first as an offensive lineman—as a backup. When Ralph Neely got hurt, Wright was pressed into his first starting assignment. And what an assignment it was. The 8–1 Cowboys were playing at the 9–0 Los Angeles Rams, against their "Fearsome Foursome" defense. Wright would be lined up across from David "Deacon" Jones, the Rams' perennial first-team All-Pro defensive end. Cowboys coaches told Wright that Jones was big, strong, and mean. "So am I," he told them.

On the Cowboys' first play from scrimmage, Roger Staubach called a play in the huddle with a snap count of two. "We go up to the line of scrimmage, and I'm looking at Deacon Jones square in his eyes," Wright once told the story. "His eyes seem to be as red as fire, he's kicking his back leg like a bull. I'm saying to myself, 'My God, what have I got myself into?'" After the first "Hut," Staubach paused. Jones asked Wright, "Does your mother know you're out here?" The question stunned Wright, and he failed to react on Staubach's second "Hut." Jones steamrolled Wright. "I rolled over, looked over at our sideline thinking that Coach Landry was going to take me out of the game," Wright said. Landry turned away from Jones. "By that time, Deacon Jones reached his big arms down and said, 'Hey, rookie, welcome to the NFL.'" Wright looked Jones in the eyes and said, "Well, Mr. Jones, you don't know my Mama, so don't talk about her. You want to play the game this way, we'll play it." Wright went toe-to-toe with Jones the rest of the game. Said offensive line coach Jim Myers, "Deacon didn't even get a smell of the quarterback that day." Wright earned a game ball for his efforts against Jones.

2. January 16, 1972

The season after the heartbreaking loss to Baltimore in Super Bowl V, the Cowboys set out for a return engagement in the championship game. "That was something we really strived to get to," Wright said, "because we knew we could win it. We worked to that effect." After a 4–3 start, they won the final seven games of the regular season and defeated the Minnesota Vikings and San Francisco 49ers in the playoffs to set up a meeting with the Miami Dolphins in Super Bowl VI. The Cowboys controlled that game on the ground, rushing for 252 yards despite not having one running back reach the 100-yard mark, and they easily defeated the Dolphins, 24–3, for the franchise's first Super Bowl championship. As the final seconds ticked off the clock, Wright was among the players who hoisted Tom Landry onto their shoulders and carried him off the field. "That was the most important game and one that I will never, ever forget," Wright said, "because the media had named us the team that couldn't win the big game." The struggle to win that first title made the victory more rewarding. "It's the sweetest feeling that you ever want to feel, to win that Super Bowl trophy."

3. January 15, 1978

The Cowboys' second Super Bowl title came six years after their first, with a 27–10 victory against the Denver Broncos in Super XII in New Orleans, Louisiana. Although a game dominated by the Dallas defense, which forced eight Bronco turnovers, the offense rebounded from a sloppy first half to put together two second-half scoring drives. "It was such a great feeling," Wright said, continuing,

> even if you've been there. . . . Every time you get to that plateau in the game itself, it's exciting. And it's something that you want to go back and get it [again], because you've been there and you know you can get it. And the only thing is, you have to bring all your teammates along with you so that they can feel the excitement and know exactly what it is once you get to a Super Bowl."

4. The 1970 season

Wright's first full season at right tackle came in 1970. Tom Landry made him the permanent starter before training camp, and he was selected as a co-captain. He started all 14 games that season, as the Cowboys went 10–4 and won the NFC East. Dallas defeated the Detroit Lions and San Francisco 49ers to qualify for their first Super Bowl, where they lost, 16–13, to the Baltimore Colts. "I was blocking Bubba Smith in that game, who was a big, tall, strong guy," Wright recalled. "I held my own against him, but we lost that game by a field goal that was kicked by [Jim] O'Brien." The loss deepened reporters' criticism of the Cowboys' inability to win in the biggest games. "The media really jumped on us about that one," he said. But the Cowboys took care of that the next season, and after establishing himself at right tackle in 1970, Wright made the Pro Bowl in 1971—the first of six consecutive invitations to the game.

5. December 31, 1967

Like many Cowboys who played in the game, Wright lists the "Ice Bowl" as one of the top memories from his playing days, even though Dallas lost 21–17, to the Green Bay Packers. The game came at the end of Wright's rookie season, when he was a backup tight end. He has cited lingering effects from frost bite suffered that day on his feet.

Statistics

Season	Team	Games	Starts
1967	Dallas	10	0
1968	Dallas	14	0
1969	Dallas	14	3
1970	Dallas	14	14
1971	Dallas	14	14
1972	Dallas	14	14
1973	Dallas	12	12
1974	Dallas	14	14
1975	Dallas	13	13
1976	Dallas	14	14
1977	Dallas	2	0
1978	Dallas	15	11
1979	Dallas	16	5
Totals		166	114

Others—Rushing: 1-minus 10; receiving: 2–27.

• *16* •

Other Contributors

$\mathcal{S}$even members of the Hall of Fame played minor portions of their careers with the Cowboys.

HERB ADDERLEY

Herbert Allen Adderley
Class: 1980 (David "Deacon" Jones, Bob Lilly, Jim Otto)
Primary NFL team: Green Bay Packers (1961–1969)
Seasons with Cowboys: 1970–1972
Other NFL teams: None
Positions: Cornerback
College: Michigan State

Herb Adderley made a career out of producing big plays on defense and special teams. He honed those skills on the offensive side of the ball.

Adderley was a running back at Michigan State when the Green Bay Packers selected him in the first round of the 1961 draft. But with Jim Taylor and Paul Hornung already holding down spots in the Packers' backfield, there seemed little opportunity for Adderley to display the dazzling speed he could unleash from his 6-foot-1, 205-pound frame.

Midway through Adderley's rookie season, however, cornerback Hank Gremminger suffered an injury, and Coach Vince Lombardi placed Adderley in Gremminger's spot. The emergency move proved to be a stroke of genius.

Adderley went on to intercept 48 passes during the regular season in his 12-year career. Twice he led the league in interceptions return yards.

Although tasked on defense with keeping opposing offensive players out of the end zone, Adderley became a scoring threat when he picked off a pass. He returned seven interceptions for touchdowns and accumulated more than 1,000 yards on interception returns for his career. He picked off five passes in the postseason, including one he returned for 60 yards for a touchdown in Super Bowl II. Adderley also returned kickoffs his first eight seasons and averaged 25.7 yards per return. He never averaged fewer than 20 yards a return for a season.

He played in the first two Super Bowls with the Packers and played on all five of Lombardi's NFL championship teams.

After the 1969 season, Adderley expressed his displeasure with the coaching staff not recommending him for what would have been his sixth Pro

Statistics

Regular Season			Interceptions				Kickoff Returns			
Season	Team	G	No.	Yds	Avg	TD	No.	Yds	Avg	TD
1961	Green Bay	14	1	9	9.0	0	18	478	26.6	0
1962	Green Bay	14	7	132	18.9	1	15	418	27.9	1
1963	Green Bay	14	5	86	17.2	0	20	597	29.9	1
1964	Green Bay	13	4	56	14.0	0	19	508	26.7	0
1965	Green Bay	14	6	175	29.2	3	10	221	22.1	0
1966	Green Bay	14	4	125	31.3	1	14	320	22.9	0
1967	Green Bay	14	4	16	4.0	1	10	207	20.7	0
1968	Green Bay	14	3	27	9.0	0	14	331	23.6	0
1969	Green Bay	14	5	169	33.8	1	0	0	0.0	0
1970	Dallas	14	3	69	23.0	0	0	0	0.0	0
1971	Dallas	12	6	182	30.3	0	0	0	0.0	0
1972	Dallas	13	0	0	0.0	0	0	0	0.0	0
Totals		164	48	1,046	21.8	7	120	3,080	25.7	2

Postseason			Interceptions				Kickoff Returns			
Season	Team	G	No.	Yds	Avg	TD	No.	Yds	Avg	TD
1961	Green Bay	1	1	14	14.0	0	0	0	0.0	0
1962	Green Bay	1	0	0	0.0	0	0	0	0.0	0
1965	Green Bay	2	1	0	0.0	0	2	32	16.0	0
1966	Green Bay	2	0	0	0.0	0	5	105	21.0	0
1967	Green Bay	3	2	75	37.5	1	1	24	24.0	0
1970	Dallas	3	0	0	0.0	0	0	0	0.0	0
1971	Dallas	3	1	8	8.0	0	0	0	0.0	0
Totals		15	5	97	19.4	1	8	161	20.1	0

Others—Fumble returns: 14–65 (playoffs 1–0); punt returns: 1–0.

Bowl. He requested a trade and did not report to training camp in 1970, saying he would retire if not traded.

The Packers shipped Adderley to the Dallas Cowboys in exchange for starting center Malcolm Walker and rookie defensive end Clarence Williams.

Adderley joined a Cowboys team that had won four consecutive division titles and stepped into a starting cornerback spot opposite Mel Renfro. Dallas advanced to their first Super Bowl in Adderley's first season in Dallas and lost, 16–13, to the Baltimore Colts. The next year, Adderley led the team with six interceptions, including three in one game against the Philadelphia Eagles, and the Cowboys defeated the Miami Dolphins, 24–3, in Super Bowl VI.

Adderley started for the Cowboys until midway through the 1972 season, when Coach Tom Landry benched him in favor of Charlie Waters. Adderley retired following the season. In three years with the Cowboys, he intercepted nine passes in the regular season and one in the playoffs.

LANCE ALWORTH

Lance Dwight Alworth
Class: 1978 (Weeb Ewbank, Alphonse "Tuffy" Leemans, Ray Nitschke, Larry Wilson)
Primary NFL team: San Diego Chargers (1962–1970)
Seasons with Cowboys: 1971–1972
Other NFL teams: None
Positions: Flanker
College: Arkansas

Lance Alworth, who received the nickname "Bambi" because of the deer-like grace with which he ran and for his leaping catches, was the first player from the AFL to be inducted into the Pro Football Hall of Fame.

Alworth, Hall of Fame Class of 1978, played nine seasons with the AFL's San Diego Chargers before spending his final two seasons with the Cowboys.

The San Francisco 49ers picked Alworth with the eighth overall pick in the 1962 NFL Draft. In that year's AFL Draft, the Oakland Raiders chose Alworth in the second round, with the ninth pick, and traded his rights to the Chargers.

Alworth had turned scouts' heads at the University of Arkansas, where as a halfback he played a key role in the freshman team's undefeated season of 1958. He also lettered that school year in baseball and as a sprinter on the track team. First eligible to play on the Razorbacks' varsity as a sophomore, he started on offense and defense, returned kicks, punted, and helped lead Arkansas to a school-record nine victories and the school's second-ever bowl win.

The Razorbacks played in the Cotton Bowl the next year, and Alworth was named the game's outstanding back. As a senior, he lettered in three sports—the first Arkansas athlete to do so in the same school year—and was named an All-American after leading the Razorbacks in rushing, receiving, punt returns, and kickoff returns.

In addition to the being drafted by AFL and NFL teams, Alworth received contract offers from baseball's Pittsburgh Pirates and New York Yankees. He opted for football and signed with the Chargers.

Beginning with his second season, Alworth topped 1,000 receiving yards for seven consecutive seasons. Six of those years, he hauled in at least nine touchdown catches. He was named All-AFL seven consecutive years and played in seven league all-star games. Before the AFL and NFL merged for the 1970 season, he played in 96 AFL games and caught at least one pass in

Statistics

Regular Season			Receiving				Rushing			
Season	Team	G	No.	Yds	Avg	TD	No.	Yds	Avg	TD
1962	San Diego	4	10	226	22.6	3	1	17	17.0	0
1963	San Diego	14	61	1,205	19.8	11	2	14	7.0	0
1964	San Diego	12	61	1,235	20.2	13	3	60	20.0	2
1965	San Diego	14	69	1,602	23.2	14	3	−12	−4.0	0
1966	San Diego	13	73	1,383	18.9	13	3	10	3.3	0
1967	San Diego	11	52	1,010	19.4	9	1	5	5.0	0
1968	San Diego	14	68	1,312	19.3	10	3	18	6.0	0
1969	San Diego	14	64	1,003	15.7	4	5	25	5.0	0
1970	San Diego	14	35	608	17.4	4	0	0	0.0	0
1971	Dallas	12	34	487	14.3	2	2	−10	−5.0	0
1972	Dallas	14	15	195	13.0	2	1	2	2.0	0
Totals		136	542	10,266	18.9	85	24	129	5.4	2

Postseason			Receiving				Rushing			
Season	Team	G	No.	Yds	Avg	TD	No.	Yds	Avg	TD
1963	San Diego	1	4	77	19.3	1	0	0	0.0	0
1965	San Diego	1	4	82	20.5	0	0	0	0.0	0
1971	Dallas	3	5	78	15.6	1	0	0	0.0	0
1972	Dallas	2	3	55	18.3	1	0	0	0.0	0
Totals		7	16	292	18.3	3	0	0	0.0	0

Others—Passing 1–2–0, minus-11 yards; kickoff returns: 10–216 (playoffs 2–47); punt returns: 29–309.

each of them. He also caught a pass in the two AFL title games and seven all-star games.

In May 1971, the Cowboys traded for Alworth, sending tight end Pettis Norman, tackle Tony Liscio, and defensive tackle Ron East to the Chargers.

The Cowboys were a run-oriented team then, and Alworth totaled four touchdown receptions in his two seasons with the franchise. By comparison, only once previously during his career had he caught fewer than four touchdown passes in any season, and that happened during his rookie year. He did, however, score the Cowboys' first touchdown in Super Bowl VI, on a seven-yard pass from Roger Staubach.

Alworth retired at age 32, with 10,266 receiving yards on 542 catches—an average of 18.9 yards per reception.

MIKE DITKA

Michael Keller Ditka
Class: 1988 (Fred Biletnikoff, Jack Ham, Alan Page)
Primary NFL team: Chicago Bears (1961–1966)
Seasons with Cowboys: 1969–1972
Other NFL teams: Philadelphia Eagles (1967–1968)
Positions: Tight end
College: Pittsburgh

Mike Ditka played the final four seasons of his 12-year playing career as a tight end with the Cowboys, but he spent a total of 13 seasons with the franchise, from 1969 to 1981.

Pennsylvania born and raised, Ditka's "Iron Mike" nickname fit the formative years he spent growing up in the state's steel country. He attended college in-state at the University of Pittsburgh, where he led the Panthers in receiving three consecutive years and also played defense and punted. Named All-American as a senior in 1960, Ditka played basketball and baseball at Pitt and won an intramural wrestling championship.

The Chicago Bears selected Ditka with the fifth pick in the 1961 NFL Draft, and in his rookie year, he caught 56 passes and turned in what would remain his career highs for receiving yards (1,076) and touchdown receptions (12). Not surprisingly, he was voted the NFL Rookie of the Year and earned his first of five consecutive Pro Bowl invitations.

Ditka caught 58 passes for 904 yards and five touchdowns in 1962, and then he caught 59 passes for 794 yards and eight touchdowns in 1963, when

Chicago won the NFL championship. The following year, he had a career-best 75 receptions for 897 yards and five touchdowns. He transformed the tight end position from an extra offensive tackle into a receiving position.

Ditka spent six seasons in Chicago and then played for the Philadelphia Eagles from 1967 to 1968. At age 29, he was traded to the Cowboys, a move that he said at the time "delighted" him.

In his four seasons in Dallas, Ditka caught 72 passes for 924 yards and five touchdowns, and played in two Super Bowls, including the Cowboys' victory in Super Bowl VI. In that game, he caught two passes for 28 yards and scored Dallas' final touchdown on a 7-yard pass from Roger Staubach.

Ditka retired following the 1972 season, with 427 career receptions for 5,812 yards and 43 touchdowns. His reception total was second-most in league history for a tight end.

Ditka did not leave football or the Cowboys, however. When he retired as a player, he did so to become an assistant coach on Tom Landry's staff. He

Statistics

	Regular Season			Receiving			
Season	Team	G	No.	Yds	Avg	TD
1961	Chicago	14	56	1,076	19.2	12
1962	Chicago	14	58	904	15.6	5
1963	Chicago	14	59	794	13.5	8
1964	Chicago	14	75	897	12.0	5
1965	Chicago	14	36	454	12.6	2
1966	Chicago	14	32	378	11.8	2
1967	Philadelphia	9	26	274	10.5	2
1968	Philadelphia	11	13	111	8.5	2
1969	Dallas	12	17	268	15.8	3
1970	Dallas	14	8	98	12.3	0
1971	Dallas	14	30	360	12.0	1
1972	Dallas	14	17	198	11.6	1
Totals		158	427	5,812	13.6	43

	Postseason			Receiving			
Season	Team	G	No.	Yds	Avg	TD
1963	Chicago	1	3	38	12.7	0
1969	Dallas	1	0	0	0.0	0
1970	Dallas	3	1	5	5.0	0
1971	Dallas	3	5	51	10.2	1
1972	Dallas	2	2	13	6.5	0
Totals		10	11	107	9.7	1

Others—Rushing: 2–2 (playoffs 1–17); kickoff returns: 3–30.

held that position through 1981, before returning to Chicago to be the Bears' head coach.

He coached the Bears for 11 years, winning 63 percent of his regular-season games and one Super Bowl (XX). He also coached the New Orleans Saints for three years.

Ditka was the first tight end enshrined in the Pro Football Hall of Fame.

FORREST GREGG

Alvin Forrest Gregg
Class: 1977 (Frank Gifford, Gale Sayers, Bart Starr, Bill Willis)
Primary NFL team: Green Bay Packers (1956, 1958–1970)
Seasons with Cowboys: 1971
Other NFL teams: None
Positions: Tackle, guard
College: Southern Methodist University

Vince Lombardi writes in his book *Run to Daylight* that Forrest Gregg was the "finest player I ever coached."

For 15 years, Gregg overcame what was considered a lack of size for an offensive lineman. At 6-foot-4 and 249 pounds, he relied on natural athletic ability, a strong work ethic (which led him to study game film seemingly endlessly), and an immeasurable amount of want-to.

He was rewarded with nine Pro Bowl berths, being chosen All-Pro eight times, and a spot on the NFL 75th Anniversary Team. Gregg also brought reliability for the Packers; he played in 187 consecutive games, a franchise record that stood until broken by quarterback Brett Favre in 2003.

Gregg played right tackle for a majority of his career, but he also played some at left guard. In the years Lombardi coached and Gregg played on the offensive line, the Packers averaged more than 2,000 rushing yards per season and won Super Bowls I and II.

Gregg was ready to give up his playing career by age 30, however. In 1963, he retired so he could become an assistant coach at the University of Tennessee, but Lombardi talked him into remaining a Packer. On two other occasions—in 1969 and 1970—he intended to retire as a player. Both times, after starting out as an assistant coach with Green Bay, he wound up playing.

He retired a fourth time when the Packers released him following the 1970 season and began working in the sporting goods industry in Dallas. But the Cowboys needed offensive linemen and convinced Gregg to sign with them.

The 1971 season was a homecoming of sorts for Gregg. A native Texan, he had attended high school in Sulphur Springs, about 80 minutes east of Dallas. He played his college football in Dallas, at Southern Methodist University. With the Mustangs, he played offensive tackle and defensive tackle, and made the All-Southwest Conference team in 1954 and 1955.

With the Cowboys, he played in only six games during the regular season, but being with Dallas gave him the opportunity to play in one more Super Bowl. The Cowboys' win in Super Bowl VI gave Gregg his third Super Bowl ring and seventh NFL championship.

Gregg, at age 38, then retired for the fifth and final time to make his long-awaited entry into the coaching ranks as offensive line coach with the San Diego Chargers. He was head coach in Cleveland (1975–77) and Cincinnati (1980–83), taking the Bengals to one Super Bowl. He then returned to the Packers as their head coach in 1984, replacing former teammate Bart Starr.

Gregg coached Green Bay for four years before going back to his alma mater to lead SMU in its return from the NCAA's so-called "death penalty." After the Mustangs' first season back on the field, he was named the university's athletic director. He held both positions for one year and then relinquished his coaching duties to focus on his administrative ones.

Statistics

Season	Team	Games
1956	Green Bay	11
1958	Green Bay	12
1959	Green Bay	12
1960	Green Bay	12
1961	Green Bay	14
1962	Green Bay	14
1963	Green Bay	14
1964	Green Bay	14
1965	Green Bay	14
1966	Green Bay	14
1967	Green Bay	14
1968	Green Bay	14
1969	Green Bay	14
1970	Green Bay	14
1971	Dallas	6
Total		193

The former lineman left SMU in 1994 and coached the Shreveport Pirates of the Canadian Football League for two seasons. Following the 1995 season, he retired from football—for good.

TOMMY MCDONALD

Thomas Franklin McDonald
Class: 1998 (Paul Krause, Anthony Muñoz, Mike Singletary, Dwight Stephenson)
Primary NFL team: Philadelphia Eagles (1957–1963)
Seasons with Cowboys: 1964
Other NFL teams: Los Angeles Rams (1965–1966), Atlanta Falcons (1967), Cleveland Browns (1968)
Positions: Wide receiver
College: Oklahoma

Tommy McDonald played one season for the Cowboys. He came to Dallas in a trade in which the Cowboys gave away a kicker, and one year later he was traded for a kicker. That seems only fitting for a receiver who scored touchdowns at a rate that kept kickers busy attempting points after touchdowns.

The Philadelphia Eagles drafted McDonald out of the University of Oklahoma in the third round of the 1957 NFL Draft. McDonald had been a touchdown-scoring halfback for Sooner coach Bud Wilkinson, finding the end zone 28 times during his junior and senior seasons.

As a junior, McDonald became the first Sooner to score a touchdown in every game. As a senior, he scored in nine of 10 games, giving him a touchdown in 20 of 21 games those two seasons.

McDonald was a first-team All-American both of those years, and as a senior he received two national player of the year honors—the Maxwell Award and *The Sporting News* College Football Player of the Year Award—and placed third in Heisman Trophy voting, finishing close behind Notre Dame quarterback Paul Hornung and Tennessee running back Johnny Majors.

The Eagles employed McDonald primarily as a kickoff and punt returner during his rookie campaign of 1957. Although he caught only nine passes that season, he did score three touchdowns. That high rate of touchdown receptions would be a hallmark of McDonald's early career. His second year, he caught 29 passes for 603 yards—and scored a league-high nine touchdowns.

Statistics

Offense

Regular Season			Receiving				Rushing			
Season	Team	G	No.	Yds	Avg	TD	No.	Yds	Avg	TD
1957	Philadelphia	12	19	228	25.3	3	12	36	3.0	0
1958	Philadelphia	10	29	603	20.8	9	3	−4	−1.3	0
1959	Philadelphia	12	47	846	18.0	10	2	−10	−5.0	0
1960	Philadelphia	12	39	801	20.5	13	0	0	0.0	0
1961	Philadelphia	14	64	1,144	17.9	13	0	0	0.0	0
1962	Philadelphia	14	58	1,146	19.8	10	0	0	0.0	0
1963	Philadelphia	14	41	731	17.8	8	0	0	0.0	0
1964	Dallas	14	46	612	13.3	2	0	0	0.0	0
1965	L.A. Rams	14	67	1,036	15.5	9	0	0	0.0	0
1966	L.A. Rams	13	55	714	13.0	2	0	0	0.0	0
1967	Atlanta	14	33	436	13.2	4	0	0	0.0	0
1968	Cleveland	9	7	113	16.1	1	0	0	0.0	0
Totals		152	495	8,410	17.0	84	17	22	1.3	0

Postseason			Receiving				Rushing			
Season	Team	G	No.	Yds	Avg	TD	No.	Yds	Avg	TD
1960	Philadelphia	1	3	90	30.0	1	0	0	0.0	0
1968	Cleveland	2	0	0	0	0	0	0	0.0	0
Totals		3	3	90	30.0	1	0	0	0.0	0

Special Teams

Regular Season		Punt Returns				Kickoff Returns			
Season	Team	No.	Yds	Avg	TD	No.	Yds	Avg	TD
1957	Philadelphia	26	127	4.9	0	11	304	27.6	0
1958	Philadelphia	18	135	7.5	0	14	262	18.7	0
1959	Philadelphia	21	115	5.5	1	24	444	18.5	0
1960	Philadelphia	1	2	2.0	0	2	45	22.5	0
1962	Philadelphia	5	8	1.6	0	0	0	0.0	0
1964	Dallas	2	17	8.5	0	0	0	0.0	0
Totals		73	404	5.5	1	51	1,055	20.7	0

Postseason		Punt Returns				Kickoff Returns			
Season	Team	No.	Yds	Avg	TD	No.	Yds	Avg	TD
1968	Cleveland	2	6	3.0	0	0	0	0.0	0
Totals		2	6	3.0	0	0	0	0.0	0

Others—Passing: 2–2, 21 yards, 1 TD.

McDonald's best two seasons with Philadelphia came in 1961 and 1962. In 1961, his 1,144 receiving yards (on 64 catches) and 13 touchdowns led the NFL. The next year, he established a new career-high with 1,146 yards on 58 receptions and scored 10 touchdowns—his fourth consecutive season with double-digit touchdowns receiving. He also made his fifth straight Pro Bowl that season.

In seven years in Philadelphia, McDonald caught 287 passes for 5,499 yards and 66 touchdowns. In the final six of those seasons, he caught 63 touchdown passes in 76 games and impressively averaged a touchdown every 4.4 receptions.

That made McDonald attractive to the Cowboys, and with the Eagles rebuilding, Dallas was able to acquire the receiver in March 1964, for a three-player package that consisted of kicker Sam Baker, guard-tackle Lynn Hoyem, and defensive tackle John Meyers. Four months earlier, the Cowboys had traded for Pittsburgh receiver Buddy Dial, and the combination of Dial and McDonald gave the franchise one of the league's most feared one–two receiver tandems.

Both Dial and the 1964 season turned out to be disappointments. McDonald caught 46 passes for 612 yards and two touchdowns, while Dial caught just 11 passes as the Cowboys finished 5–8–1. In the final game of that campaign, McDonald's streak of consecutive games with at least one catch ended at 93 because he played defense in that contest.

The following off-season, the Cowboys shipped McDonald to the Los Angeles Rams for kicker Danny Villanueva. He had two productive seasons with the Rams, including his third 1,000-yard season in 1965, earning him his sixth Pro Bowl invite. He played for the Atlanta Falcons in 1967 and the Cleveland Browns in 1968, and then retired with career totals of 495 receptions, 8,410 yards, and 84 touchdowns—a touchdown every 5.9 catches.

BILL PARCELLS

Duane Charles "Bill" Parcells
Class: 2013 (Larry Allen, Cris Carter, Curley Culp, Jonathan Ogden, Dave Robinson, Warren Sapp)
Primary NFL team: New York Giants (1983–1990)
Seasons with Cowboys: 2003–2006
Other NFL teams: New England Patriots (1993–1996), New York Jets (1997–1999)
Positions: Coach
Colleges: Colgate, Wichita State

Bill Parcells subscribed to a belief that he was famous for telling reporters who covered his teams: "You are what your record says you are." Parcells's coaching record was 172–130–1 in his 19 seasons as a head coach. His .569 winning percentage, however, does not say all that he was as a coach. Not even the three Super Bowl appearances and the two Super Bowl championships tell the whole story.

Parcells was the master of the turnaround, coaching four different teams and quickly reversing the fortunes of each franchise. The following is a look at the before and after of each of his coaching stops:

1. New York Giants (77–49–1): The season before Parcells became the Giants head coach in 1983, New York had a 4–5 record in a strike-shortened season. The Giants had made the playoffs once in the previous 19 seasons. Parcells's first team started 2–2 but finished the season at 3–12–1. But the franchise had a winning record in six of the next seven seasons under him. A 9–7 record in 1984 put New York back into the playoffs, where it won in the wild-card round. A 10–6 mark and another wild-card victory followed in 1985. Then, in 1986, the Giants went 14–2, won the NFC East, and defeated the Denver Broncos in Super Bowl XXI. Four years later, in Parcells's final season with the team, the Giants edged the Buffalo Bills, 20–19, in Super Bowl XXV. Parcells then retired because of health concerns.

2. New England Patriots (32–32): The Patriots had missed the postseason six consecutive years and won only nine games in the previous three seasons, including a 2–14 record in 1992. Parcells left his job as a television commentator to return to the sidelines to take over in New England in 1993. The Patriots improved to 5–11 in Parcells's first season. The next year, 1994, they won 10 games and made the playoffs. In 1996, Parcells led them to their first Super Bowl in 11 years. He left New England after the Super Bowl to return to the Big Apple.

3. New York Jets (29–19): The Jets were coming off a 1–15 season when Parcells took over. They went 9–7 in his first season and missed out on ending their five-year postseason drought on a tiebreaker. In 1998, New York finished 12–4 and earned the franchise's first playoff victory since 1986. Parcells coached the Jets one more season—to an 8–8 mark—and retired from coaching again. He served as the Jets' general manager for one year.

4. Dallas Cowboys (34–30): Owner Jerry Jones lured Parcells out of retirement in 2003 to take over a Dallas team that had finished 5–11 for three consecutive seasons. Parcells had the Cowboys back in the playoffs that same year after posting a 10–6 record in the regular sea-

Statistics

Season	Teams	Regular Season			Postseason		Round Reached
		W	L	T	W	L	
1983	N.Y. Giants	3	12	1			
1984	N.Y. Giants	9	7	0	1	1	Divisional
1985 (B)	N.Y. Giants	10	6	0	1	1	Divisional
1986 (A)	N.Y. Giants	14	2	0	3	0	Super Bowl (won)
1987	N.Y. Giants	6	9	0			
1988 (B)	N.Y. Giants	10	6	0			
1989 (A)	N.Y. Giants	12	4	0	0	1	Divisional
1990 (A)	N.Y. Giants	13	3	0	3	0	Super Bowl (won)
1993	New England	5	11	0			
1994 (B)	New England	10	6	0	0	1	Wild Card
1995	New England	6	10	0			
1996 (A)	New England	11	5	0	2	1	Super Bowl (lost)
1997	N.Y. Jets	9	7	0			
1998 (A)	N.Y. Jets	12	4	0	1	1	AFC Championship
1999	N.Y. Jets	8	8	0			
2003	Dallas	10	6	0	0	1	Wild Card
2004	Dallas	6	10	0			
2005	Dallas	9	7	0			
2006	Dallas	9	7	0	0	1	Wild Card
Totals		172	130	1	11	8	

Note: A indicates the team won its division; B indicates the team tied for first place.

son. Dallas lost at Carolina in the Wild-Card round. The Cowboys failed to make the postseason the next two years, finishing 6–10 and 9–7. In 2006, however, a 9–7 record was good enough to give the Cowboys a wild-card spot. They lost their playoff game, 21–20, at Seattle. That was Parcells's last season in Dallas and as a head coach. But his influence remained, because he had signed undrafted free agent quarterback Tony Romo in 2003, and developed him into a Pro Bowler during his final season in charge.

JACKIE SMITH

Jackie Larue Smith
Class: 1994 (Tony Dorsett, Bud Grant, Jimmy Johnson, Leroy Kelly, Randy White)
Primary NFL team: St. Louis Cardinals (1963–1977)
Seasons with Cowboys: 1978
Other NFL teams: None
Positions: Tight end
College: Northwestern State (Louisiana)

When Jackie Smith retired in 1979, he had caught more passes than any tight end in NFL history. Cowboys fans still wish he had caught one more.

Smith played 15 years for the St. Louis Cardinals before ending his career with one season in Dallas. It was that one year in Dallas that provided him his only opportunity to play in a Super Bowl, and it was that one game that has tended to overshadow a stellar career.

St. Louis drafted Smith in the 10th round of the 1963 draft out of Northwestern State in Louisiana. He became a starter during his rookie season and turned in a nine-reception, 212-yard, two-touchdown game against the Pittsburgh Steelers in the Cardinals' fifth game of the season.

In his second year in the league, Smith's speed—he ran track in college—enabled him to become a focal point of the St. Louis passing game, and he caught 47 passes for 657 yards and four touchdowns. In 1967, he made the second of five Pro Bowl appearances after recording career highs with 56 receptions, 1,205 yards, and nine touchdowns.

A knee injury in 1971 ended his string of 121 consecutive games played, but Smith was a mainstay in the St. Louis starting lineup into the 1975 season.

Because of injuries, he caught a total of only 21 passes in 1975, 1976, and 1977, before retiring from the Cardinals.

Despite Smith's personal success, he did not experience the postseason until his 12th season in the league, in 1974. The Cardinals lost their first-round game that season and again the following postseason. In those two games, Smith caught a total of two passes for eight yards.

In his 15 seasons with St. Louis, Smith played in 210 games and caught 480 passes for 7,918 yards and 40 touchdowns.

The Cowboys' postseason success enabled them to draw him out of retirement to join them in 1978, at age 37, as a blocking tight end. Smith did not catch a pass during the regular season, but in a first-round playoff game against the Atlanta Falcons, he had three receptions for 38 yards and caught a touchdown pass from Danny White in the third quarter that tied the score at

Statistics

Regular Season			*Receiving*				*Rushing*			
Season	*Team*	*G*	*No.*	*Yds*	*Avg*	*TD*	*No.*	*Yds*	*Avg*	*TD*
1963	St. Louis	14	28	445	15.9	2	0	0	0.0	0
1964	St. Louis	14	47	657	14.0	4	0	0	0.0	0
1965	St. Louis	14	41	648	15.8	2	0	0	0.0	0
1966	St. Louis	14	45	810	18.0	3	1	8	8.0	0
1967	St. Louis	14	56	1,205	21.5	9	9	86	9.6	0
1968	St. Louis	14	49	789	16.1	2	12	163	13.6	3
1969	St. Louis	14	43	561	13.0	1	4	0	0.0	0
1970	St. Louis	14	37	687	18.6	4	5	43	8.0	0
1971	St. Louis	9	21	379	18.0	4	1	10	10.0	0
1972	St. Louis	14	26	407	15.7	2	5	31	6.2	0
1973	St. Louis	14	41	600	14.6	1	1	−14	−14.0	0
1974	St. Louis	14	25	413	16.5	3	0	0	0.0	0
1975	St. Louis	9	13	246	18.9	2	0	0	0.0	0
1976	St. Louis	12	3	22	7.3	0	0	0	0.0	0
1977	St. Louis	14	5	49	9.8	1	0	0	0.0	0
1978	Dallas	10	0	0	0.0	0	0	0	0.0	0
Totals		210	480	7,918	16.5	40	38	327	8.6	3
Postseason			*Receiving*				*Rushing*			
Season	*Team*	*G*	*No.*	*Yds*	*Avg*	*TD*	*No.*	*Yds*	*Avg*	*TD*
1974	St. Louis	1	1	7	7.0	0	0	0	0.0	0
1975	St. Louis	1	1	1	1.0	0	0	0	0.0	0
1978	Dallas	3	3	38	12.7	1	1	-9	-9.0	0
Totals		5	5	46	9.2	1	1	-9	-9.0	0

Others—Passing: 0–3–2; kickoff returns: 5–103; punting: 127–4,971, 39.1 avg.

20–20. The Cowboys won, 27–20, and shut out the Los Angeles Rams, 28–0, the next week to advance to Super Bowl XIII.

In that game, against the Pittsburgh Steelers, the Cowboys trailed, 21–14, late in the third quarter. On third-and-three from the Pittsburgh 10-yard line, Smith slipped into the end zone uncovered. Roger Staubach spotted him. Staubach has said in the years since then that he underthrew Smith. The veteran tight end adjusted by slowing and sliding to the ground. The pass hit him in the chest and caromed to the ground. Dallas had to settle for a field goal and, after rallying for two touchdowns in the final three minutes, came up four points shy of the Steelers in a 35–31 loss.

When Smith entered the Hall of Fame in 1994, he did so with two teammates from his one season with the Cowboys: Tony Dorsett and Randy White.

Bibliography

CHAPTER 1: TROY AIKMAN: A WINNER

Archer, Todd. "Two Cowboys Get Claim to Fame: Aikman, Wright Make Cut for Hall; Irvin Shut Out Again." *Dallas Morning News*, February 5, 2006.

Aron, Jaime. "Troy Aikman Retires, Broadcasting Career Likely Next Step." *Bangor (Maine) Daily News*, April 10, 2001. Accessed October 6, 2014. http://news.google.com/newspapers?nid=2457&dat=20010410&id=9qRJAAAAIBAJ&sjid=ng0NAA AAIBAJ&pg=1609,2443679.

Associated Press. "Suspense Ends; Cowboys Sign UCLA's Aikman." *Observer-Reporter (Washington, Pennsylvania)*, April 21, 1989. Accessed October 6, 2014. http://news.google.com/newspapers?nid=2519&dat=19890419&id=kmZiAAAAIBAJ&sjid=t3 YNAAAAIBAJ&pg=2744,3908590.

Blinebury, Fran. "Dallas Earns San Francisco Treat: Aikman Answers Questions with an Exclamation Point." *Houston Chronicle*, January 9, 1995.

Buck, Ray. "Blast Off! Rocket Launch in Overtime Caps Cowboys' Wild Opening-Day Comeback." *Fort Worth Star-Telegram*, September 13, 1999.

Cowlishaw, Tim. "It's Hall Good: Troy Now Thankful for Gap He Was Forced to Bridge." *Dallas Morning News*, August 5, 2006.

———. "Two More Cowboys Get The Call." *Dallas Morning News*, February 5, 2006.

Farmer, Sam. "Aikman's Journey Ends in Canton." *Los Angeles Times*, August 5, 2006.

Fisher, Mike. "Cowboys Bowl over 49ers: Aikman Carries Dallas 'Long Way.'" *Fort Worth Star-Telegram*, January 18, 1993.

Goldstein, Jody. "Cowboys Log Classic Comeback: Up 21 in 4th, Redskins Succumb 41–35 in OT." *Houston Chronicle*, September 13, 1999.

Mell, Randall. "Walsh, J. J. a Team Again." *Sun Sentinel (Fort Lauderdale, Florida)*, July 8, 1989. Accessed October 6, 2014. http://articles.sun-sentinel.com/1989-07-08/sports/8902190746_1_troy-aikman-steve-walsh-cowboys.

Reeves, Jim. "Hall Fixes Wrong with Wright, Aikman." *Fort Worth Star-Telegram*, February 5, 2006.

———. "Mr. January's Hot Hand Leaves Playoff Pretenders Out in Cold." *Fort Worth Star-Telegram*, January 9, 1995.

Tramel, Berry. "Aikman the Best Cowboy QB of Them All." *Oklahoman*, August 7, 2006.

Wangrin, Mark. "One Great Win Elevates Aikman to King's Throne: Quarterback Receives Keys to More Stardom." *Austin American-Statesman*, February 1, 1993.

Williams, Charean. "Aikman: A Look Back." *Fort Worth Star-Telegram*, August 5, 2006.

———. "Star Attraction: No Matter Where He Was—Oklahoma, California, or Texas—Aikman Always Played a Leading Role." *Fort Worth Star-Telegram*, August 5, 2006.

CHAPTER 2: LARRY ALLEN: QUIET STRENGTH

Associated Press. "Allen Released by Cowboys." *Victoria (Texas) Advocate*, March 22, 2006.

———. "Sonoma State's Allen Excels in Cowboys Debut." *San Francisco Chronicle*, October 13, 1994.

Branch, Eric. "Standouts in the Trenches Dominate Class of 2013." *San Francisco Chronicle*, February 3, 2013.

Brown, Roger B. "The Class of '94: Larry Allen Is Starting, but the Rest of the Cowboys' Rookie Draft Picks Have Had Little Chance to Play." *Fort Worth Star-Telegram*, December 7, 1994.

Canning, Whit. "An Eye for Talent." *Fort Worth Star-Telegram*, October 19, 1994.

"Cowboys Part Ways with SSU's Allen: Lineman, Called 'Sure-Fire Hall of Famer' by Dallas Owner, Becomes Free Agent." *Press Democrat (Santa Rosa)*, March 22, 2006.

Cowlishaw, Tim. "Allen Flashes His Speed." *Dallas Morning News*, December 20, 1994.

———. "Allen Left the Way He Spent His Time Here–Quietly." *Dallas Morning News*, March 24, 2006.

———. "Cowboys Keep Harper as McGinest Gets Away." *Dallas Morning News*, April 25, 1994.

Davis, Dave. "Allen Glad to Be Coming Home to Play." *Chico (California) Enterprise-Record*, March 26, 2006.

Dixon, Schuyler. "Cowboys' Allen Takes Quiet Path to Hall of Fame." *Associated Press State Wire: Ohio*, July 30, 2013.

Fisher, Mike. "Cowboys Miss Out on Coveted Lineman." *Fort Worth Star-Telegram*, April 25, 1994.

Gosselin, Rick. "Jones: Cutting Allen Not an Easy Choice to Make." *Dallas Morning News*, March 29, 2006.

Hill, Clarence E., Jr. "Cowboys Great Larry Allen's Path to Hall of Fame Marked by Perils, Good People." *Fort Worth Star-Telegram*, August 2, 2013.

———. "Cowboys' Larry Allen Was Big, Strong, Fast, and Now Headed to the Hall of Fame." *Fort Worth Star-Telegram*, July 27, 2013.

———. "Football Journey Is Complete for Cowboys Great Larry Allen." *Fort Worth Star-Telegram*, August 3, 2013.

———. "Larry Allen Hall of Fame Blitz." *Fort Worth Star-Telegram*, July 27, 2013.

———. "Larry Allen Is a No-Brainer for the NFL Hall of Fame." *Fort Worth Star-Telegram*, February 2, 2013.

———. "Lett Still in Awe of the Way Allen Played." *Dallas Morning News*, August 2, 2013.

Jenkins, Jim. "Allen's Effectiveness Doesn't Surprise UCD Coaches." *Sacramento Bee*, November 13, 1994.

"Larry Allen 700-Pound Bench Press—Hall of Famer," YouTube video, posted by "Allen, Larry," February 1, 2013. Accessed June 9, 2015. https://www.youtube.com/watch?v=aX-YuvQkSRE.

Maiocco, Matt. "After 14 Seasons, Allen to Retire: Sonoma State Product a Certain Hall of Fame Lineman." *Press Democrat (Santa Rosa)*, August 30, 2008.

Mihoces, Gary. "Larry Allen: My Super Bowl." *USA Today*, February 3, 2013. Accessed July 2, 2015. http://www.usatoday.com/story/sports/nfl/2013/02/03/larry-allen-my-super-bowl-memory-dallas-cowboys/1886737/.

Orsborn, Tom. "Hall of Fame Cements Pair of Greats' Place: Mammoth Lineman Allen Earns Bust with Parcells." *San Antonio Express-News*, August 4, 2013.

———. "Mother Never Far from Allen's Thoughts." *San Antonio Express-News*, August 3, 2013.

Padecky, Bob. "Allen's Road: From SSU to Hall of Fame." *Press Democrat (Santa Rosa)*, February 3, 2013.

Price, Dwain. "Rookie's Life Takes Positive Turn." *Fort Worth Star-Telegram*, July 26, 1994.

Rattie, Jim. "Garcia Improves His Stock: San Jose QB Wins Shrine Game with Three Late TDs." *Sacramento Bee*, January 16, 1994.

"The Rivalry: 2000 and Beyond." *Washington Post*. Accessed June 10, 2015. http://www.washingtonpost.com/wp-srv/sports/redskins/history/rivalry/articles/2000sdec.htm.

Sabin, Rainer. "His Play Spoke Volumes." *Dallas Morning News*, February 2, 2013.

Swan, Gary. "Sonoma State Star Takes Hard Road to NFL." *San Francisco Chronicle*, April 23, 1994.

Taylor, Jean-Jacques. "Allen's Exit Leaves Unit without Any Sure Things." *Dallas Morning News*, March 22, 2006.

———. "End of the Line: Final Link to Franchise's Glory Days of '90s Is Cut." *Dallas Morning News*, March 22, 2006.

Townsend, Brad. "Man of Steel." *Dallas Morning News*, July 28, 2013.

Williams, Charean. "Cowboys' Allen, Parcells Voted to Pro Football Hall of Fame." *Fort Worth Star-Telegram*, February 2, 2013.

———. "Larry Legend: Offensive Lineman Larry Allen Joins Bill Parcells in 2013 Hall of Fame Class." *Fort Worth Star-Telegram*, February 3, 2013.

CHAPTER 3: TONY DORSETT: "TD," FOR SURE

Associated Press. "Bartender Drops Fight Complaint." *Victoria (Texas) Advocate*, August 19, 1977. Accessed August 30, 2015. https://news.google.com/newspapers?nid=8 61&dat=19770819&id=_y4PAAAAIBAJ&sjid=ZoUDAAAAIBAJ&pg=3768,381 8103&hl=en.

———. "Cowboys Ride Colts Roughshod, 38–0." *Victoria (Texas) Advocate*, September 5, 1978. Accessed June 28, 2015. https://news.google.com/newspapers?nid=8 61&dat=19780905&id=vV4dAAAAIBAJ&sjid=w1oEAAAAIBAJ&pg=7145,1150 446&hl=en.

———. "Dallas Shatters Colts, 38–0." *Ellensburg (Washington) Daily Record*, September 5, 1978. Accessed June 28, 2015. https://news.google.com/newspapers?nid=860& dat=19780905&id=3YRUAAAAIBAJ&sjid=MI8DAAAAIBAJ&pg=6891,445105 5&hl=en.

———. "Dorsett, White Make College Hall of Fame: Former Cowboy Teammates Join 13 Other Inductees. *Austin American-Statesman*, January 18, 1994.

———. "It's Official: Dorsett Gets His Wish When Deal Is Made with Broncos." *Houston Chronicle*, June 4, 1988.

———. "Staubach, Dorsett Destroy Colts." *Reading (Pennsylvania) Eagle*, September 5, 1978. Accessed June 14, 2015. https://news.google.com/newspapers?nid=195 5&dat=19780905&id=BsotAAAAIBAJ&sjid=JaEFAAAAIBAJ&pg=4429,3272318 &hl=en.

———. "Tony Dorsett, Famous Friends Head for Canton: Cowboys' Running Back Lets Out a Hoot after Hearing the Good News." *Akron (Ohio) Beacon Journal*, January 30, 1994.

Bires, Mike. "Once in a Lifetime: 25 Years Ago, Dorsett Wowed 'Em at Hopewell High." *Beaver County (Pennsylvania) Times*, August 26, 1997. Accessed June 13, 2015. https://news.google.com/newspapers?nid=2002&dat=19970826&id=pCN WAAAAIBAJ&sjid=8kANAAAAIBAJ&pg=3624,6586317&hl=en.

Bouchette, Ed. "Dorsett Makes Hall." *Pittsburgh Post-Gazette*, January 30, 1994.

Campbell, Steve. "Hall Final Link for Two Greats: White, Dorsett Increase to Six Number of Cowboys Enshrined." *Fort Worth Star-Telegram*, July 31, 1994.

"Dorsett's Special Day: 10,000 Yards, 2 Scores, and 1 Win vs. Steelers." *Los Angeles Times*, October 14, 1985. Accessed June 14, 2015. http://articles.latimes. com/1985-10-14/sports/sp-14936_1_nfl.

Dulac, Gerry. "Dorsett Scores Big on His Day at Canton: Ex-Pitt, Dallas Star Pays Hall of Fame Tribute to His Parents." *Pittsburgh Post-Gazette*, July 31, 1994.

Finder, Chuck. "Tony Dorsett's Hopewell High Coaches Celebrate His Hall of Fame Induction." *Pittsburgh Post-Gazette*, August 4, 1994.

Gosselin, Rick. "Dorsett, White Elected to Hall." *Dallas Morning News*, January 30, 1994.

Harasta, Cathy. "Dorsett's Former Teammates Express Regrets about Trade." *Dallas Morning News*, June 4, 1988.

Manoloff, Dennis. "The Class of 1994: Profiles of the People to Be Inducted into the Pro Football Hall of Fame in Canton Tomorrow." *Plain Dealer (Cleveland)*, July 29, 1994.

Miklasz, Bernie. "Dorsett Has Rare Gifts, Plus Heart." *Dallas Morning News*, June 5, 1988.

"Pitt Retired Jerseys: #33 Tony Dorsett." *University of Pittsburgh*. Accessed June 13, 2015. http://www.pittsburghpanthers.com/sports/m-footbl/dorsettretiredjersey.html.

Rose, Tom. "Davis and Dorsett: Like It or Not, Comparison Unavoidable." *Observer-Reporter (Washington, Pennsylvania)*, October 17, 1985. Accessed June 13, 2015. https://news.google.com/newspapers?nid=2519&dat=19851017&id=ooZiAAAAI BAJ&sjid=pHcNAAAAIBAJ&pg=4567,2549407&hl=en.

Seaburn, John. "Another Shining Moment: Running Back Dorsett and Dallas Mentor Landry Are Reunited for Hall Induction." *Akron (Ohio) Beacon Journal*, July 28, 1994.

United Press International. "Raiders, Cowboys Win 'Wild Card': Dorsett Sets Dallas Playoff Rush Record." *Sarasota (Florida) Herald-Tribune*, December 29, 1980.

Werder, Ed. "The Ultimate Rush: Tony Dorsett's Run to Hall of Fame Wasn't All Daylight." *Dallas Morning News*, July 17, 1994.

CHAPTER 4: CHARLES HALEY: FIVE RINGS

Archer, Todd. "In Addition to Ability, Charles Haley Brought Attitude to Cowboys." *ESPN*, August 6, 2015. Accessed August 18, 2015. http://espn.go.com/blog/nflnation/post/_/id/173500/in-addition-to-ability-charles-haley-brought-attitude-to-cowboys.

Associated Press. "Bad Back Forces Haley, Novacek into Retirement." *Dallas Morning News*, July 16, 1997.

———. "Fumble Puts Dallas in Frenzy." *Moscow-Pullman Daily News*, January 31, 1994. Accessed August 18, 2015. https://news.google.com/newspapers?nid=2026&dat=1 9940131&id=9cAjAAAAIBAJ&sjid=89AFAAAAIBAJ&pg=4837,3053448&hl=en.

———. "Relieved Aikman Looks to Future." *Gainesville (Florida) Sun*, January 29, 1996. Accessed August 18, 2015. https://news.google.com/newspapers?nid=132 0&dat=19960129&id=KSVkAAAAIBAJ&sjid=CusDAAAAIBAJ&pg=1606,63398 38&hl=en.

Didinger, Ray. "Haley Reconsiders, Might Return in '96." *Philadelphia News*, December 6, 1995. Accessed August 18, 2015. http://articles.philly.com/1995-12-06/sports/25668466_1_charles-haley-jerry-jones-and-coach-dallas-cowboys-locker-room.

Dixon, Schuyler. "Haley Takes Five Titles to Hall after Gruff Years in Dallas, SF." *Big Story*, August 5, 2015. Accessed August 18, 2015. http://bigstory.ap.org/urn:publicid:ap.org:3cd231d7ba6e4cfba79db002eff6360e.

Domowitch, Paul. "Steeler on Erik: We Can Play Dirty, Too." *Philadelphia Daily News*, January 24, 1996. Accessed August 18, 2015. http://articles.philly.com/1996-01-24/sports/25654177_1_dirty-tactics-questionable-tactics-john-jurkovic.

Gosselin, Rick. "Armed with New Maturity, Medication, Charles Haley's Bitterness over Hall Wait Is Gone." *Dallas Morning News*, August 6, 2015. Accessed August 18, 2015. http://www.dallasnews.com/sports/columnists/rick-gosselin/20150806-gosselin-armed-with-new-maturity-medication-charles-haleys-bitterness-over-hall-wait-is-gone.ece.

———. "Pressure to Shield O'Donnell from Haley, Cowboys Falls on Steelers' Offensive Line. *Cedartown (Georgia) Standard*, January 25, 1996. Accessed August 18, 2015. https://news.google.com/newspapers?nid=365&dat=19960125&id=Gh5IA AAAIBAJ&sjid=5D8DAAAAIBAJ&pg=4845,1593803&hl=en.

Hill, Clarence E., Jr. "Mostly Disliked, but Respected, Cowboys Great Haley Enters Hall of Fame." *Fort Worth Star-Telegram*, August 7, 2015. Accessed August 18, 2015. http://www.star-telegram.com/sports/nfl/dallas-cowboys/article30415554.html.

Hitzges, Norm. *Greatest Team Ever: The Dallas Cowboys Dynasty of the 1990s.* Nashville, TN: Thomas Nelson, 2007.

Inman, Cam. "Charles Haley Says He Can Use Hall Status to Help Others." *San Jose Mercury News*, July 23, 2015. Accessed August 18, 2015. http://www.mercurynews.com/49ers/ci_28529368/charles-haley-says-he-can-use-hall-status.

Jardine, Jeff. "Big D for Another with a Big Mouth." *Modesto (California) Bee*, August 27, 1992.

Karp, Josie. "Haley Sees Doctor Today in Step to Decide Future." *Fort Worth Star-Telegram*, January 15, 1997.

Lisko, B. J. "Charles Haley: Always Outworking the Competition." *Repository (Canton, Ohio)*, August 4, 2015. Accessed August 18, 2015. http://www.cantonrep.com/article/20150730/SPORTS/150739911.

———. "Charles Haley: Traveling Down the 'Road Of Destruction' before Bipolar Treatment." *Repository (Canton, Ohio)*, August 4, 2015. Accessed August 18, 2015. http://www.cantonrep.com/article/20150730/SPORTS/150739912.

———. "Charles Haley Notebook: The One That Got Away." *Repository (Canton, Ohio)*, August 4, 2015. Accessed August 18, 2015. http://www.cantonrep.com/article/20150730/SPORTS/150739914.

Michael, Gary. "Charles Haley: JMU Standout to NFL Hall of Famer—Part 1." *James Madison University*, August 4, 2015. Accessed August 18, 2015. http://www.jmusports.com/news/2015/8/3/Football_0803152625.aspx.

———. "Charles Haley: JMU Standout to NFL Hall of Famer—Part 2." *James Madison University*, August 5, 2015. Accessed August 18, 2015. http://www.jmusports.com/news/2015/8/5/Football_0805155605.aspx.

———. "Charles Haley: JMU Standout to NFL Hall of Famer—Part 3." *James Madison University*, August 6, 2015. Accessed August 18, 2015. http://www.jmusports.com/news/2015/8/6/Football_0806152552.aspx.

Moore, David. "Wait Was Tough but Worth It for New HOF Members Charles Haley, Tim Brown." *Dallas Morning News*, January 31, 2015. Accessed August 18, 2015. http://www.dallasnews.com/sports/dallas-cowboys/headlines/20150131-

moore-wait-was-tough-but-worth-it-for-new-hof-members-charles-haley-tim-brown.ece.

Prisuta, Mike. "Steelers Had No Remedy for Cowboys' Sack Attack." *Beaver County (Pennsylvania) Times*, September 6, 1994. Accessed August 18, 2015. https://news.google.com/newspapers?nid=2002&dat=19940906&id=brsiAAAAIBAJ&sjid=fbUFAAAAIBAJ&pg=1417,1074818&hl=en.

Robinson, Alan, Associated Press. "Defending Champs Look Super in Impressive Win." *Deseret (Salt Lake City) News*, September 5, 1994. Accessed August 17, 2015. https://news.google.com/newspapers?nid=336&dat=19940905&id=A-0vAAAAIBAJ&sjid=wOwDAAAAIBAJ&pg=3370,2997276&hl=en.

Schultz, Jeff. "49ers Are Hoping That This Haley's Comet Is No Joke." *San Jose Mercury News*, August 9, 1986.

Schumacher, John. "Cowboys Ride High Again: Dallas Rushes Past Buffalo, 30–13." *Ellensburg (Washington) Daily Record*, January 31, 1994. Accessed August 18, 2015. https://news.google.com/newspapers?nid=860&dat=19940131&id=PKNUAAAAIBAJ&sjid=J48DAAAAIBAJ&pg=6319,3034105&hl=en.

Silverstein, Tom, and Tom Mulhern. "Smith Carried Load for Offense." *Milwaukee Sentinel*, January 31, 1994. Accessed August 18, 2015. https://news.google.com/newspapers?nid=1368&dat=19940131&id=AqxRAAAAIBAJ&sjid=_hIEAAAAIBAJ&pg=6747,7440360&hl=en.

Wangrin, Mark. "Cowboys Get Haley from 49ers: Three-time Pro-Bowler Will Bolster Dallas Defense." *Austin American-Statesman*, August 27, 1992.

Werder, Ed. "Explosive Talent: Despite Incidents, Cowboys Like Charles Haley." *Dallas Morning News*, September 6, 1992.

Whitt, Richie, and Mike Fisher. "Pass-Rushing Standout Obtained from 49ers for Multiple Draft Picks." *Fort Worth Star-Telegram*, August 27, 1992.

Williams, Charean. "Former Cowboys Star Charles Haley among Eight Headed to Hall." *Fort Worth Star-Telegram*, January 31, 2015.

Wright, Branson. "An NFL and Hall of Fame career was not an early dream for Charles Haley." *Plain Dealer (Cleveland)*, July 24, 2015. Accessed August 18, 2015. http://www.cleveland.com/ohio-sports-blog/index.ssf/2015/07/hall_of_fame_de_charles_haley.html.

CHAPTER 5: BOB HAYES: A GAME-CHANGER

Aron, Jaime, Associated Press. "Cowboys' Hayes Finally Gets Hall of Fame Spot." *Lubbock Avalanche-Journal (Texas)*, August 6, 2009.

Associated Press. "Bob Hayes Bounces Back." *Daytona Beach (Florida) Morning Journal*, December 23, 1970. Accessed June 18, 2015. https://news.google.com/newspapers?nid=1873&dat=19701223&id=sk0fAAAAIBAJ&sjid=mNEEAAAAIBAJ&pg=3476,6385223&hl=en.

———. "Cowboys 'Bomb' Giants, 42–14; Long Passes Break Game Open." *Daytona Beach (Florida) Morning Journal*, December 12, 1971. Accessed June 18, 2015. https://

news.google.com/newspapers?nid=1873&dat=19711212&id=vfsoAAAAIBAJ&sjid =vNEEAAAAIBAJ&pg=2876,4677865&hl=en.

———. "Dallas Bombs Oilers, 52–10." *Spartanburg (South Carolina) Herald*, December 21, 1970. Accessed June 18, 2015. https://news.google.com/newspapers?nid=187 6&dat=19701221&id=54wsAAAAIBAJ&sjid=JMwEAAAAIBAJ&pg=5606,42430 51&hl=en.

———. "Thinking Man Bob Hayes Proves Tough for Foes." *Spartanburg (South Carolina) Herald*, November 16, 1966. Accessed June 18, 2015. https://news.google. com/newspapers?nid=1876&dat=19661116&id=OYEsAAAAIBAJ&sjid=Yc0EAA AAIBAJ&pg=7334,2455222&hl=en.

"Bob Hayes." *USA Track and Field Hall of Fame.* Accessed June 18, 2015. http://www. usatf.org/HallOfFame/TF/showBio.asp?HOFIDs=70.

"Bob Hayes's Enshrinement Speech Transcript." *Pro Football Hall of Fame*, August 8, 2009. Accessed June 18, 2015. http://www.profootballhof.com/story/2009/8/8/ bob-hayes-enshrinement-speech-transcript/.

Cantu, Rick. "'Bullet Bob' Changed the Game of Football." *Austin American-Statesman*, September 20, 2002.

Fraley, Gerry. "'His Speed Was Beautiful': Among the Cowboys' Three Greatest Receivers, Bob Hayes Had a Gift That Was Unmatched." *Dallas Morning News*, September 23, 2001.

Frenette, Gene. "Borderline Bob's Wait Finally Over." *Florida Times-Union*, February 1, 2009.

———. "Late Justice for Bullet: Hayes's Family Anticipates a Mix of Tears, Cheers." *Florida Times Union*, August 2, 2009.

Gosselin, Rick. "Statistics Have Kept Hayes from Hall." *Dallas Morning News*, September 21, 2001.

Habib, Hal. "Path to Greatness." *Palm Beach (Florida) Post*, August 7, 2009.

Hill, Clarence E., Jr. "Racing to the Finish." *Fort Worth Star-Telegram*, September 23, 2001.

Litsky, Frank. "Bob Hayes, Stellar Sprinter and Receiver, Is Dead at 59." *New York Times*, September 20, 2002. Accessed June 18, 2015. http://www.nytimes. com/2002/09/20/sports/bob-hayes-stellar-sprinter-and-receiver-is-dead-at-59. html.

Lowitt, Bruce. "Cowboys Get That Big One (Super Bowl), 24–3. *Owasso (Michigan) Argus-Press*, January 17, 1972. Accessed June 18, 2015. https://news.google.com/ newspapers?nid=1978&dat=19720117&id=gz0iAAAAIBAJ&sjid=56oFAAAAIBAJ &pg=1165,1490416&hl=en.

Luksa, Frank. "For Bob Hayes, It's Time to Celebrate." *Dallas Morning News*, September 22, 2001.

Nichols, Bill. "Game-Breaking Speed: Whether It Was a High School Meet, the Olympics, or the NFL, Bob Hayes Distinguished Himself with Unparalleled Speed." *Dallas Morning News*, August 7, 2009.

Robertson, Linda. "Addiction and a Prison Term Sent the World's Fastest Man into a Lonely and Bitter Descent to Failing Health and Dreams Unfulfilled." *Miami Herald*, December 23, 2001.

Schwartz, Larry. "Hayes Sets 100-Yard Dash World Record." *ESPN Classic*, June 21, 1963. Accessed June 18, 2015. http://espn.go.com/classic/s/moment010621_hayes_100worldrecord.html.

"Staubach: Hayes 'Fought a Tough Fight.'" *Miami Herald*, September 6, 2002.

Stellino, Vito. "'Bullet' Back on Target for Hall: Proponents Outspoken in Their Support for Hayes, but His Bid for Enshrinement Still Has Detractors." *Florida Times-Union*, January 25, 2009.

Tays, Alan. "Enduring Greatness: Hayes's Legend Took Root, Blossomed in Florida." *Palm Beach (Florida) Post*, September 20, 2002.

United Press International. "Cowboys Are 'Super VI-Shooters' as They Gun Down Dolphins, 24–3." *Sarasota (Florida) Herald-Tribune*, January 17, 1972. Accessed June 18, 2015. https://news.google.com/newspapers?nid=1755&dat=19720117&id=GD0gAAAAIBAJ&sjid=gGYEAAAAIBAJ&pg=5227,957957&hl=en.

Wright, Teneshia L. "Bob Hayes: 1942–2002: City Loses Its 'Fastest Man.'" *Florida Times-Union*, September 20, 2002.

———. "Hometown Tribute: 'Bullet Bob' Hayes Remembered for His Talent and His Struggles." *Florida Times-Union*, September 26, 2002.

———. "Unfulfilled Wish: Hall of Fame Never Called for Hayes." *Florida Times-Union*, September 20, 2002.

CHAPTER 6: MICHAEL IRVIN: CONTAGIOUS CONFIDENCE

Archer, Todd. "Irvin Finally Gets His Hands on Hall Invite." *Dallas Morning News*, February 4, 2007.

Associated Press. "Irvin Finally Makes Mark." *St. Petersburg (Florida) Times*, December 13, 1988.

———. "Judge Decides It Was Just Horseplay by the Cowboys." *Toledo (Ohio) Blade*, August 20, 1998.

———. "Wait Over: Irvin among Six New Hall of Famers." *Longview (Texas) News-Journal*, February 4, 2007.

Carlton, Chuck. "Fame Maker." *Dallas Morning News*, February 4, 2007.

Casstevens, David. "Irvin's Act Will Catch on in Dallas." *Dallas Morning News*, April 26, 1988.

D'Angelo, Tom. "The Wait Is Over." *Palm Beach (Florida) Post*, February 4, 2007.

Freeman, Denne, Associated Press. "Cowboys' Irvin Has Career Day: Receiver Frustrates Cardinals." *Los Angeles Daily News*, September 21, 1992.

Gosselin, Rick. "Gift of Gab: Irvin Made His Mark without the Benefit of a Complementary Wideout." *Dallas Morning News*, August 4, 2007.

Habib, Hal. "Reaching the Pinnacle." *Palm Beach (Florida) Post*, August 3, 2007.

Hall, Dennis. "Irvin Catches Packers Unprepared: Playmaker Exploits Single Coverage for 100 Yards and Two Touchdowns." *Fort Worth Star-Telegram*, January 15, 1996.

Hill, Clarence E., Jr. "Delay of Fame." *Fort Worth Star-Telegram*, February 3, 2007.

Hyde, Dave. "A Flawed Man of the Street Rises to a Flawless Finish." *Sun-Sentinel (Fort Lauderdale, Florida)*, August 1, 2007.

Irvin, Michael. "Interview with Yahoo Sports Radio." *Talk of Fame*, April 27, 2015. Accessed June 24, 2015. http://sports.yahoo.com/video/radio-michael-irvin-revisits-1988-123000033.html;_ylt=A0SO8xgGIItVfzAAJGRXNyoA;_ylu=X3oD MTByYnR1Zmd1BGNvbG8DZ3ExBHBvcwMyBHZ0aWQDBHNlYwNzcg--.

Luttermoser, John. "Irvin's Draft Decision Could Prove Costly." *St. Petersburg (Florida) Times*, April 24, 1988.

"Michael Irvin Enshrinement Speech." *Pro Football Hall of Fame*, April 4, 2007. Accessed June 24, 2015. http://www.profootballhof.com/hof/member. aspx?PlayerId=246&tab=Speech.

Miklasz, Bernie. "Cowboys' 10-Game Skid Ends vs. Redskins, 24–17." *Dallas Morning News*, December 12, 1988.

———. "Hot Dog? Irvin Says He's Just Having Fun." *Dallas Morning News*, April 25, 1988.

Myers, Gary. "Piece of Their Heart: Cowboys Find Out What It Feels Like to Lose the Big One." *Austin American-Statesman*, via *New York Daily News*, January 16, 1995.

Orsborn, Tom. "Irvin Says Arrest Should Gain Him Hall of Fame Votes." *San Antonio Express-News*, February 4, 2006.

Sefko, Eddie. "'I Beat Everybody': Miami Receiver Irvin's Favorite Subject Is Himself." *Houston Chronicle*, December 30, 1987.

Sherrington, Kevin. "Family Matters: Flashy Irvin, a Clan's Hope, Has Firm Foundation." *Dallas Morning News*, May 8, 1988.

———. "Triangular Foundation: Aikman, Smith, and Irvin: Youthful Cornerstones of Cowboys' Dynasty Dreams." *Dallas Morning News*, February 3, 1993.

United Press International. "Hurricanes Defeat Sooners 20–14 to Capture National Championship." *Lodi (California) News-Sentinel*, January 2, 1988. Accessed June 24, 2015. https://news.google.com/newspapers?nid=2245&dat=19880102&id=kqxA AAAAIBAJ&sjid=sDIHAAAAIBAJ&pg=6911,95208&hl=en.

Wangrin, Mark. "Splitting Defenses, Lips: Irvin Cuts Up Cardinals, Leaves Johnson Bleeding." *Austin American-Statesman*, September 21, 1992.

Williams, Charean. "Receiving His Due: Passionate Irvin Always the Straw That Stirred the Cowboys' Championship Teams of the '90s." *Fort Worth Star-Telegram*, August 4, 2007.

CHAPTER 7: TOM LANDRY: THE MAN BEHIND THE IMAGE

Associated Press. "Dallas Finally Wins One; Steelers Are the Victim." *Daytona Beach (Florida) Morning Journal*, September 18, 1961. Accessed June 26, 2015. https://news.google.com/newspapers?nid=1873&dat=19610918&id=NlsrAAAAIBAJ&sji d=2ZwFAAAAIBAJ&pg=5074,3328507&hl=en.

Blair, Sam. "End of an Era: For 29 Years, Landry Ran Cowboys the Way He Ran Life—with Faith." *Dallas Morning News*, February 26, 1989.

Bohls, Kirk. "Tom Landry, 1994–2000: Recalling 'a Holy Man' Who Coached." *Austin American-Statesman*, February 18, 2000.

Cantu, Rick. "Tom Landry Dies: Dignified Yet Demanding Coach Led Dallas Cowboys into Legend." *Austin American-Statesman*, February 13, 2000.

Cowlishaw, Tim. "Landry Joins Elite in NFL: Ex-Cowboys Coach One of Seven New Hall of Famers." *Dallas Morning News*, August 5, 1990.

———. "Landry's New Title: Hall of Fame Coach." *Dallas Morning News*, January 28, 1990.

———. "A Legend Reflects: Landry's Road to Hall of Fame Ran True after a Bumpy Start." *Dallas Morning News*, July 29, 1990.

Doclar, Mary. "Farewell, Coach: Landry Public Memorial Draws 1,200 Football Fans, Celebrities." *Fort Worth Star-Telegram*, February 18, 2000.

Feigen, Jonathan. "Landry in Retirement: Image Takes a Backseat to Reality." *Houston Chronicle*, July 29, 1990.

Finger, Mike. "Mission's Favorite Son: City Proud of the Man, the Legend." *San Antonio Express-News*, February 13, 2000.

Gosselin, Rick. "Innovations Left Imprint on Game: Flex Defense, Shotgun among Ideas That Put Landry in Hall of Fame." *Dallas Morning News*, February 14, 2000.

Halliburton, Suzanne. "The Landry Years." *Austin American-Statesman*, February 26, 1989.

Horn, Barry. "Tom Landry Dies: Leukemia Claims Cowboys Legend, 75." *Dallas Morning News*, February 13, 2000.

Landry, Tom, with Gregg Lewis. *Tom Landry: An Autobiography*. Grand Rapids, MI: Zondervan; New York: HarperCollins, 1990.

LeBreton, Gil. "America's Coach." *Fort Worth Star-Telegram*, February 13, 2000.

McClain, John. "Legendary Dallas Cowboys Coach Landry Dies: Hall of Famer, 75, Loses Battle with Leukemia." *Houston Chronicle*, February 13, 2000.

Meyer, Ed. "Landry Stands Tall as a Man as Well." *Akron (Ohio) Beacon Journal*, July 29, 1990.

Miklasz, Bernie. "Tears Flow Freely as Cowboys Legend Bids Team Farewell." *Dallas Morning News*, February 28, 1990.

Moore, David. "Building America's Team: Cowboys' Architect Constructed Foundation on Faith, Leadership." *Dallas Morning News*, February 14, 2000.

"Remembering the Coach." *Fort Worth Star-Telegram*, February 18, 2000.

Riggs, Randy. "Landry Bids Farewell." *Austin American-Statesman*, February 28, 1989.

Stone, Mike. "Tom Landry Says He's Put Firing behind Him, Doesn't Miss Dallas." *Rocky Mountain News (Denver, Colorado)*, August 22, 1990.

CHAPTER 8: BOB LILLY: "MR. COWBOY"

"10 Things to Know about Cowboys Legend Bob Lilly, Including His Super Bowl Legacy, Famous Photography." *SportsDayDFW.com*, July 13, 2015. Accessed August 3, 2015. http://cowboysblog.dallasnews.com/2015/07/10-things-to-know-about-cowboys-legend-bob-lilly-including-his-super-bowl-legacy-famous-photography. html/.

Archer, Todd. "Cowboys' Top Plays: Bob Lilly Sack of Griese." *ESPN,* July 3, 2014. Accessed August 3, 2015. http://espn.go.com/blog/dallas/cowboys/post/_/id/4729749/cowboys-top-plays-bob-lillys-sack.

Associated Press. "Bob Lilly—Calling It Quits." *Times Daily (Florence, Alabama),* July 15, 1975. Accessed August 3, 2015. https://news.google.com/newspapers?nid=1842&dat=19750715&id=6Q4sAAAAIBAJ&sjid=TMgEAAAAIBAJ&pg=969,3295989&hl=en.

———. "Bob Lilly Plans Thanksgiving Blitz." *Eugene (Oregon) Register-Guard,* November 23, 1966. Accessed August 3, 2015. https://news.google.com/newspapers?nid=1310&dat=19661123&id=ZqtVAAAAIBAJ&sjid=COEDAAAAIBAJ&pg=7030,4926534&hl=en.

Bortstein, Larry. "Seven NFL Stars Recall: Playing Thrills of the Super Bowl." *Sarasota (Florida) Herald-Tribune,* January 7, 1973. Accessed August 3, 2015. https://news.google.com/newspapers?nid=1755&dat=19730107&id=LEg0AAAAIBAJ&sjid=pmYEAAAAIBAJ&pg=4912,3004318&hl=en.

Cantu, Rick. "Lilly's Era a Freeze Frame of Simplicity." *Austin American-Statesman,* August 4, 1996.

Dent, Jim. "Lilly Credits Father, Coaches." *Dallas Times Herald,* August 3, 1990. Section C, page 1.

Landry, Tom, with Gregg Lewis. *Tom Landry: An Autobiography.* Grand Rapids, MI: Zondervan; New York: HarperCollins, 1990.

Lilly, Bob. "Interview with John Canzano." *Bald-Faced Truth,* 750-AM, the Game. Accessed August 3, 2015. http://www.oregonlive.com/sports/oregonian/john_canzano/index.ssf/2012/02/bald-faced_truth_with_john_can_204.html.

Lilly, Bob, with Kristine Setting Clark. *Bob Lilly: A Cowboy's Life.* Chicago: Triumph, 2008.

"Mr. Cowboy." *Pro Football Hall of Fame,* October 12, 2009. Accessed August 3, 2015. http://www.profootballhof.com/story/2009/10/12/mr-cowboy/.

Olderman, Murray. "Now Bob Lilly Can Sit Back and Relax—Until Next Year." *Times-News (Hendersonville, North Carolina),* February 7, 1972. August 3, 2015. https://news.google.com/newspapers?nid=1665&dat=19720207&id=wy8aAAAAIBAJ&sjid=gSQEAAAAIBAJ&pg=5714,2642998&hl=en.

Poyner, Jim. "Laurels for a Cowboys Legend." *Dallas Morning News,* August 3, 1980. Section B, page 1.

"Ring of Honor, Chuck Howley." *Dallas Cowboys.* Accessed August 6, 2015. http://www.dallascowboys.com/ring-of-honor/chuck-howley.

"Six Pros Tougher Than Tough." *LIFE Magazine,* October 6, 1972, 81. Accessed August 7, 2015. https://books.google.com/books?id=aVUEAAAAMBAJ&pg=PA81&dq=%22bob+lilly%22&hl=en&sa=X&ved=0CDsQ6AEwA2oVChMIhYTykqOYxwIVgYINCh3JFQMb#v=onepage&q=%22bob%20lilly%22&f=false.

United Press International. "Bob Lilly Retires from Football." *Beaver County (Pennsylvania) Times,* July 21, 1975. Accessed August 3, 2015. https://news.google.com/ne

wspapers?nid=2002&dat=19750721&id=URsvAAAAIBAJ&sjid=U9sFAAAAIBAJ
&pg=6220,5044397&hl=en.

CHAPTER 9: MEL RENFRO: NATURAL ATHLETICISM

Associated Press. "Landry Says Win Was 'Best Ever.'" *Daytona Beach (Florida) Morning Journal*, December 26, 1970. Accessed June 29, 2015. https://news.google.com/ne wspapers?nid=1873&dat=19701226&id=tE0fAAAAIBAJ&sjid=mNEEAAAAIBAJ &pg=4190,6989577&hl=en.

———. "Mel Renfro Convicted." *Daytona Beach (Florida) Morning Journal*, March 11, 1981. Accessed June 29, 2015. https://news.google.com/newspapers?nid=1870& dat=19810311&id=c3ApAAAAIBAJ&sjid=1tEEAAAAIBAJ&pg=3595,5731275& hl=en.

Brandt, Gil. "1964 Draft Left Lasting Impact on Dallas Cowboys, NFL." *NFL.com*, April 9, 2014. Accessed June 29, 2015. http://www.nfl.com/news/story/0ap1000000340099/article/1964-draft-left-lasting-impact-on-dallas-cow-boys-nfl.

Canning, Whit. "Wait Off His Shoulders." *Fort Worth Star-Telegram*, July 27, 1996.

"Finally, Canton Is the Call: The Class of '96 Offers Plenty Of Hard-Nosed Success Stories." *Orlando Sentinel*, July 28, 1996.

Forbes, Gordon. "Cowboys Will Never Forget Renfro's '63 Mirror Move." *USA Today*, July 26, 1996.

Goddard, Lee. "The Greatest Cowboys: Renfro Back on His Feet." *Corpus Christi (Texas) Caller-Times*, August 4, 2004. Accessed June 28, 2015. http://www.caller.com/sports/greatest-cowboys-renfro-back-his-feet.

Gosselin, Rick. "Renfro's Wait Finally Over with Induction into Hall." *Dallas Morning News*, July 28, 1996.

Lee, Mike. "Renfro Hurdles Travails, Bitterness at Cowboys." *Corpus Christi (Texas) Caller-Times*, October 6, 1996.

Leutzinger, Dick. "18 Webfoots' Football Careers Ending." *Eugene (Oregon) Register-Guard*, November 28, 1963. Accessed June 29, 2015. https://news.google.com/ne wspapers?nid=1310&dat=19631128&id=W_xVAAAAIBAJ&sjid=UuMDAAAAI BAJ&pg=4947,5187566&hl=en.

Luksa, Frank. "Bad Break 30 Years Ago May Have Been Renfro's Best." *Dallas Morning News*, July 27, 1996.

"Mel Renfro, Class of 1996." *Pro Football Hall of Fame*, June 10, 2014. Accessed June 28, 2015. http://www.profootballhof.com/hof/2014/6/10/mel-renfro-class-of-1996/.

"Mel Renfro Heads East." *Eugene (Oregon) Register-Guard*, December 5, 1962. Accessed June 29, 2015. https://news.google.com/newspapers?nid=1310&dat=19621 205&id=Iv9VAAAAIBAJ&sjid=1uIDAAAAIBAJ&pg=5131,927022&hl=en.

Morgan, David Lee, Jr. "Renfro Heads to Hall Focused on Higher Goal." *Akron (Ohio) Beacon-Journal*, July 27, 1996.

Strite, Dick. "Absence of Renfro Puts Oregon State in Favorite's Role." *Eugene (Oregon) Register-Guard*, November 25, 1963. Accessed June 29, 2015. https://news.google.com/newspapers?nid=1310&dat=19631125&id=WPxVAAAAIBAJ&sjid=UuMDAAAAIBAJ&pg=4045,4687763&hl=en.

Taylor, Jean-Jacques. "Long, Winding Road: Mel Renfro's Travels Reach Hall of Fame." *Dallas Morning News*, July 23, 1996.

United Press International. "Mel Renfro Wins Bias Settlement." *Afro American*, January 10, 1970. Accessed June 29, 2015. https://news.google.com/newspapers?nid=2211&dat=19700110&id=ESEmAAAAIBAJ&sjid=Bv4FAAAAIBAJ&pg=2578,169735&hl=en.

Wheeler, Ken. "Renfro Finally Completes His Journey." *Oregonian*, July 28, 1996.

CHAPTER 10: DEION SANDERS: CREATED FOR PRIMETIME

Aron, Jaime, Associated Press. "Sanders Never Lacked in Style, Substance in Prime." *Augusta (Georgia) Chronicle*, August 4, 2011.

Associated Press. "Cowboys in Prime, Rout Eagles: Deion's Touchdown Sparks Dallas to Easy 30–11 Victory." *Observer-Reporter (Washington, Pennsylvania)*, January 7, 1996. Accessed July 2, 2015. https://news.google.com/newspapers?nid=2519&dat=19960107&id=2YReAAAAIBAJ&sjid=CGINAAAAIBAJ&pg=5448,1952253&hl=en.

———. "Primetime: Sanders, Cowboys Clobber New York Giants 31–7." *Ludington (Michigan) Daily News*, September 22, 1998. Accessed July 2, 2015. https://news.google.com/newspapers?nid=110&dat=19980922&id=bvhOAAAAIBAJ&sjid=f0wDAAAAIBAJ&pg=4864,2014774&hl=en.

Barnes, Craig. "Multitalented Sanders Is Having a Ball at FSU." *Sun Sentinel (Fort Lauderdale, Florida)*, August 14, 1986. Accessed June 30, 2015. http://articles.sun-sentinel.com/1986-08-14/sports/8602180243_1_football-season-punt-deion-sanders.

"Bobby Bowden Takes Part in Dadgum Q&A on Reddit." *Fox Sports Florida*, August 19, 2014. Accessed July 1, 2015. http://www.foxsports.com/florida/story/bobby-bowden-takes-part-in-q-a-session-on-social-media-081914.

Caldwell, Dave. "Sanders Makes Eagles Pay." *Dallas Morning News*, November 3, 1998. Section B, page 5.

Cantu, Rick. "Cowboys Unveil Their Prize Catch." *Austin American-Statesman*, September 12, 1995.

Cowlishaw, Tim. "Zero Resistance: Dallas Walks While Eagles Lay an Egg." *Dallas Morning News*, November 3, 1998. Section B, page 1.

"Deion Sanders Timeline." *News-Press (Fort Myers, Florida)*, February 3, 2011. Accessed June 30, 2015. http://archive.news-press.com/article/99999999/SPORTS/110203024/Deion-Sanders-timeline.

Faust, Pete. "Mandarich Hit the Bank, but Other Rookies Broke It." *Milwaukee Journal*, September 17, 1989. Accessed July 1, 2015. https://news.google.com/newspapers?nid=1499&dat=19890917&id=BmYaAAAAIBAJ&sjid=-SsEAAAAIBAJ&pg=6909,270322&hl=en.

Freeman, Mike. "Behind the Swagger, Deion Was the Picture of Professionalism." *CBSSports.com*, August 6, 2011. Accessed July 1, 2015. http://www.cbssports.com/nfl/story/15402713/behind-the-swagger-deion-was-the-picture-of-professionalism.

Gosselin, Rick. "Sanders Is 'Proud, Thankful.'" *Dallas Morning News*, August 7, 2011.

———. "The Total Package." *Dallas Morning News*, August 4, 2011.

Hill, Clarence E., Jr. "Man of Many Faces: Deion Sanders Always Dreamed Big, and Realized Those Dreams." *Fort Worth Star-Telegram*, August 6, 2011.

———. "Prime Time for All Time: Deion Went from Rough Streets to Prime Spot in Canton." *Fort Worth Star-Telegram*, August 6, 2011.

———. "Prime's Time: Deion Sanders Takes Call to Hall amid Prayer, Family, Youth Team." *Fort Worth Star-Telegram*, February 6, 2011.

Kaufman, Ira. "Deion: Primed to Star." *Tampa Tribune*, January 30, 2009. Accessed June 30, 2015. http://tbo.com/ap/sports/pro_football/deion-primed-to-star-128668.

Luksa, Frank. "Strong to the Finish: Deion's Debut Leaves Cowboys Waiting for More." *Dallas Morning News*, October 30, 1995. Section B, page 8.

Marvel, John. "Sanders, Jones Put on Show under Big Top." *Contra Costa (California) Times*, September 12, 1995.

Meyer, Paul. "Deion Dances Away from Tackles." *Pittsburgh Post-Gazette*, January 29, 1996. Accessed July 2, 2015. https://news.google.com/newspapers?nid=1129&dat=19960129&id=7uJRAAAAIBAJ&sjid=QW8DAAAAIBAJ&pg=6553,7563644&hl=en.

Nohe, Patrik. "FSU All-Time Countdown: No. 1—Deion Sanders." *Miami Herald*, August 4, 2013. Accessed June 30, 2015. http://miamiherald.typepad.com/florida-state/2013/08/fsu-all-time-countdown-no-1-deion-sanders.html.

Poole, Monte. "Deion Was 49ers' One-Year Wonder(Ful)." *San Jose Mercury News*, August 7, 2011.

Shuler, Roger, Scripps Howard News Service. "'Neon Deion' Doesn't Shine So Bright: These Days, FSU's Deion Sanders Doesn't Relish Being in the Spotlight." *Miami News*, December 31, 1988.

Werder, Ed. "Deion Says He's Primed for Title Run: Newest Cowboy Visits, but Return Date Unclear." *Dallas Morning News*, September 12, 1995.

———. "Right on the Money: Deion, Crisp Offense Fill the Bill as Cowboys Deposit Atlanta, 28–13. *Dallas Morning News*, October 30, 1995. Section B, page 1.

Wilner, Barry, Associated Press. "Prime Time Now Golden Piece of Hall: Sanders, Sharpe, Faulk, Dent Headline Inductions at Canton." *Pittsburgh Post-Gazette*, August 7, 2011.

CHAPTER 11: TEX SCHRAMM: MASTER INNOVATOR

Associated Press. "Cowboys' Executive Gains Hall of Fame." *Kentucky New Era*, July 26, 1991. Accessed July 5, 2015. https://news.google.com/newspapers?nid=266&

dat=19910726&id=gtwrAAAAIBAJ&sjid=jWQFAAAAIBAJ&pg=5371,2328016 &hl=en.

———. "Schramm a Pillar of Cowboys." *St. Louis Post-Dispatch*, July 27, 1991.

Blair, Sam. "End of an Era: For 29 Years, Landry Ran Cowboys the Way He Ran Life—with Faith." *Dallas Morning News*, February 26, 1989.

Brandt, Gil. "1964 Draft Left Lasting Impact on Dallas Cowboys, NFL." *NFL. com*, April 9, 2014. Accessed June 29, 2015. http://www.nfl.com/news/story/0ap1000000340099/article/1964-draft-left-lasting-impact-on-dallas-cowboys-nfl.

Burch, Jimmy. "Schramm, Campbell Join Immortals in Hall of Fame." *Fort Worth Star-Telegram*, January 27, 1991.

Casstevens, David. "Farewell to a Legend: Mourners Pay Final Tribute to Tex Schramm." *Fort Worth Star-Telegram*, June 19, 2003.

Cowlishaw, Tim. "Schramm Surprised by Election to Hall: Campbell Also One of Five to Be Inducted." *Dallas Morning News*, July 24, 1991.

———. "Segregation among Obstacles That Fail to Deter Schramm." *Dallas Morning News*, July 22, 1991.

———. "The Stage Is Cast Away: Schramm Became More of a Leading Man in '80s, but the Last Act Was a 'Nightmare.'" *Dallas Morning News*, July 24, 1991.

———. "The Writer Reverses His Field: In This LA Story, Ex-journalist Schramm Becomes Fast Climber in Football." *Dallas Morning News*, July 21, 1991.

Engel, Jennifer Floyd. "Tex Schramm: Innovative Leader Leaves Mark on Cowboys." *Fort Worth Star-Telegram*, July 16, 2003.

Finney, Peter. "Peter Finney's Super Bowl Memories, 1978: Dallas 27, Denver 10." *Times-Picayune (New Orleans, Louisiana)*, January 26, 2013. Accessed July 5, 2015. http://www.nola.com/superbowl/index.ssf/2013/01/peter_finneys_super_bowl_memor_8.html.

Gosselin, Rick. "Cowboys' Big Star: Catalyst for Merger Brought Football into Prominence." *Dallas Morning News*, July 16, 2003.

Luksa, Frank. "Architect of a Dynasty: Scorning Business as Usual, Tex Aimed for 'Something Special.'" *Dallas Morning News*, July 16, 2003.

Maher, John. "Schramm's Vision Turned NFL into a Sports Goliath." *Austin American-Statesman*, July 16, 2003.

Orsborn, Tom. "Tex Made NFL Better: Schramm's Innovations Are a Big Reason for the League's Popularity." *San Antonio Express-News*, July 16, 2003.

Rabun, Mike, United Press International. "A Dynasty in Dallas?" *Beaver County (Pennsylvania) Times*, July 6, 1972. Accessed July 5, 2015. https://news.google.com/newspapers?nid=2002&dat=19720706&id=87IiAAAAIBAJ&sjid=eLMFAAAAIBAJ&pg=815,1012765&hl=en.

Riggs, Randy. "Texas E. Schramm, 1920–2003: He Made the Cowboys 'America's Team.'" *Austin American-Statesman*, July 16, 2003.

Rollow, Cooper, Knight-Ridder Tribune News Service. "Schramm: A Shrewd and Colorful Showman." *Austin American-Statesman*, July 26, 1991.

"Schramm Reaction." *Spokesman-Review (Spokane, Washington)*, July 16, 2003. Accessed July 3, 2015. https://news.google.com/newspapers?nid=1314&dat=20030716&id=BtVYAAAAIBAJ&sjid=wPIDAAAAIBAJ&pg=2404,4127617&hl=en.

Seaburn, John. "Schramm's Loyalty Is with the NFL: He Also Ran Cowboys and Was Great Innovator." *Akron (Ohio) Beacon Journal*, July 25, 1991.

Taylor, Jean-Jacques. "Tex Schramm: 1920–2003—Architect of a Dynasty: Innovative GM Put His Enduring Stamp on the Cowboys and the NFL." *Dallas Morning News*, July 16, 2003.

"Tex Schramm: Producer of Dallas' Hit Show." *Palm Beach (Florida) Post*, December 29, 1979. Accessed July 4, 2015. https://news.google.com/newspapers?nid=1964&dat=19791229&id=AAEtAAAAIBAJ&sjid=zc0FAAAAIBAJ&pg=2590,6665800&hl=en.

Wilkins, Galyn. "Schramm Built Team, Respect." *Fort Worth Star-Telegram*, July 26, 1991.

Williams, Charean. "NFL Visionary: Schramm's Innovations Sparked League's Success." *Fort Worth Star-Telegram*, July 16, 2003.

CHAPTER 12: EMMITT SMITH: RUSHING CHAMPION

Abrams, Alex. "Happy Trails: Cowboy Emmitt Runs into Retirement with Rushing Record." *Florida Times-Union (Jacksonville)*, February 4, 2005.

Andreu, Robbie. "No Question about It: Emmitt Happy to Be a Cowboy." *Sun-Sentinel (Fort Lauderdale, Florida)*, April 23, 1990.

Associated Press. "Smith Runs Wild as Cowboys Roll: Back's 237 Yards Key in 23–10 Win." *Milwaukee Sentinel*, November 1, 1993. Accessed July 9, 2015. https://news.google.com/newspapers?nid=1368&dat=19931101&id=SZsWAAAAIBAJ&sjid=BRMEAAAAIBAJ&pg=5340,87957&hl=en.

Bock, Hal, Associated Press. "Success Follows Smith: MVP Takes Charge in Second Half." *Free Lance Star (Fredericksburg, Virginia)*, January 31, 1994. Accessed July 9, 2015. https://news.google.com/newspapers?nid=1298&dat=19940131&id=ouYyAAAAIBAJ&sjid=lwcGAAAAIBAJ&pg=5413,5390384&hl=en.

Bohls, Kirk. "No. 22 Will Always Be No. 1 among Dallas Fans." *Austin American-Statesman*, February 4, 2005.

Cowlishaw, Tim. "Flashback: Emmitt Smith Carries Cowboys to Super Bowl XXVIII Win." *Dallas Morning News*, January 30, 2013. Accessed July 9, 2015. http://www.dallasnews.com/sports/dallas-cowboys/headlines/20130130-flashback-emmitt-smith-carries-cowboys-to-super-bowl-xxviii-win.ece.

Fraley, Gerry. "Still a Hometown Hero." *Dallas Morning News*, February 5, 2010.

Freeman, Denne H., Associated Press. "Smith, Cowboys Corral the Redskins, 21–10: Dallas, Washington Now Tied for First." *Kingman (Arizona) Daily Miner*, November 29, 1996. Accessed July 9, 2015. https://news.google.com/newspapers?nid=932&dat=19961129&id=upNPAAAAIBAJ&sjid=RFMDAAAAIBAJ&pg=6182,4015493&hl=en.

George, Dave. "'Slow-Motion' Style Carries Emmitt Smith into Hall." *Palm Beach (Florida) Post*, February 5, 2010.

Goodall, Fred, Associated Press. "Smith to Bypass Final Year at UF to Play in NFL." *Times-News (Hendersonville, North Carolina)*, February 1, 1990. Accessed July 10,

2015. https://news.google.com/newspapers?nid=1665&dat=19900201&id=K-VP AAAAIBAJ&sjid=OCQEAAAAIBAJ&pg=4721,81705&hl=en.

Hill, Clarence E., Jr. "Emmitt Smith's Dream Came True on an October Day at Texas Stadium." *Fort Worth Star-Telegram*, July 25, 2010.

———. "Former Teammates Bask in the Glow of Emmitt Smith's Induction." *Fort Worth Star-Telegram*, August 7, 2010.

———. "Star Attraction: Emmitt Smith Always Knew Which Way to Run, from Pensacola to Dallas." *Fort Worth Star-Telegram*, August 7, 2010.

Mooney, Roger. "So Long, Cowboy: Emmitt Smith Leaves a Lasting Legacy." *Bradenton (Florida) Herald*, February 4, 2005.

Moore, David. "Fame Awaits." *Dallas Morning News*, February 6, 2010.

Oliver, Richard. "The Emmitt Era Ends: Cowboys Drop NFL's Top Career Rusher." *San Antonio Express-News*, February 28, 2003.

Orsborn, Tom. "Captain Courageous." *San Antonio Express-News*, August 7, 2010.

Schwartz, Kris. "Emmitt Gives New Meaning to Sweetness." *ESPN Classic.* Accessed July 10, 2015. http://espn.go.com/classic/biography/s/Smith_Emmitt.html.

Smith, Brian. "Smith Has Career Day with 237 Rushing Yards." *Reading (Pennsylvania) Eagle*, November 1, 1993. Accessed July 9, 2015. https://news.google.com/newspapers?nid=1955&dat=19931101&id=rfghAAAAIBAJ&sjid=kqIFAAAAIBAJ&pg=1455,159766&hl=en.

Taylor, Jean-Jacques. "His Legacy Carries On: Running Back Leaves a Trail of Records, Long Runs, and Big-Time Performances." *Dallas Morning News*, February 4, 2005.

Whitney, David. "Emotional Emmitt Calls It Quits." *Orlando Sentinel*, February 4, 2005.

CHAPTER 13: ROGER STAUBACH: HALL OF FAME PERSON

Associated Press. "Navy's Roger Staubach Wins Heisman Trophy." *Pittsburgh Post-Gazette*, November 27, 1963. Accessed August 3, 2015. https://news.google.com/newspapers?nid=1129&dat=19631127&id=lp1RAAAAIBAJ&sjid=YGwDAAAAIBAJ&pg=4979,4202270&hl=en.

Bishop, Greg. "Roger Staubach's Journey from Cowboys Star QB to Real Estate Mogul." *Sports Illustrated*, October 13, 2014. Accessed August 3, 2015. http://www.si.com/nfl/2014/10/08/profiles-roger-staubach-cowboys-quarterback-real-estate-entrepreneur.

Casstevens, David. "For Hall Ceremonies, Inductees Wear Emotions on Their Sleeves." *Dallas Morning News*, August 4, 1985.

Deindorfer, Robert G. "Big Gun in the Backfield." *Boys' Life*, November 1963, 14–17, 69. Accessed August 30, 2015. https://books.google.com/books?id=JBdMc4ZrPesC&pg=PA15&dq=%22roger+staubach%22&hl=en&sa=X&ved=0CDsQ6AEwAjgKahUKEwjU2q3aq9LHAhUElA0KHclyDZM#v=onepage&q=%22roger%20staubach%22&f=false.

Elderkin, Phi. "Staubach Chooses to Bow Out a Winner." *Christian Science Monitor*, April 14, 1980.

Flowers, Jack. "Roger Staubach: From Vietnam to the Super Bowl." *Palm Beach (Florida) Post*, January 13, 1971. Accessed August 3, 2015. https://news.google.com/newspapers?nid=1964&dat=19710113&id=koIyAAAAIBAJ&sjid=dLcFAAAAIBAJ&pg=5789,5293794&hl=en.

Fox, Larry. "Roger Staubach: Never Defeated." *Boys' Life*, November 1977, 20–22. Accessed August 8, 2015. https://books.google.com/books?id=JojSZh4KJVsC&pg=PA20&dq=%22roger+staubach%22&hl=en&sa=X&ved=0CFkQ6AEwB2oVChMItsnOmvuZxwIViv2ACh1TdAMx#v=onepage&q=%22roger%20staubach%22-&f=false.

Hollandsworth, Skip. "Navy Keeps Quarterback on Even Keel." *Dallas Times Herald*, April 1, 1980. Section G, page 4.

Horn, Barry. "Staubach, Pearson Discuss Genesis of 'Hail Mary' Pass." *Dallas Morning News*, January 17, 2010. Accessed August 10, 2015. http://www.dallasnews.com/sports/dallas-cowboys/headlines/20100117-Staubach-Pearson-discuss-genesis-of-7095.ece.

Justice, Richard. "Two Super Bowl Victories Highlight Career." *Dallas Times Herald*, April 1, 1980. Section G, page 10.

Lassiter, Jim. "Is There Anything Staubach Couldn't Do?" *Oklahoman*, June 27, 1985.

Luksa, Frank. "Another Miracle for Crown." *Dallas Times Herald*, December 17, 1979. Section C, page 1.

———. "Cowboys Hijack 49er Gold, 30–28." *Dallas Times Herald*, December 24, 1972. Section B, page 1.

———. "NFL Coaches Praise Staubach." *Dallas Times Herald*, March 30, 1980. Section C, page 1.

———. "Roger Staubach Makes It Official; Ends Era as Cowboys Quarterback." *Dallas Times Herald*, March 31, 1980. Section C, page 1.

"Opponents: Roger Was Tough Competitor." *Dallas Times Herald*, April 1, 1980. Section G, page 5.

Perkins, Steve. "Desire, Consistency Made Staubach Great." *Dallas Times Herald*, April 1, 1980. Section G, page 9.

———. "Staubach Got Off to a Fast Start." *Dallas Times Herald*, March 1, 1980. Section D, page 1.

"Roger Staubach: Football Star Turned Business Titan." *New Mexico Military Institute*. Accessed August 9, 2015. http://www.nmmi.edu/athletics/broncofootball/Roger-Staubach.htm.

Sheppard, Jack. "From Heisman to Hall of Fame: Staubach, Simpson Break Long Jinx." *Dallas Times Herald*, August 3, 1985. Section C, page 1.

Sherrod, Blackie. "Cowboys' Win Could Have Been Runaway." *Dallas Times Herald*, January 16, 1978. Section D, page 1.

St. John, Bob. "Staubach, Up Close and . . ." *Dallas Morning News*, April 1, 1980. Section B, page 1.

"Staubach Began as End: Cincinnati Kid Had Moves in High School." *Dallas Morning News*, April 1, 1980. Section B, page 3.

"Staubach Dreamed of Playing for Reds." *Lexington Herald-Banner*, January 25, 1985.

"Teammates: Staubach Would Never Give Up." *Dallas Times Herald*, April 1, 1980. Section G, page 5.

Wojciechowski, Gene. "Passing into History: Roger Staubach Prepares for Hall of Fame Induction." *Dallas Morning News*, August 2, 1985. Section B, page 1.

Wolfe, Alexandra. "Roger Staubach, America's Quarterback." *Wall Street Journal*, August 29, 2014. Accessed August 3, 2015. http://www.wsj.com/articles/roger-staubach-americas-quarterback-1409329809.

CHAPTER 14: RANDY WHITE: COMPLETE DOMINANCE

Associated Press. "Cowboys Knock Off Cardinals." *Tuscaloosa News*, November 12, 1984. Accessed August 4, 2015. https://news.google.com/newspapers?nid=1817& dat=19841112&id=RTUdAAAAIBAJ&sjid=pqUEAAAAIBAJ&pg=3364,3431625&hl=en.

———. "Cowboys Stop Seahawks, Warner 35–10." *Palm Beach (Florida) Post*, December 5, 1983. Accessed August 4, 2015. https://news.google.com/newspapers?nid=1964&dat=19831205&id=wAEtAAAAIBAJ&sjid=xs4FAAAAIBAJ&pg=1459,5842833&hl=en.

———. "Neck Injury Forces Cowboys' White to Retire." *Houston Chronicle*, April 14, 1989.

———. "White Says Firing of Landry Influenced Decision to Retire." *St. Louis Post-Dispatch*, April 15, 1989.

Blair, Sam. "White Goes Quietly: He's the Same after 14 Years as a Cowboy." *Dallas Morning News*, April 15, 1989.

Bohls, Kirk. "A Legend Born at Maryland." *Austin American-Statesman*, December 10, 2014.

Campbell, Steve. "Hall Final Link for Two Greats: White, Dorsett Increase to Six Number of Cowboys Enshrined." *Fort Worth Star-Telegram*, July 31, 1994.

Casstevens, David. "Another Cowboy Hero Rides Off into the Sunset." *Dallas Morning News*, April 15, 1989.

———. "Bliss of State Passes to Only a Chosen Few." *Dallas Morning News*, December 20, 1986.

Cowlishaw, Tim. "Rhythm and Bruise: Ex-Cowboy Randy White Mashed Force and Finesse into a Hall of Fame Career." *Dallas Morning News*, July 24, 1994.

Dent, Jim. "Dallas Front Four Revive Memories of Doomsday." *Dallas Times Herald*, December 5, 1983. Section C, page 6.

Didinger, Ray. "The Price Is Right as White Returns to Dallas Defense." *Philadelphia Daily News*, August 28, 1984.

———. "White Cherishes Hallmark Career: Ex-Cowboy among Six Inductees." *Philadelphia Daily News*, August 1, 1994.

Gosselin, Rick. "Dorsett, White Elected to Hall." *Dallas Morning News*, January 30, 1994.

Halliburton, Suzanne. "Randy White Calls It Quits: Neck Injury Forces Retirement." *Austin American-Statesman*, April 14, 1989.

Lucas, Bick. "Dallas Cowboys Came Out of Super Bowl Chute with Guns Blazing vs. Denver Broncos." *Denver Post*, January 16, 1978. Accessed July 11, 2015. http://www.denverpost.com/broncos/ci_24970766/dallas-cowboys-denver-broncos-super-bowl-1978.

Luksa, Frank. "Cowboys Basics Rattle Seattle: Seahawk Mistakes Costly." *Dallas Times Herald*, December 5, 1983. Section C, page 1.

———. "Stautner's Defense Rolled Dice, New England Paid the Price." *Dallas Times Herald*, November 23, 1984. Section C, page 8.

Miklasz, Bernie. "Randy White Quits after 14 Years: 'Pounding Caught Up to Me,' He Says." *Dallas Morning News*, April 14, 1989.

"Randy 'The Manster' White." *College Football Hall of Fame*. Accessed July 25, 2015. http://www.cfbhall.com/inductees/?ps=true&playername=Randy+White&fromDate=&toDate=&school=&yearInducted=&position=&submit=Search.

"Randy White Chases Receiver from Behind." YouTube video, posted by Zack Speranza, December 27, 2010. https://www.youtube.com/watch?v=W2r-0tOrvtk.

"So They Say . . ." *Austin American-Statesman*, February 17, 1990.

Sullivan, Bill. "Quiet White Leaves Smiling: Tackle Ends 14 Seasons as Cowboy." *Houston Chronicle*, April 15, 1989.

Underwood, John. "He'll Tackle Anything." *Sports Illustrated*, October 22, 1984. Accessed July 11, 2015. http://www.si.com/vault/1984/10/22/620785/hell-tackle-anything.

White, Randy. "Interview with David Spada and Elliott Harris." *Sports and Torts*. Accessed July 11, 2015. https://www.youtube.com/watch?v=E1Nz2KlFGwQ.

Wojciechowski, Gene. "NFL Strike: 1982: A History Lesson Not Learned." *Los Angeles Times*, September 23, 1987. Accessed July 27, 2015. http://articles.latimes.com/1987-09-23/sports/sp-6303_1_nfl-strike.

CHAPTER 15: RAYFIELD WRIGHT: LONG ROAD TO CANTON

Archer, Todd. "Is It Time? Some Former Opponents, Teammates Say Honor Overdue for Cowboys Great." *Dallas Morning News*, February 1, 2006.

———. "Two Cowboys Get Claim to Fame: Aikman, Wright Make Cut for Hall; Irvin Shut Out Again." *Dallas Morning News*, February 5, 2006.

Aron, Jaime, Associated Press. "Landry Was Right about Wright; Dallas RT Headed for Hall." *Midland (Texas) Reporter-Telegram*, August 3, 2006. Accessed August 2, 2015. http://www.mrt.com/import/article_3ce43620-8aee-56f6-bb65-5a04a16a1850.html.

Buck, Ray. "A Man of Faith: Wright Counts His Blessings after His Long Wait for Fame." *Fort Worth Star-Telegram*, August 5, 2006.

———. "Speech Hits All Wright Notes." *Fort Worth Star-Telegram*, August 6, 2006.

———. "Wright Stuff: After 22 Years, Ex-Cowboy Talks It All Out." *Fort Worth Star-Telegram*, August 6, 2006.

Gaffney, Tom. "Waiting Comes to Fruition: Dallas' Rayfield Wright Finally Gets Call to Hall." *Akron (Ohio) Beacon Journal*, July 31, 2006.

Kendall, Josh. "Football Just Happened to Be the Vehicle That Led to Rayfield's Success." *Macon (Georgia) Telegraph*, July 30, 2006.

Ledbetter, D. Orlando. "Hall of Famer Wright Almost Missed Shot at NFL." *Atlanta Journal-Constitution*, August 5, 2006.

Lough, Michael A. "Fort Valley State in Front Row with Hall's 'Names.'" *Macon (Georgia) Telegraph*, August 7, 2006.

Mosley, Matt. "Meet the Presenters: Stan Lomax—in Georgia, This Man Needs No Introduction." *Dallas Morning News*, July 30, 2006.

———. "New Life: All Seemed Lost Long Ago, but in Time Wright Found His Way Home Again." *Dallas Morning News*, July 30, 2006.

———. "Two More Cowboys Get the Call." *Dallas Morning News*, February 5, 2006.

———. "The Wright Stuff." *Dallas Morning News*, July 30, 2006.

Orsborn, Tom. "Aikman, Wright Answer Hall's Call." *San Antonio Express-News*, February 5, 2006.

Renfro, Mel, and Rayfield Wright. "Mel Renfro and Rayfield Wright Recall Super Bowls VI and XII." Interview with Pro Football Hall of Fame. Accessed August 5, 2015. https://www.youtube.com/watch?v=8GIA_Yjdzcs.

Ridenour, Marla. "Emotional Moments: Aikman Credits Talented Cowboys Teammates as He Enters Hall." *Akron (Ohio) Beacon Journal*, August 6, 2006.

Williams, Tom. "Cowboys Clubbers Laugh with Tom." *Dallas Times Herald*, March 17, 1967, Section C, page 2.

Winkeljohn, Matt. "Griffin Native Overwhelmed and Relieved." *Atlanta Journal-Constitution*, February 5, 2006.

Wright, Rayfield. "Interview with David Spada and Elliott Harris." *Sports and Torts*. Accessed August 2, 2015. https://www.youtube.com/watch?v=bWo9wnaSXyk.

CHAPTER 16: OTHER CONTRIBUTORS

Associated Press. "Ditka Delighted to Be a Cowboy." *Sumter (South Carolina) Daily Item*, January 27, 1969. Accessed August 19, 2015. https://news.google.com/news papers?nid=1979&dat=19690127&id=vI4iAAAAIBAJ&sjid=wqkFAAAAIBAJ&pg=3212,2233313&hl=en.

———. "McDonald a Maybe: Pro Grid Star Considers Crucial Move to Dallas." *Milwaukee Journal*, April 22, 1964. Accessed August 19, 2015. https://news.google.com/newspapers?nid=1499&dat=19640422&id=_98jAAAAIBAJ&sjid=eCcEAAA AIBAJ&pg=3207,966743&hl=en.

Belock, Joe. "Super Bowl XIII: Dallas Cowboys' Jackie Smith's Key Drop Helps Steelers Win." *New York Daily News*, December 29, 2013. Accessed August 24, 2015. http://www.nydailynews.com/sports/football/super-bowl-xiii-sickest-man-america-article-1.1561166.

"Forrest Gregg: Class of 1977." *Green Bay Packers*. Accessed August 19, 2015. http://www.packers.com/history/hall-of-famers/gregg-forrest.html.

"Herb Adderley: Class of 1980." *Green Bay Packers*. Accessed August 19, 2015. http://www.packers.com/history/hall-of-famers/adderley-herb.html.

Hoffman, Dale. "Gregg Cherishes Past." *Milwaukee Sentinel*, February 10, 1975. Accessed August 19, 2015. https://news.google.com/newspapers?nid=1368&dat=19750210&id=44FRAAAAIBAJ&sjid=tREEAAAAIBAJ&pg=7187,1821945&hl=en.

Lea, Bud. "Packers Trade Adderley to Dallas." *Milwaukee Sentinel*, September 2, 1970. Accessed August 19, 2015. https://news.google.com/newspapers?nid=1368&dat=19700902&id=E6RRAAAAIBAJ&sjid=vhAEAAAAIBAJ&pg=7274,217477&hl=en.

Lombardi, Vince. *Run to Daylight: Vince Lombardi's Diary of One Week with the Green Bay Packers*. New York: Simon & Schuster, 1989.

"Tommy 'Shoo-Fly' McDonald." *College Football Hall of Fame*. Accessed August 19, 2015. http://www.cfbhall.com/inductees/?ps=true&playername=Tommy+McDonald&fromDate=&toDate=&school=&yearInducted=&position=&submit=Search.

United Press International. "Cowboys Bench Herb Adderley." *Star-News (Wilmington, North Carolina)*, November 2, 1972. Accessed August 19, 2015. https://news.google.com/newspapers?nid=1454&dat=19721102&id=ebgsAAAAIBAJ&sjid=2wkEAAAAIBAJ&pg=3366,399663&hl=en.

Van Sickle, Gary. "King of the Forrest: Gregg Always Gave the Best He Could; Now He Has Taught the Bengals to Do the Same." *Milwaukee Journal*, January 17, 1982. Accessed August 19, 2015. https://news.google.com/newspapers?nid=1499&dat=19820117&id=i-AjAAAAIBAJ&sjid=LyoEAAAAIBAJ&pg=7014,2606174&hl=en.

Index

About the Author

David Thomas is author/cowriter of 10 books, including two *New York Times* best sellers. A former sports journalist, he worked more than two decades with the *Fort Worth Star-Telegram* and the *Dallas Morning News*. He still considers Roger Staubach his favorite athlete.